THE BATTLE OF THE
SOMME

OSPREY
PUBLISHING

THE BATTLE OF THE
SOMME

EDITED BY

MATTHIAS STROHN

First published in Great Britain in 2016 by Osprey Publishing,
PO Box 883, Oxford, OX1 9PL, UK
PO Box 3985, New York, NY 10185-3985, USA
E-mail: info@ospreypublishing.com
Osprey Publishing, part of Bloomsbury Publishing Plc

A CIP catalogue record for this book is available from the British Library

Hew Strachan, Lothar Höbelt, Gerhard Groß, Georges-Henri Soutou, James Corum, Stuart
Mitchell, Christopher Pugsley, Michael Neiberg, Christian Stachelbeck, Bill Mitchinson, Matthias
Strohn, Jonathan Krause and Mungo Melvin have asserted their right under the Copyright,
Designs and Patents Act, 1988, to be identified as the Authors of this Work.

ISBN: 978 1 4728 1556 9
PDF ISBN: 978 1 4728 1557 6
ePub ISBN: 978 1 4728 1558 3

Index by Zoe Ross
Cartography by Peter Bull Map Studios
Typeset in Garamond, Gill Sans and Trajan
Originated by PDQ Digital Media Solutions, UK
Printed in China through World Print Ltd.

16 17 18 19 20   10 9 8 7 6 5 4 3 2 1

Front cover: Troops attacking over barbed wire. (© Ullsteinbild / TopFoto)

Osprey Publishing supports the Woodland Trust, the UK's leading woodland conservation
charity. Between 2014 and 2018 our donations will be spent on their Centenary Woods project in
the UK.

www.ospreypublishing.com

Imperial War Museum Collections
Many of the photos in this book come from the Imperial War Museum's huge collections which
cover all aspects of conflict involving Britain and the Commonwealth since the start of the
twentieth century. These rich resources are available online to search, browse and buy at www.
iwmcollections.org.uk. In addition to Collections Online, you can visit the Visitor Rooms where
you can explore over 8 million photographs, thousands of hours of moving images, the largest
sound archive of its kind in the world, thousands of diaries and letters written by people in
wartime, and a huge reference library. Imperial War Museum www.iwm.org.uk

Acknowledgements

I was reading a German account of the battle of the Somme. I had read the account several times before, and I had learned about the suffering, the endless waiting in the dugouts before the enemy attack, and the relentless, seemingly never-ending enemy artillery bombardment. But now this account had gained a new perspective. I was reading it lying on my worn mattress in a rocket-proof shelter in Afghanistan. That day, we had been attacked by indirect fire – rockets and mortars. This had been the third or fourth time that I had come under attack during my deployments to Afghanistan and Iraq. Some of these attacks were more dangerous than others, but there are certain things I still remember about all of them: hearing the grenades whizz towards me, waiting for the impact and explosion. Every time thinking 'Will it hit me' while my body is pressed against the ground and all I see is the grass (or sand, more often) right in front of me. The relief after the explosion when I realize 'this one was not for me' and then all this again as the next round comes in. The attacks I endured seldom lasted longer than half an hour and, most of the time, the frequency of explosions was not particularly high and the accuracy low. And then, that night, I read about relentless enemy artillery fire on the Somme that the soldiers had to endure for days and weeks. It was probably only then when I realized what constant horror, pain, fear and also silent heroism was experienced by the soldiers of all nations on the Western Front in World War I, and it is important that these lessons are not forgotten. This was my motivating factor for this book.

First and foremost, I would like to thank the contributors to this book. Absolutely everybody worked with a high level of professionalism and sometimes to very tight deadlines. This made my work as the editor an enjoyable task. This is more the book of the contributors than it is mine.

My role as the editor was made even easier by the outstanding support provided by Laura Callaghan, Marcus Cowper and the team at Osprey. I would also like to thank the design team, Stewart Larking and Beth Cole, who produced such a well-finished book and Peter Bull Map Studio, who prepared the maps.

I am particularly pleased that Sir Hew Strachan agreed to write the foreword to the book. Not only is he the most eminent World War I historian, but I have known him for many years, since I started my DPhil at Oxford under his supervision. Without Sir Hew and his support over the years, I would not be where I am today.

I would also like to thank the Royal Military Academy Sandhurst, in particular the Director of Studies Sean McKnight, for the ongoing support of this project, which falls into my wider role as Sandhurst coordinator for the World War I centenary commemorations.

There is one person who deserves a very special thank you: my wife Rocio. This book project was not the only one I was working on at the time and, as a consequence, there were far too many lonely days and nights for her while I was typing and editing in my study. She endured all this without complaining. I know it was not an easy time for her and I owe her a great deal.

This book is dedicated to Wilhelm. I wish that he will never have to face the same experiences that the soldiers on both sides did during the battle of the Somme.

Matthias Strohn

CONTENTS

CONTRIBUTORS

Sir Hew Strachan is professor of International Relations at the University of St Andrews, having previously held the post of Chichele Professor of the History of War at the University of Oxford. He is an emeritus fellow of All Souls College, Oxford and a life fellow of Corpus Christi College, Cambridge. He is a member of the Chief of Defence Staff's Strategic Advisory Panel, the Defence Academy Advisory Board, and the Council of the International Institute for Strategic Studies. A trustee of the Imperial War Museum and a Commonwealth War Graves Commissioner, he also serves on the advisory panels of the UK and Scotland for the centenary of World War I. Recent publications include *The First World War: Volume 1: To Arms* (2001), *The First World War: An Illustrated History* (2003; related to a multi-part documentary series), *Clausewitz's On War: a Biography* (2007), and *The Direction of War* (2013). He is the editor of *The Oxford Illustrated History of the First World War* (revised edition, 2014), and of various books arising from his directorship of the Oxford Changing Character of War Programme from 2004 to 2015.

Professor Lothar Höbelt was born in Vienna 1956 and graduated with honours from University of Vienna 1982. He was assistant visiting professor at the University of Chicago in 1992, associate professor of Modern History at the University of Vienna since 1997 and lecturer at Military Academy Wiener Neustadt since 2001. The main focus of his research is the history of Austria(-Hungary) in the 19th and 20th centuries. His publications include *Franz Joseph I: Der Kaiser und sein*

Reich: Eine politische Geschichte (2009), and *Die Habsburger: Aufstieg und Glanz einer europäischen Dynastie* (2009). His latest work is '*Stehen oder Fallen?' Österreichische Politik im Ersten Weltkrieg* (2015).

Dr Gerhard P. Groß is a colonel at the Bundeswehr Centre of Military History and Social Sciences in Potsdam, Germany, where he has been working as a military historian since 1996. From 1988 to 1996 he was lecturer for military history at the army military academy, Hannover. He was chief of the World War I research section, head of the department for military history of the GDR in the Warsaw Treaty Organization and the Bundeswehr, and is now head of the department of German military history to 1945. He is author of a number of books and articles dealing with the Imperial German Army and Navy, including *Mythos und Wirklichkeit: Geschichte des operativen Denkens im deutschen Heer von Moltke d.Ä. bis Heusinger* (2012), *Der Schlieffenplan: Analysen und Dokumente* (ed., with Hans Ehlert and Michael Epkenhans) (2006), *Die vergessene Front – der Osten 1914/15: Ereignis, Wirkung, Nachwirkung* (2006) and *Der Krieg zur See 1914–1918, Abteilung Der Krieg in der Nordsee, Band 7: Vom Sommer 1917 bis zum Kriegsende 1918* (2006).

Georges-Henri Soutou is emeritus professor at Paris-Sorbonne (Paris IV) University, member of the Institut de France, and chairman of ISC (Institut de Stratégie et des Conflits).

He belongs to the Diplomatic Archives Commission of the French Foreign Ministry. He is a member of the editorial board of several journals, including *Relations internationales* and *Revue historique des Armées*; he is co-editor of the *Revue d'histoire diplomatique*.

Professor Soutou works in the field of international history during the 20th century, particularly World War I, Franco-German relations and East–West relations after 1945. He has published, besides numerous articles, *L'Or et le Sang: Les buts de guerre économiques de la première guerre mondiale* (1989); *L'Alliance Incertaine: Les rapports politico-stratégiques franco-allemands, 1954–1996* (1996); *La Guerre de Cinquante Ans: Les relations Est-Ouest 1943–1990* (2001); *L'Europe de 1815 à nos jours* (2007); and *La Grande Illusion: Quand la France perdait la paix 1914–1920* (2015).

Dr James Corum teaches military history at Salford University UK, having been dean of the Baltic Defence College 2009–2014. From 1991 to 2004 he was a professor at the US Air Force School of Advanced Air and Space Studies at Maxwell Air Force Base, Alabama. In 2005 he was a visiting fellow at All Souls College, Oxford, where he held a Leverhulme Fellowship, and then an associate professor at the US Army Command and General Staff College, Fort Leavenworth, Kansas. Dr Corum is the author of several books on military history, including *The Roots of Blitzkrieg: Hans von Seeckt and German Military Reform* (1992); *The Luftwaffe: Creating the Operational Air War, 1918–1940* (1997); *The Luftwaffe's Way of War: German Air Doctrine, 1911–1945*, with Richard Muller (1998); *Airpower in Small Wars: Fighting Insurgents and Terrorists*, with Wray Johnson (2003); and *Fighting the War on Terror: A Counterinsurgency Strategy* (2007). His eighth book on Cold War history is *Rearming Germany* (2011). He is the editor in chief of the translation (from German) of the *Encyclopedia of the First World War* (2 volumes) (2012). He has also authored more than 60 major book chapters and journal articles on a variety of subjects related to air power and military history. Dr Corum served in Iraq in 2004 as a lieutenant colonel in the US Army Reserve. He holds a master's degree from Brown University, a Master of Letters from Oxford University, and a PhD from Queen's University, Canada.

Dr Stuart Mitchell is a senior lecturer in war studies at the Royal Military Academy Sandhurst where he specializes in learning, transformation and leadership in the British Army during World War I. He completed his PhD at the University of Birmingham in 2014 which looked at the learning process at the divisional level of the British Army between 1916 and 1918. Stuart's recent publications include co-editing the volume: *A Military Transformed? Adaptation and Innovation in the British Military 1792–1945* (Helion Press, 2014) and 'Jan Smuts, Paul von Lettow-Vorbeck and the Great War in East Africa' in Jonathan Krause *The Greater War: Other Combatants and Other Fronts 1914-1918* (2014). He is an associate editor of the *British Journal for Military History*, as well as a member of the British Commission for Military History, Western Front Association and the Institute for Historical Research.

Lieutenant Colonel (Ret'd) Christopher Pugsley ONZM, formerly of the New Zealand Army, has held appointments at universities in New Zealand and Australia and worked in the Department of War Studies, Royal Military Academy Sandhurst. He received his PhD from the University of Waikato with a thesis on the discipline and morale of the New Zealand Expeditionary Force in World War I. He is an adjunct professor in the School of Humanities, University of Canterbury, New Zealand and is a recipient of the Distinguished Alumni Award of the University of Waikato. He received an ONZM (Officer of the New Zealand Order of Merit) for service as a military historian in the 2015 New Year Honours List.

His publications include *Gallipoli: The New Zealand Story* (shortlisted Watties New Zealand Book of the Year 1984); *From Emergency to Confrontation: The New Zealand Armed Forces in Malaya and Borneo 1949–1966* (shortlisted Templer Medal 2004); *The Anzac Experience: New Zealand, Australia and Empire in the First World War* (shortlisted Templer Medal 2005, finalist in History, Montana New Zealand Book Awards 2005). His most recent book is *A Bloody Road Home: World War Two and New Zealand's Heroic Second Division* (shortlisted Templer Medal 2014 and Ernest Scott Prize 2015).

Professor Michael S. Neiberg is the inaugural Chair of War Studies in the Department of National Security and Strategy at the United States Army War College. His published work specializes on World Wars I and II, notably the American and French experiences. His most recent book on World War I is *Dance of the Furies: Europe and the Outbreak of World War I* (2011). The *Wall Street Journal* recently named it one of the five best books ever written about the war. In October, 2012 Basic Books published his *The Blood of Free Men*, a history of the liberation of Paris in 1944. In May, 2015 Basic published his *Potsdam: The End of World War II and the Remaking of Europe*. He is currently at work on a history of American responses to the Great War, 1914–1917.

Dr Bill Mitchinson is employed by King's College London and teaches at the Joint Services Command and Staff College, Shrivenham. He studied at the University of Leeds in the 1970s and has written and lectured extensively on the Great War for over forty years. His books include *Gentlemen and Officers* (1995), *Amateur Soldiers* (1999) and *Pioneer Battalions in the Great War* (1997). His most recent publications have concentrated on Britain's early twentieth century auxiliary forces. *Defending Albion*, which was shortlisted for the 2005 Templer Prize, examined the political and military problems created by the emergence of the Volunteer Force between 1914 and 1918; *England's Last Hope* (2008) analysed the relationship between the War Office and the Territorial Force County Associations; and *The Territorial Force at War 1914–1916* (2014) offered an assessment of the performance and contribution of the auxiliary in the first two years of the war. He is a frequent contributor at academic seminars and regularly leads staff rides of senior military personnel to the European battlefields.

Oberstleutnant Dr Christian Stachelbeck is a staff member of the German Armed Forces Office for Military History and Social Sciences in Potsdam, Germany. He was a lecturer in military history at the German officer training academy in Dresden and served as a company commander in Afghanistan (ISAF). He holds an MA from the German armed forces university Hamburg and a PhD from the Humboldt-University Berlin. His research interests are currently learning processes in the German armed forces 1871–1945. His publications include *Militärische Effektivität im Ersten Weltkrieg: Die 11. Bayerische Infanteriedivision 1915 bis 1918* (2010) (Zeitalter der Weltkriege, 6) and *Deutschlands Heer und Marine im Ersten Weltkrieg, (4) (2013)* (Militärgeschichte kompakt, 5).

Dr Jonathan Krause is a research associate at the University of Oxford working on the ARHC-funded project *Rebellion and Mobilization in French and German colonies, 1914–1918*. This project is a collaboration with scholars from France, the US and UK examining the widespread unrest that wracked France's overseas colonies during World War I, with a comparative look at German colonies. It seeks to expand our understanding of the political, social, cultural and geographic boundaries of World War I, whilst also repositioning the war as a crucial moment in the long struggle for decolonization. Jonathan is the winner of a 2014 Moncado Prize for his article 'The French Attack on Vimy Ridge, Spring 1915' (*Journal of Military History*, 2013), author of *Early Trench Tactics in the French Army: the Second Battle of Artois, May–June 1915* (2013) and editor of *The Greater War: other combatants and other fronts, 1914–1918* (2014).

Dr Matthias Strohn was educated at the universities of Münster (Germany) and Oxford. He has lectured at Oxford University, the German Staff College (Führungsakademie der Bundeswehr) and the Joint Services Command and Staff College at Shrivenham. Since 2006 he has been a senior lecturer in the Department of War Studies at the Royal Military Academy Sandhurst, and in 2011 he was also made a senior research fellow at the University of Buckingham. He holds a commission in the German army and is currently a member of the military attaché reserve. He has published widely on 20th century German and European military history and is an expert on the German Army in World War I and the inter-war period. He has advised British and German government bodies on the World War I centenary commemorations.

Major General (Ret'd) Mungo Melvin CB OBE is the author of *Manstein: Hitler's Greatest General*, first published to critical acclaim in 2010. In 2011 it was runner-up in the prestigious Westminster Prize; in 2012, it won a distinguished book award as best biography of the year from the US Society for Military History. Now retired from the British Army, General Melvin was commissioned into the Royal Engineers in 1975, saw operational service in Northern Ireland, the Middle East and the Balkans. During the latter part of his 37-year career as a member of the General Staff he specialized in strategic analysis, professional military education and doctrine. President of the British Commission for Military History, he is currently advising the British Army on the World War I centenary commemorations, and has edited the Army's battlefield guide to the Western Front (2014). He is author of the forthcoming *Sevastopol's Wars: Crimea from Potemkin to Putin* (2016), also published by Osprey. He is a senior associate fellow of the Royal United Services Institute and a senior visiting research fellow of the war studies department of King's College London. He lectures widely on strategy and military history in both the public and commercial sectors.

FOREWORD

Professor Sir Hew Strachan

The year 1916 both defined how we see World War I and redefined how warfare itself was understood. It did so because of two titanic battles, Verdun and the Somme. The latter is the subject of this book, but the former is also central to its arguments. Both were fought on the Western Front. The Great War of 1914–18 was a global war and its fronts were integrated and interdependent. Yet the epicentre of its strategic arguments and of its memorialization lies in France. Modern scholarship rightly rejects the use of words like 'sideshow' or 'indirect approach' to capture what was going on in Italy, Salonika, the Middle East or Africa – let alone in Russia, the war's other major front – but that vocabulary still conveys something important about the war's mental map, both then and now. Nowhere today remains as continuously and visibly marked by World War I as do the battlefields of north-western Europe.

We call Verdun and the Somme 'battles': the fact that we do so captures the challenges of definition which they posed for warfare itself. In 1914 a battle was still a climactic event, often lasting only a single day, and had demonstrable outcomes, at least at the tactical level and ideally at the strategic. Verdun began in February 1916 and ended in December; the Somme began in late June and ended in November. Their duration embraced months, not days, and neither could be construed as a battle in the same sense as Waterloo in 1815 or even Tannenberg in 1914.

According to those standards, Verdun and the Somme were more campaigns: chronologically extended over the 'campaigning season' and geographically contained. And yet the Napoleonic ideal of a campaign culminated with a decisive battle. Neither Verdun nor the Somme did. They ended with a whimper, not a bang, closing as the days shortened, and because they had proved more indecisive than decisive.

All three nations engaged on the Somme, the British, French and German, adopted the same nomenclature for the battle (unlike the British and German navies, who gave a different name – Jutland for the British and Skaggerak for the Germans – to the clash of their battle fleets at the end of May 1916). They were united in calling it 'the battle of the Somme'. Given that the Somme at this stage of its journey to the sea is hardly one of the great rivers of France, the choice may seem surprising, not least when the fighting sought to avoid the river rather than to use it. John Buchan, the British writer and propagandist, called it 'a curious river which strains, like the Oxus, "through matted rushy isles," and is sometimes a lake and sometimes an expanse of swamp'. For the British, the river Ancre, flowing from the north-east to Albert before it joins the Somme at Corbie, and for Buchan 'such a stream as may be found in Wiltshire, with good trout in its pools', would have provided a more apposite name. If the battle deserves the title of the Somme, it was more because it was also that of the département, the local administrative area within which the fighting occurred. Perhaps the Marne, the battle which had saved France in 1914, acted as precedent. Called the battle of the Somme virtually from its inception, nobody thought to rename it after its extent had become evident.

The French official history, Les Armées Françaises dans la Grande Guerre, devoted 'Tome IV', itself divided into three volumes, to Verdun and the Somme. The foreword to the second recognized the challenge for warfare which they created: 'these two great battles often transformed themselves into detailed fighting which tended to obscure the lines of direction'. Today's visitors have the same problem. As they follow narrow roads through rolling landscape, they struggle to place individual locations in an overall scheme or to make connections between attacks in one sector and those in another. The battlefield tourist here – more than say at Ypres or at Gallipoli, where the town and the sea provide fixed points – focuses on vignettes rather than grand designs. The connections between the two were often no clearer to the participants. Historians have sought to give greater shape to the battle, but run the risk that in doing so they may misrepresent the operational realities. In any case they have failed to find consensus, and consequently they can add to the confusion rather than clarify it.

The official historians of Germany and Britain responded to the problem identified by their French peers by sub-dividing the battle of the Somme into component parts. In 1927 the series designed for the popular market by the Reichsarchiv in Berlin, Schlachten des Weltkrieges ('battles of the world war'), produced a two-volume account of what it called Somme-Nord. It embraced the battles fought north of the river and up to the Albert–Bapaume road, and for July only. There were no comparable volumes for the fighting astride and south of the river against the French, and none for the British offensives in the subsequent months up to November. In his introduction to Somme-Nord Georg Soldan, the series editor, divided the whole battle into four phases, but the book embraced only the first and part of the second. The British official history (Military Operations: France and Belgium 1916, published in 1938) responded differently. It identified five battles within the big one: those of Albert in early July, Flers-Courcelette in mid-September, Morval and Thiepval Ridge in late September, and the Ancre in November. The battle of the Somme was now, according to the volume's title page, no longer a singular event but a plural one: 'the battles of the Somme'.

As the essays in this book make clear, the issue of whether the Somme could really be called a 'battle' was not the end of the matter. Far more important to the subsequent debates and their escalating temperature have been the other associations with the term: the idea that a great battle is inherently 'decisive' and so has demonstrable outcomes. The objectives of the Anglo-French offensive of 1916 were not obvious to several senior officers at the time, were the subjects of dispute while the battle was being fought, and have remained contentious ever since. At their heart lies the balance between futility and utility, and both sides can produce strong evidence in support of either position. Neither, however, can gainsay the fundamental ambiguity which underpinned the purposes of the offensive, and on which their arguments depend.

In terms of what would be called 'grand strategy' today (but was not then), the solution ought to be clear. At Chantilly in December 1915 the allies agreed to mount a series of linked offensives on all the fronts facing the Central Powers, so stretching the German and Austro-Hungarian reserves as they simultaneously fought in the west, east and south. Although this plan was geographically determined, in that the Entente Powers were distributed around the periphery of Europe, and so were operating on what strategists would call 'exterior lines' (while the Central Powers in Europe's heartland were on interior lines), its results would be measured less by the gaining of ground and more by the depletion of enemy resources. Its underlying assumption, therefore, was that Germany and its allies would be defeated through their exhaustion and not through battle. This did not mean there would be no battles, but it did suggest that they would be the means to another end, not ends in themselves.

On 21 March 1919, Douglas Haig subscribed at least in part to the Chantilly plan when he wrote his final despatch on leaving the command of the British Expeditionary Force. He described the fighting which began on the Somme and ended on the Sambre in November 1918 as 'a single great battle'. This was indeed one way of looking at the Western Front, at least in retrospect, but it was one whose broad brushstrokes obscured the details, the bumps on the road whose effects on the overall direction of travel created the confusion to which the French official history alluded. There were those who were prepared to countenance a longer battle for these sorts of results in the summer of 1916, although Haig was not among them. They included Ferdinand Foch, who was both French army group commander in 1916 and allied generalissimo in 1918, but neither he nor anyone else was talking about a battle which would last more than two years.

Those looking for strategic benefits from the Somme before the German surrender had to address a mixed bag. Principal among them, to the extent that it is often wrongly cited as the reason for the offensive in the first place, was the relief it provided the French Army at Verdun. This was not an outcome which could have been anticipated in December

1915, given that the German attack in February 1916 was a surprise. Undoubtedly, however, the two battles interacted. Verdun reduced the French commitment to the Somme but their commander-in-chief, Joseph Joffre, safeguarded it sufficiently to deliver the one unequivocal success on 1 July and to maintain France's contribution until November. In terms of the strategy developed in December 1915, the effects of the Somme were more mixed. At the beginning of June, almost a month before the Somme opened, the Brusilov Offensive in the east provided direct aid to the Italians, as well as to the defenders of Verdun. The Central Powers were forced to rush reserves to Galicia. Moreover, the Russian victory persuaded Romania to enter the war on the Entente side. By September 1916, with the chief of the Prussian general staff, Erich von Falkenhayn, dismissed, it looked as though Chantilly was working despite Verdun, and that for this both the French and Russians should take the bulk of the credit. And yet in the winter of 1916–17 these successes unravelled. In 1917 Russia and France confronted crises at home and in their armies. One of the most pressing reasons for a joint offensive in 1916 had been the need to support the Russians in the east with greater activity in the west, and yet, despite the strains on the Meuse and the Somme, the Germans and their allies had overrun most of Romania by December. The military problem facing Russia on its south-western front was exacerbated, not resolved. After July 1917, the month of the last Russian offensive in the east, 'the Chantilly strategy' was in ruins.

Moreover, the Chantilly strategy does not get us very far when we look at the battle of the Somme in its own terms. Its planning acquired a momentum which subsumed the overarching goals meant to underpin it. Almost immediately generals began looking for territorial objectives to give the offensive direction. However, the Somme had been chosen because it was where the British and French armies met, not because it possessed any obvious geographical aiming points. Repeatedly in 1916–18 Entente generals would target the railway junctions which sustained the German Army in France, but on the Somme the principal hubs were too distant to be realistic. Péronne became the default objective, at least for the French. The lack of clarity as to the objects of any attack, and how distant they might be and yet remain realistic, divided both the French and British command chains. Fayolle, the commander of the French 6e Armée, protested that the battle which Foch had in mind had no goal, and Foch himself frequently seemed to agree. Henry Rawlinson, commanding the British Fourth Army, worked to limit Haig's ambitions, which favoured a breakthrough – even if it was not always clear where it might be going if it were achieved.

The battle was unlikely to be guided by a single conception when its command structure was unclear. In the British memory of the war, Douglas Haig commanded at the Somme, and yet he delegated considerable responsibility to Rawlinson and later to the commander of the Reserve Army, Hubert Gough. Moreover, he was certainly not the commander if the battle is seen in alliance terms. That was Joffre: the British were still France's junior partners at the beginning of 1916, and although the balance of power changed on the Somme the command arrangements did not. Formally Joffre was Haig's principal interlocutor, but should it actually have been Foch? And how in reality could a commander command? The armies of all three nations, either before the Somme or during it, realized that in the tactical conditions of 1916 effective leadership was exercised at the level of the section, squad or platoon, not that of the army or corps. In these circumstances tactical control trumped strategic intent, and so the challenge for the general was to shape the latter in the light of the former, not vice versa.

Attrition was the expression of this effort to reconnect strategy and tactics, but it was both differently and indifferently understood. It was never clear whether it was the means to another operational end, breakthrough, or an end in itself. With their doctrines in flux, generals oscillated along this spectrum, rarely cleaving to either attrition or breakthrough with any consistency. If attrition were an end, it could be brought into harmony with the allied strategy of December 1915, and it could reintegrate the idea of battle within the war as a whole. But the only tool by which to measure the exhaustion of the enemy was the number of his casualties. It is symptomatic of the controversies surrounding the Somme that, one hundred years on, we are still no nearer agreement on the one yardstick by which its outcome might be measured.

Front lines, July to November 1916

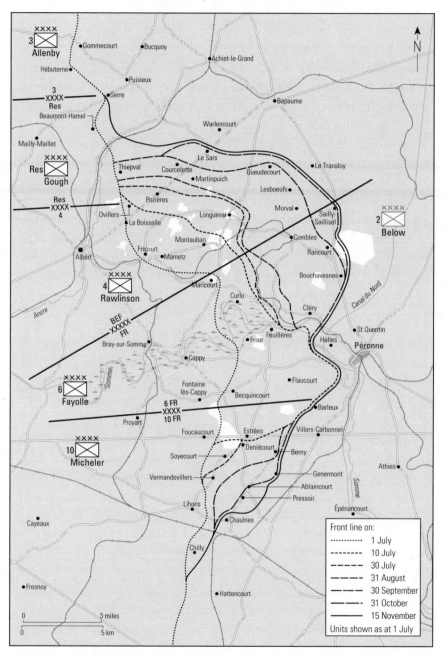

Front line on:

.... 1 July
- - - - - - - 10 July
— — — — 30 July
— — — 31 August
— · — 30 September
— · · — 31 October
——— 15 November

Units shown as at 1 July

The German and British official histories each claimed that their enemies lost more than they did. Their academic successors are not much the wiser. And were the million or so total casualties on the Somme what the Entente had meant by exhaustion in December 1915? Or had it meant economic exhaustion of the sort which prompted the German generals to call the Somme a 'battle of matériel', and caused Falkenhayn's successor, Paul von Hindenburg, to reduce his field army not by fighting but by returning men to the factories so as to increase productivity?

For some, if blood-letting had become the sole definition of victory in battle, it was not worth the price. Yet, despite the Somme, that was not a conclusion to which statesmen were drawn in December 1916. For their populations the 'blood sacrifice' deepened the commitment to the war more than undermined it. Their soldiers could not have died in vain. In Britain, as elsewhere, loss legitimized conscription precisely because the war demanded equality of sacrifice. Battle had been unable to resolve the issues dividing the two sides, and yet neither was able to take the opportunities for negotiation offered at the end of the year, first by Germany and then by the United States, to forfeit its use. The pursuit of victory remained more important than the pursuit of peace.

CHAPTER 1

THE CONTEXT OF THE SOMME

The Pripet Marshes to the Federal Reserve

Professor Dr Lothar Höbelt

The Somme was the biggest battle of 1916, and also the bloodiest. If the jury is still out as to who actually won, then that makes it a perfect symbol of what was widely seen as the futility and the senseless slaughter of the Great War. It reinforces the image of the war in 1916 as one characterized by stalemate – a stalemate that prompted the leading combatants to either find an unsatisfactory compromise solution, or to double their efforts to achieve a 'knock-out blow'.

The Central Powers go their separate ways

The Central Powers had made the most of their 'window of opportunity' that lasted until Kitchener's armies reached the trenches and as long as Germany could still boast a certain technical superiority, especially in terms of heavy artillery. Despite the dangers posed by the Italian 'intervento', the Central Powers had managed to overrun Russian Poland in the summer of 1915 and – together with their new-found Bulgarian allies – Serbia and Montenegro in the autumn. On top of this, the Western Allies had suffered a reverse in Mesopotamia in November and withdrawn from Gallipoli around the turn of the year.

The war effort in the eastern Mediterranean shifted from Gallipoli to Salonika where a few French divisions landed on 5 October 1915, the very day that the pro-Entente Venizelos government that had secretly invited them was summarily dismissed by King Constantine (who was the Kaiser's brother-in-law). Constantine wanted the Germans to either totally dislodge the Armée Française d'Orient from Salonika, or keep out of Greece. What he did not want was Greece turned into a theatre of war. Unfortunately, that is what he got. In May 1916 the Central Powers advanced a few miles into Greece. When the Greeks surrendered a fort without fighting, they unleashed a French drive to disarm the Greek army loyal to Constantine. The French encouraged the formation of a rival government in Salonika under Venizelos. An attempt to get rid of the king himself was only temporarily halted by British misgivings and French Prime Minister Aristide Briand's intimate relations with Constantine's daughter-in-law. However, Entente interference still led to fighting in Piraeus in December 1916, to anti-French guerrilla operations in the north and to a massacre of Greek villagers by Senegalese *tirailleurs* in retaliation.[1]

In military terms, the malaria-infested Macedonian theatre of war – including Albania – had become a backwater. Kaiser Wilhelm is said to have called Salonika his biggest prisoner-of-war camp, whereas Clemenceau scathingly talked about the 'gardeners of Salonika'. The British would have liked to cut their losses and leave, but French politics prevented any withdrawal.[2] Conspiracy theories had it that the Germans in turn wanted to keep the Bulgarian army busy guarding the Greek border lest it turn its energies in unwanted directions. It is more likely that the Central Powers did not pursue the Salonika angle simply because the chiefs of staff of Germany and Austria-Hungary had different plans – unfortunately for the Central Powers, they really were different plans, not just from the Salonika venture, but from each other.

The Austro-Hungarian Chief of Staff, Franz Conrad von Hötzendorf, did not succeed in persuading his German opposite number, General Erich von Falkenhayn, that they continue to eliminate the weakest links in the ring of enemies surrounding them, i.e. deliver the next blow against Italy, their treacherous ex-ally and Conrad's pet hate. Falkenhayn had already set his mind on the Verdun Offensive that started on 21 February. Germany and Austria-Hungary thus went their separate ways. Falkenhayn has long been regarded as the perfect scapegoat. In his favour it is argued that at least he realized there were no longer any easy options. The war could not be won by operational means, by some stroke of genius. It had turned into a struggle of national economies. Conrad held the opposite view, continuing to believe in a classic 'winner takes all' campaign. The Austrians would mount an offensive from the Tyrolean mountains, break through into the Venetian plains and simply cut off all the Italian armies fighting along the Isonzo. (In addition, the Austrians even planned an early exercise in strategic bombing to destroy the Italian bridges over the Piave River, but the planes got lost in the fog.) Diplomat Friedrich von Wiesner commented, 'Conrad's ideas are brilliant as such; their only fault is they don't work because he takes insufficient notice of the realities on the ground'. Chief amongst those realities was the fact that numerically the Italians were still vastly superior to the Austrians on their front – 46 against the Austrians' 32 divisions – even if on the sector chosen for the attack the Austrians achieved a temporary superiority of 16 to 10 divisions.

The Austrians did score a tactical success, advancing for about 15 miles, and taking 30,000 prisoners and 300 guns before the offensive ground to a halt.[3] Politically, the so-called 'Strafexpedition' shocked the Italian public enough to lead to the fall of the Salandra government. It was replaced by a more broadly based coalition, including the odd Socialist and Catholic politician, led by the octogenarian Piero Boselli, a personal friend of Salandra's rival, ex-Prime Minister Giolitti.[4] In retrospect, the Austrians liked to claim that they had only stopped their advance because of the unfortunate news from the Eastern Front. That was an overstatement, to say the least, if not an outright perversion of the truth; while 'unfortunate news' was a massive understatement. In the swamplands of Volhynia, a terrain in stark contrast to the Alps, dozens of miles of the Austrian front had simply collapsed.

The Somme's companion campaign: the Brusilov Offensive

Launched on 4 June, the Brusilov Offensive was probably the crucial battle of 1916. In the end, it did not turn into a great Russian success story. However, it was certainly a massive defeat for the Austrians, and a massively embarrassing one, too.

The stereotype of the fighting on the Eastern Front was of Russian steam-rolling, crudely led masses, foiled by the superior skill and equipment of the Central Powers. Generalfeldmarschall Paul von Hindenburg's and General Erich Ludendorff's reputations were built on that image. If Hindenburg's formidable public relations machine had something to do with that perception, there was still solid statistical evidence to back up most of their claims.[5] From Tannenberg onwards, Hindenburg had rarely enjoyed numerical superiority; German 6-inch howitzers were the backbone of the Eastern Front; Germans had weathered the shell crisis of 1915 better than their rivals, the Russians worst of all (often their troops even lacked rifles). On the southern half of the Eastern Front, however, the Russians facing the Austrians did not enjoy the advantage of the bigger battalions. Yet, Russian theatre commander Alexei Brusilov's forces managed to overrun the Austrian front with surprisingly little resistance.

It is estimated that the Austrians lost no less than 400,000 prisoners that summer, more than half their fighting strength on the Eastern Front. The Russians advanced more than 50 miles on a broad front. Initially, the Germans tried to organize a counterstroke from the railway junction of Kowel in the north; however, the Russians managed to punch new holes into the Austrian front further south along the Dnjestr River and retook Czernowitz, the capital of the Bukovina, on 18 June. The Austrians desperately needed German support.

Brusilov's surprise meant the Somme hit Falkenhayn while he was busy filling gaps on the Eastern Front. In 1915, for the Gorlice-Tarnów Offensive, or in 1917, for Caporetto, seven or eight German divisions

The advantage of interior lines and impact of the Brusilov Offensive

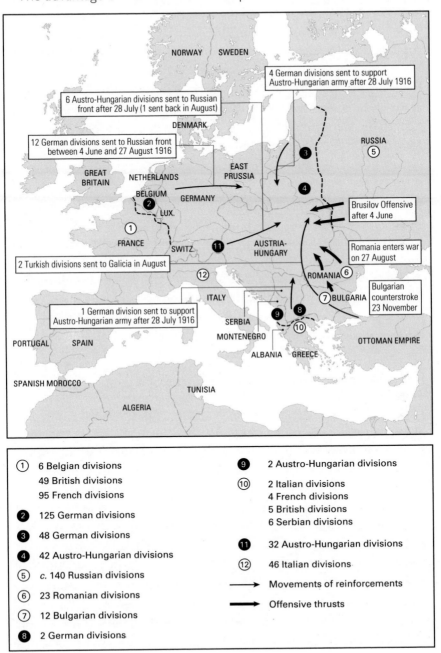

①	6 Belgian divisions	● 9	2 Austro-Hungarian divisions
	49 British divisions	○ 10	2 Italian divisions
	95 French divisions		4 French divisions
● 2	125 German divisions		5 British divisions
● 3	48 German divisions		6 Serbian divisions
● 4	42 Austro-Hungarian divisions	● 11	32 Austro-Hungarian divisions
⑤	c. 140 Russian divisions	⑫	46 Italian divisions
⑥	23 Romanian divisions	→	Movements of reinforcements
⑦	12 Bulgarian divisions	➤	Offensive thrusts
● 8	2 German divisions		

sent to stiffen the Austrians sufficed to win signal victories. In the summer of 1916, the hole in the front had already swallowed more than twice that many German divisions, and yet the Russians kept coming. From 4 June to 27 August no fewer than 12 German divisions were shifted from the Western Front to the East, the biggest contingent following further Austrian reverses after 28 July, with the Russians once again threatening Lvov; a further ten were sent from the northern, exclusively German-held part of the Eastern Front (plus one from Macedonia). Two dozen divisions, which almost equalled the size of the German General Headquarters reserve of *c*. 30 divisions, had all been spent by the middle of July. The batch of reinforcements sent in early August was thus scraped together from units that had already been severely mauled at the Somme or from newly established divisions. Even the Ottomans sent a corps to Galicia in the autumn. In turn, the Austrians themselves managed to contribute only five or six of their divisions, withdrawn from the Italian front.[6] Even the movements of those reinforcements was thrown into reverse gear once the Italians took their revenge for the 'Strafexpedition' and won their first real victory by taking Gorizia on 9 August.[7]

Romania: the unintended consequences of an untimely attack

Even once the military crisis had been more or less weathered, political disaster struck the Central Powers. The Brusilov battle had been fought on Romania's doorstep. The year before, Romania had scornfully declined to enter the war when the Russians continued to retreat during the summer of 1915. Now, the apparent Austrian collapse in Galicia finally made up their minds for them. Russia had already promised Transylvania to the Romanians if Austria-Hungary lost the war, but that offer would be withdrawn if their help arrived when it was no longer needed.[8] That is why on 27 August, Romanian Prime Minister Ion Bratianu finally declared war. In military terms, Romanian intervention did come too late to deliver the coup de grâce to the Austrians. 'If Romania had entered the war in late June instead of procrastinating until the end of August, it is conceivable that this would have proved one front too many for the Central Powers.'[9] But Romania lacked sufficient reserves of munitions to start earlier; its army of no fewer than 23 divisions 'was large in numbers but weak in training, experience, leadership and equipment, especially firepower at all levels.'[10]

By the time Romania declared war, the Central Powers had regained their ability to react adequately to the new threat facing them. Fortunately for them, August did not see any big British attack on the Somme. True, the Hungarians in Transylvania faced a few anxious moments; but just as the Austrians presented an open flank to the Romanian advance in the south-east, the Romanians, too, presented an open flank in the south-east to their eternal rivals, the Bulgarians. Hopes that Bulgaria might be scared off by the sight of Russian troops facing them turned out to be wishful thinking. Tsar Ferdinand hesitated and hedged his bets for 48 hours, then decided to stick with the Central Powers. German Generalfeldmarschall August von Mackensen managed to turn Bulgarian and Turkish troops, with just a handful of Germans and some Austrian ships, into an effective force to stab the Romanians in the back. On 23 November he crossed the Danube at Sistovo (using predecessors of World War II landing craft for the horses), thus threatening Bucharest from the rear. The Bratianu government withdrew to Jassy; British experts saw to the prior demolition of the Romanian oil wells. Within three months, Romania had been soundly defeated. Recently, the campaign has even been labelled 'the prelude to the Blitzkrieg'.[11]

Yet, despite the Central Powers' military triumph, Romanian entry into the war in 1916 had unfortunate consequences for the Central Powers. The Allied blockade was slowly taking its toll on their reserves of raw materials, but on food in particular. In the first half of 1916, more than 80 per cent of Austrian grain supplies had come from Romania. All that stopped when Romania declared war. It was not until the late spring of 1917 that supplies started flowing again. In the meantime, the Central Powers experienced their first real hunger crisis. The Christmas season of 1916 became known as the winter of the turnips. War enthusiasm reached an all-time low in the early part of 1917 (morale only fell lower in the last few weeks of the war in 1918).[17]

The Romanian campaign proved to be the high-water mark of inter-allied cooperation on the part of the Central Powers. A grand-sounding Supreme War Council was created, with Kaiser Wilhelm at the head. Austrians have long bewailed the supposed loss of independence that German overall command of the war entailed for them. But appearances were deceptive: the Central Powers' version of the Supreme War Council was first and foremost a device to make it palatable for the Bulgarians to fight alongside the Turks. The Italian front remained outside its remit. Austrian politicians in general were not at all unhappy to see Conrad's wings clipped. Kaiser Franz-Josef retained a power of veto over any decision he thought threatened the vital interests of the Austro-Hungarian Empire; needless to say, the Bulgarian tsar or the Turkish sultan did not boast any such privilege.[13]

Yet, there was one part of the leadership re-shuffle that did prove crucial in the long run. That part was a purely German, nay Prussian affair. Chancellor Theobald von Bethmann-Hollweg had long relied on playing off Falkenhayn, the technocratic 'Westerner', against Hindenburg, the wizard from the East. Encouraging the formation of a unified command in the East under Hindenburg's formal and Ludendorff's de facto leadership was part of that tactic. However, the unexpected Romanian entry sparked a crisis of nerves with the Kaiser who blamed Falkenhayn for not alerting him to that danger in time. In fact, Falkenhayn seems to have dismissed talk of a Romanian attack as Austrian scare tactics designed to wring a few more divisions out of German reserves for their pet projects; alternatively, some people have it that the Central Powers were correctly informed about the crucial date but forgot to take into account the Orthodox calendar. Thus, a wily Balkan politician like Bratianu came to push Hindenburg into the top job.[14]

Bethmann had wanted to take cover behind Hindenburg's popularity. Alas, for him Hindenburg turned out to be the proverbial sorcerer's apprentice. After the appointment of this so-called Third OHL, there was no longer anyone whom Bethmann could play off against Ludendorff or his front-man Hindenburg, as a threat of resignation by Hindenburg was enough to turn almost any argument in his favour.

The fateful decision to turn the tables on the British blockade

Gerhard Groß once compared the strategy of the Third OHL with that of a party that breezily promises tax cuts while in opposition but once they get into government discovers there is simply no money left. Hindenburg had created the impression he could win the war on his own with old-fashioned military fortitude and with none of Falkenhayn's gloomy attrition schedules. Because of his pessimistic long-term outlook Falkenhayn had begun to vehemently demand unrestricted submarine warfare in the spring of 1916 as the only way to hit back at Britain, as the cornerstone of the enemy alliance. On the face of it, the proper way to use U-boats after all was a technical matter far removed from civilian politics; but then it was probably also the most crucial foreign policy decision of the 20th century. As Supreme Commander, Kaiser Wilhelm held the key to that decision, but he was clearly unable to integrate the military and the civilian sphere properly. As a result, unpredictable Imperial moods dictated the course of strategy.[15]

In the spring of 1916, Imperial Chancellor Theobald von Bethmann-Hollweg was still successfully resisting pressure from the military to adopt unrestricted submarine warefare. The navy Chief of Staff, Admiral Henning von Holtzendorff, even agreed with him that unrestricted submarine warfare was not worth the risk of the United States entering the war. Maybe it was no coincidence that the German High Seas Fleet ventured out soon after this decision to put the U-boats on a back-burner. The unintentional result was the battle of Jutland on 31 May, a triumph for German marksmanship and engineering (as their battle-cruisers could take a lot more punishment than those of the British) but a near-disaster for the German fleet. After their battle-cruisers' initial success against Admiral David Beatty, the German High Seas Fleet got into more than one tight scrape, with the British twice 'crossing the T' in front of their battle-line, the most disadvantageous position possible in naval warfare.[16] Nightfall blinded both commanders and on its way home the German navy passed the Grand Fleet with only a few miles separating them. One damaged German battle-cruiser was even said to have been 'wandering drunkenly through the Grand Fleet' during the early hours. Indeed, for the Grand Fleet – as distinct from Beatty's unfortunate battle-cruisers – 'Jutland hardly justifies the term "battle". It had only a few intermittent minutes of shooting at shadowy silhouettes.'[17]

On the whole, the Germans were lucky to escape with a hollow tactical victory to their credit: three British dreadnoughts (out of 37) sunk versus one German (out of 21) scuttled, 6,000 sailors killed or drowned versus 2,500. The Germans won on points but nearly suffered a knock-out blow. With most of their ships heavily damaged they were not likely to repeat the performance.[18] Churchill once quipped that Admiral John Jellicoe, as the Grand Fleet's commander, 'was the only man on either side who could lose the war in one afternoon'.[19] But the battle had proven that, with all the bad luck in the world, a decisive naval defeat for Britain was still an extremely unlikely outcome.

On the other hand, Jutland was instrumental in re-directing German naval strategy towards the U-boats with a vengeance. Admiral Reinhard Scheer, commanding the German High Seas Fleet, said so in his report on 4 July.[20] Towards the end of 1916, Holtzendorff possessed at least 100 U-boats (compared to only 40 in the spring). The navy drew up huge tables of statistics to prove its assertion that within six months they would be able to starve Britain into submission, if only they were allowed to use U-boats to maximum effect.[21] To do so, they would have to gain the cooperation of what was clearly the senior service in Germany – the army leadership. The admirals had earlier managed to persuade Falkenhayn of their case. Hindenburg and Ludendorff, the lords from the Eastern marches, were non-committal, at first. However, once Hindenburg sided with the navy, Bethmann would no longer find it that easy to say no. (Even more so, as the Reichstag, or rather the Catholic Centre Party that commanded the swing votes in the German parliament, had also agreed to rely on expert advice, i.e. Hindenburg's judgment, in that respect.) It needs to be emphasized that it was not at all the famous Junker arrogance that prompted the German army leaders to provoke the United States; on the contrary, it was their pessimism that persuaded them to rely on the navy's miracle weapons. Seen in its proper perspective, for proud Prussian generals, turning the fate of the German Reich over to a few high-tech naval enthusiasts certainly was a decision born of desperation.

In Vienna, on 21 November 1916, the 86-year-old Kaiser Franz-Josef succumbed to pneumonia, having worked at his desk until a few hours before his death. His successor and great-nephew, the young Kaiser Karl, was very much taken by the sense of crisis prevalent in Vienna ever since Brusilov had launched his offensive, topped as it was by the winter of discontent. While the supply crisis persuaded Ludendorff to risk the gamble of unrestricted submarine warfare, it persuaded Karl and his Foreign Secretary Graf Ottokar Czernin that Austria-Hungary could not stand another winter of war. As a result, they were looking for a peace based on the status quo ante bellum but found that there were few kindred spirits in a position of power in either the German, or even more so, the Allied camp. In turn, the apparent unreliability of the Austrians probably further prompted the German army leadership to risk the leap into the dark. With hindsight, both sets of assumptions were wrong, as neither of them reckoned with the Russian collapse they were about to witness during 1917. Many years later, Karl's peace initiatives at least earned him beatification by Pope John Paul II, who happened to be the son of one of his NCOs. Ludendorff's decision, however, as one American author put it, managed to snatch defeat from the jaws of victory right then and there.[22]

Beyond Europe

For the Austrians, 1916 had provided a rude awakening after the euphoria of 1915. They had to be rescued by the Germans; even the Turks rushed to their help. Part of the reason that the Ottoman Empire sent whole corps of its army to different parts of Europe – Salonika, Galicia, Romania – was that Enver Pasha, the Ottoman Minister of War and the guiding spirit of the Young Turk movement, wanted to throw his weight about politically. Moreover, the withdrawal of the Allied forces from Gallipoli in January had left the Ottomans with more than half their army concentrated in the neighbourhood of Constantinople. In Mesopotamia, 'mission creep', fuelled by concern for British prestige, had led the Indian army to go for Baghdad without waiting for the necessary 'massive commitment of infrastructure resources', in particular river transport.[23] Since December 1915, its isolated spearhead division had been besieged in Kut-el-Amara, 100 miles downstream from Baghdad. Relief expeditions and half-hearted attempts to bribe the Turkish commanders both failed. After 147 days the siege ended with the surrender of *c.* 10,000 combatants on 29 April, the first time since Yorktown that such a large British force had been forced to capitulate.

However, the Ottomans were unable to turn their defensive victories into offensive strategies. Hardly any of the fantastic operations propagated by armchair strategists in Constantinople (or Berlin) turned out to be feasible: a push towards the Suez Canal in August 1916 ended in failure. Even with 16,000 camels gathered from the desert tribes, Turkish supply lines were no match for steamships, supplemented by the railway the British started to build towards Palestine next year. In Persia, an Ottoman corps escaped the stultifying heat and insect plagues of the Mesopotamian lowlands during the 'summer quarters' of 1916 to advance from Baghdad to Kermanshah and Hamadan, hundreds of miles from the nearest railheads, to re-establish the pro-German 'provisional government' of Iran.[24] Even further east, a German mission had signed a treaty with Afghanistan in January 1916 that 'nearly succeeded in involving Afghanistan in the war' –'nearly' was the operative word as the Emir was only willing to join the fight once there was a rebellion in India and Turkish troops had penetrated as far as Baluchistan.[25]

On the other hand, Turkey was faced with a new and serious challenge almost immediately after fighting ended on the Gallipoli peninsula. Russian forces began their advance in eastern Anatolia in January 1916. This offensive proved to be their most enduring success. Erzurum fell in February, Erzingjan in the summer. Logistical challenges prevented the Turks from reacting in force – the reserves sent to Armenia did not enter combat until early autumn. There were no proper rail links between Constantinople and the Eastern theatre of war. The Black Sea might have provided an alternative way to supply reinforcements, but the German battle-cruiser, *Goeben*, which had been turned over to the Turks at the war's beginning, no longer ruled the waves between the Straits and the Crimea because the Russian Black Sea fleet, laid down in 1911, had finally come of age. In 1916, it was the Russians who made use of seaborne supply lines.[26] What passed for front lines in Asia Minor stabilized in an arc equally distant from the Russian-held port of Trabzon and the fragments of the Baghdad railway.

The year 1916 is also famous for the Arab rising. In June 1916, Sherif Huseyn, ruler of Mecca and protector of the holy places of Islam, finally broke with the Ottoman government. Yet, for all the romance of Lawrence of Arabia and his *Seven Pillars of Wisdom*, the military effects of the rebellion can easily be overstated. Within the Arab peninsula, the Sherif was supported by the British authorities in Egypt; his rivals, the Saudis, were wooed by the Indian government but remained neutral; the Shammar tribe supported the Ottomans.[27] In late 1916, the Turks were only stopped from eliminating the Arab strongholds on the Red Sea by British naval gunnery. Lawrence's guerrillas did not succeed in permanently interrupting the Hejaz railway until August 1918; they proved unable to conquer Medina until January 1919.[28]

The Ottomans actually intended to cut their losses and evacuate Medina in the spring of 1917 but were thwarted by the obstinacy of their local commander. However, in terms of pinning down Ottoman forces, numbers alone did not count. What the Ottoman Empire lacked was equipment, munitions, and infrastructure, not recruits. If anything, in terms of the numbers game, the Ottomans themselves proved to be a most effective magnet for Allied troops. Their Austrian and German allies always used to look down at the sloth, corruption and mismanagement that was endemic to the Ottoman Empire. Yet, the fact remains that the Ottoman Empire kept a lot of British and Russian forces occupied, meaning that they could not be used elsewhere. At the end of the war, the British had employed more than 1 million men to keep their 20 divisions in the Middle East in fighting condition.

A debate has recently started as to the diversionary effects of the African campaigns of Paul von Lettow-Vorbeck. After February 1916, Lettow-Vorbeck's East African *askaris* were the only German forces left in Africa. During 1916, they faced a South African force, much larger though weakened by malaria and mounted on horses threatened by tse tse flies. In August, Lettow-Vorbeck was forced to give up the central highlands of Tanganyika and withdraw to the jungle in the southern corner of the colony. Lettow-Vorbeck always justified his determination to keep fighting by the overriding need to help the home front by drawing off enemy forces. Detractors have argued that the sort of troops employed against him – Indians, South Africans, the newly recruited King's African Rifles – were unlikely to be sent to Europe. However, in terms of both money and shipping the East African campaign did prove to be disproportionally costly for London.[29]

In between East Africa and the Ottoman Empire, the Sanussi brotherhood's initial advance into the Western Desert had been stopped by the British at the battle of Agagia near Sidi Barani on 24 February. The Sanussi held on to a few oases in the interior of Egypt until October; above all they and their allies continued to dominate most of Italian-claimed Libya, supported every now and then by German U-boats and Turkish officers.[30] Further south, in the Ogaden, Mohammed ben Abdallah Hassan, nicknamed the 'Mad Mullah', had proved an irritant to both the Italians and the British in Somaliland since the turn of the century. Apart from the Ottomans and their forces in Yemen, close to Aden, he was also supported by the deviant Ethiopian Emperor Ligg Jasu who had converted to Islam and celebrated the alliance by marrying one of the Mad Mullah's daughters. In September 1916, however, Ligg Jasu was deposed by his French-supported nephew Ras Tafari, the future Emperor Haile Selassie, who joined the fight against the Mad Mullah.

Incidentally, African considerations played a big part in the attitudes of the Iberian states towards the Great War. Portugal had been engaged in occasional fighting against German forces in Angola since 1914. It was not until March 1916 that Lisbon actually decided to break off relations with Germany and declare war. At the same time, the Spanish authorities enraged the French by their hospitable treatment of the German forces who had crossed into their Riu Muni colony from the Cameroons.[31] The Spanish king Alfonso XIII was the son-in-law of the nominal Austrian Commander-in-Chief, Archduke Frederick; he was the monarch most often mentioned when people looked for someone who could plausibly start negotiations for a compromise peace. For Portugal, however, a compromise peace between the great powers was exactly what she had most reason to be afraid of. Once Britain and

Germany compromised, they might easily do so at the expense of the Portuguese colonial empire. Germany might well be compensated for Alsace with all sorts of African territories. Portugal thus had an incentive to reinsure herself against any such plans by openly siding with Britain. As an unsolicited extra, the republican Costas government somewhat recklessly also offered to send two divisions to Flanders (and as a result was toppled by a coup d'état of disgruntled army officers in late 1917).

Wilson and Warburg

In terms of neutrals who had yet to make up their minds, Portugal – like everybody else – was of course dwarfed by the United States. Washington had come close to a break with Germany because of the *Lusitania* in May 1915; in 1917, Wilson finally entered the war when the Germans returned to unrestricted submarine warfare. Most of 1916, however, was characterized by quite a different trend, one that was far from favourable to the Allies. On the one hand, relations between Berlin and Washington improved after Bethmann had won his round of sparring with Falkenhayn and Tirpitz in May. For a few months, the U-boat campaign was stopped altogether; in late summer, U-boat commanders were told to follow the rules of cruiser warfare, with no sinking of ships on sight, even within British territorial waters. On the other hand, friction between the Allies and the US soared. 'Black lists' of US firms suspected of trading with the Germans and 'bunkering agreements' that forced US ships on conform to blockade procedures did not go down well with the US public.

Above all, there was an election campaign going on in the United States. Wilson had only won the presidency in 1912 because the Republicans had split and fielded two rival candidates. This time, they agreed on a compromise candidate, Charles Hughes, but were still caught on the horns of a dilemma as far as the war was concerned. Republican supporters included the bulk of pro-British East Coast interventionists like ex-President Theodore Roosevelt, but also the bulk of pro-German isolationists in the mid-West like Mayor Thompson ('Kaiser Bill') of Chicago. Wilson, with his power base in the solid South, united by the memory of the War between the States, magisterially rose above these feuds with his slogan: 'He kept us out of the War'. As a result, he lost New York but narrowly won the election in the West.

Wilson had been rebuffed when the British cabinet voted against his confidant Colonel House's initiative for a compromise peace in May.[32] The President wanted to wait until his re-election before he tried again, with no better results, in mid-December. Even before he launched his new initiative, however, the US had directed a potentially crippling blow at the Allied war effort. On 28 November, the Federal Reserve Board advised American banks that 'it was not in the interest of the country at this time that they invest' in British treasury bills.[33] Some saw the circular as the result of a wicked pro-German (and Jewish) conspiracy.[34] After all, German-born Paul Warburg figured prominently among the board members of the 'Fed'. In fact, the Fed's statement was mild compared to the draft prepared by Wilson, who wanted to put extra pressure on the Allies to listen to his peace proposals. The circular simply represented sound financial advice: Britain, as the Allies' banker, was no longer a sound investment. Within the first two years of war, exports to the Allies had already succeeded in wiping out the whole of the external debt the US had accumulated over the last century. It was extremely doubtful whether any further advances towards British war costs would ever be re-paid (as indeed they weren't). Britain needed at least 75 million dollars a month to maintain its war effort. The Chancellor of the Exchequer reckoned they would run out of cash around April 1917, unless they could secure fresh loans from the US. Thus, just as the Lloyd George government was taking over, committed to a knock-out blow against Germany, the financial props of any prolonged war effort were about to be knocked from under their feet.

Prospects for 1917

Thus, at the end of 1916, the Allies faced a rather grim prospect. Fortunately for them, so did the Central Powers, who could not foresee that within a few weeks Russia would be gripped by revolution. In the end, it was Ludendorff who lost his nerve first and undid all of Wilson's and Warburg's splendid work by fatally provoking the USA. The Russian Revolution and the American debut on the world stage combined to turn 1917 into a dramatic '*Weltwende*', a turning point of world history. None of these developments could have been predicted during 1916, maybe the most typical and emblematic year of the Great War, characterized by trench warfare at its worst (maybe excepting Passchendaele), growing shortages of food and political indecision.

The dissatisfaction with the inability of either side to achieve a real breakthrough in 1916 gave rise to two opposing schools of thought. On the one hand, the idea of a compromise peace gained ground: from McKenna and Lord Lansdowne to Bethmann (hamstrung as he was by his generals), Charles I and Briand (with all the caveats provoked by the murky state of French politics).[35] On the other hand Ludendorff and Lloyd George, later on also Clemenceau, argued for more focused, better organized, more ruthless, maybe even slightly totalitarian, versions of the war effort. This kind of 'war socialism' was spearheaded by conventional patriots, yet far removed from the cosy and libertarian conservatism of the pre-war years. In the end, the proponents of the knock-out blow had their way; yet, to some extent, they still had to dance to the tune of the Wilsons and Lenins, very different in their way of thinking, yet united by their anti-imperialist agenda.

CHAPTER 2

ATTRITION OR ANNIHILATION?

The battle of the Somme in the context
of German strategy in 1916

Oberst Dr Gerhard Groß

At first glance, 1915 was the most successful year of World War I for the
Central Powers. In the West, the German troops had successfully warded
off French offensives in the Artois and the Champagne regions. In the East,
the breakthrough at Gorlice-Tarnów had brought the Russian western
front to a collapse, and the subsequent offensive penetrated far into Russia.
Even though Russia was not forced into making peace, the victories in the
East had a great strategic impact on the overall conduct of the war. Not
only was Romania dissuaded from following Italy into the war on the side
of the Allies, but Bulgaria was encouraged to join the Central Powers. This
secured victory in the campaign against Serbia and, consequently, the land
connection to the Ottoman Empire. Furthermore, the Central Powers' ally
Turkey had succeeded in warding off the Allied attacks on Gallipoli.

These successes, on a multitude of fronts, were achieved thanks to masterful exploitation of the interior lines of communication – the well-developed railway system which allowed the fast transportation of forces between geographically distant fronts, granting them the element of surprise and enabling them to achieve temporary local superiority.

While many Germans foresaw a bright future based on these successes, the Chief of the Oberste Heeresleitung (Supreme Army Command, OHL), General Erich von Falkenhayn, evaluated the situation more soberly. Though the Central Powers had achieved the greatest success of World War I on the Eastern Front, the Russian army had not been annihilated, and continued to be a force to be reckoned with.[1] This left Germany fighting a two-front war, a war that Falkenhayn thought they could not win due to the Allies' superiority of resources in terms of economy, equipment, and personnel. He was convinced that Germany should aim to form a centre of gravity to force a decision on one front. He assumed that the Allies would better coordinate their attacks in the coming year, thus significantly complicating or even making impossible the movement of troops on the interior lines of communications.

The overall situation for the Central Powers was therefore tense: the successes achieved in 1915 were only of operational nature and not strategic. In order to achieve a decisive victory, the successes of 1915 needed to be exploited as quickly as possible.[2] Based on the economic and internal situation of the Central Powers in the coming year, Falkenhayn was determined to force a decision in the West in favour of the Central Powers, either of political or military nature.

At a briefing with the Chief of Staff of 6. Armee, Generalleutnant Hermann von Kuhl, at the end of November 1915, Falkenhayn brought up the question of plans for 2016:

> In what way will we continue our operations? The Serbian matter is finished, connection with Turkey has been established, some of our divisions are already in redeployment. We do not consider chasing any phantastic projects like Egypt. Attack on France? Hardly, which means, not very promising. Attack on Italy will also not be too advantageous. Another attack against Russia? Low chances, no objective, they will evade further. So what to do?[3]

These words contain neither any clear statements on the future plans of the OHL for the upcoming year – which Kuhl had certainly expected from his superior – nor any clear guidance on future conduct to one of the most important Western Front commanders. Falkenhayn's elaborations become understandable when set against the background of his position within the empire's power structure.

Despite the indisputable military successes of the previous months, Falkenhayn was under great pressure in late 1915. Since the defeat at Ypres in 1914, his conduct of the war had come under criticism from both the political leadership, through Imperial Chancellor Theobald von Bethmann-Hollweg, and the high-ranking army leadership. The Commander-in-Chief of 6. Armee, Prince Rupprecht von Bayern, one of the most prominent commanders in the West, simply thought him the wrong appointment.[4] The OberOst (Supreme Commander East) Generalfeldmarschall Paul von Hindenburg and General Erich Ludendorff had continually questioned Falkenhayn's leadership since his takeover of command. They accused him of planning a lengthy war of attrition that could not be won. They called him a waverer, accusing him of lacking the will and the daring to make a decisive strike – where was the strategic breakthrough, the great operational decision-making battle in the East or West that had been at the core of German military thinking for so many years?

While Falkenhayn did not believe in the possibility of a war-deciding victory over Russia, Hindenburg and Ludendorff considered the Eastern Front not a mere sideshow, but the main theatre of war. The dispute over where to place the operational strategic focus continued to smoulder even after the 1915 success in the East.[5]

Unlike Hindenburg and Ludendorff, Falkenhayn was formulating strategy that integrated military and political elements. In the aftermath of the failed German breakthrough in Flanders in 1914 he had realized that the army could not enforce a 'victory-based' peace against the Allies by military means alone. Because of the Allies' superiority of resources he considered the only possible peace to be one based upon negotiations, and in anticipation of this, Germany needed to be in a strong military position. 'If we don't lose the war, we have won it.'[6] It was these or similar words that he used in mid-November 1914 to give the Chancellor an update of the situation. Brutally honest, Falkenhayn told Bethmann that the army would not be able to ensure a military victory, and so a political solution to the conflict had to be urgently sought.

Falkenhayn even went a step further and proposed to the Chancellor a way to implement his political and strategic concepts. As he considered Russia – due to its size and available manpower – to be unconquerable, the only option was to force Russia into a separate peace, after which France would be likely to make peace. This would leave Great Britain isolated, at which point it could be defeated by the German Navy.

But Bethmann did not trust Falkenhayn's assessment of the political or military situation, and he personally wanted military successes. Since Falkenhayn did not promise him military success, he turned to the men who seemed to be offering it on a silver platter – Hindenburg and Ludendorff. Over the following months, the chancellor and OberOst jointly worked towards getting Falkenhayn replaced.[7] Falkenhayn was therefore in charge of the Central Powers' overall conduct of war, but was trying to defend himself against internal conspiracies. Falkenhayn's plans did receive decisive support from the Kaiser himself, who had thus far withstood all attempts to dismiss Falkenhayn from his position as the Chief of OHL. But if Falkenhayn's plans failed in 1916, the question would not be whether but when he would be replaced. It is therefore unsurprising that in late 1915, Falkenhayn was discussing his operational planning with only his closest confidants.

In winter 1915, Falkenhayn realized that a separate peace with Russia was not feasible; as a consequence, and despite his doubts that this could be achieved, he now concentrated on achieving a military success that would, hopefully, bring the war to an end within a year. His plan was to conduct a decisive offensive in the West. The forces for this were to be created by transferring troops from the Eastern and Balkan fronts. As a consequence, he again refused the OberOst's plan to shift the strategic focus to the East. This also applied to offensives in the other secondary theatres of war. At the end of 1915, Falkenhayn's strategic priorities led to a disagreement with the Austrian Commander-in-Chief, Franz Conrad von Hötzendorf, who suggested a joint Balkans offensive or even an offensive against Italy.[8] For

Falkenhayn, there was no alternative to an offensive in the West. As far as he was concerned the only decisions left to make were about when, where, and how the offensive in the West should be launched.

Taking the offensive

How was the offensive to be conducted using the existing forces? An obvious option was a large-scale breakthrough. For this purpose, however, it was necessary to form an operational army reserve. As a result of reorganization and establishment processes, 159 infantry divisions were subordinate to the OHL in late 1915; 118 of which – about 2,400,000 soldiers – were deployed on the Western Front. Twenty of these formed the army reserve, which could be increased to 25.5 divisions through the withdrawal of formations from other fronts. This was not as many as Falkanhayn would have wished, but it was enough to enable an offensive in the West.

The OHL, in collaboration with the armies in the West, had been planning for a decisive breakthrough in the West since early 1915. The army commanders had made several suggestions. In the summer of 1915 Falkenhayn seems to have given preference to a breakthrough at the common boundary between the Allied forces between Arras and Albert, to separate the British and French formations. This was not least because he considered the British to be the Empire's main opponent. He wanted to break their will in order to achieve a military solution as a basis for peace negotiations. Furthermore, he estimated the British formations in France were weaker than the French forces, anticipating that the newly established British formations would not yet be fully operational due to their lack of training.

Falkenhayn's plan was that a diversionary attack against Belfort (Operation *Schwarzwald*) would fix the French reserves far away from the Somme River before an offensive was launched against the British. But he began to lose confidence in the plan when the intelligence service of the OHL illustrated the Allies' superior numbers in France. According to their intelligence, approximately 2.4 million German soldiers were facing approximately 3.5 million Allied soldiers, who also had better equipment. In the face of the Allied superiority and against the backdrop of the successful defence in the Champagne region despite a clear local inferiority of numbers, could a mass breakthrough through the enemy's lines be successful? This question was the focus of the OHL's considerations at the end of 1915.

The endeavours of the Central Powers to at least balance the enemy's superior numbers by forming a joint centre of gravity in the West in 1916, as they had done in 1915, did not succeed. The German suggestion to move the released Austro-Hungarian divisions in France was rejected by Conrad. Against Falkenhayn's explicit objection, Conrad planned an attack in South Tyrol. In planning for their separate offensives, both Conrad and Falkenhayn mistakenly assumed the Russian army would not be able to conduct a large-scale offensive in the near future. The Central Powers had made neither political nor military use of their 1915 victories. Instead of forming a clear centre of gravity, as had worked so well the year before, they were pursuing separate and uncoordinated strategic objectives which supported only their own individual interests.

The battle of Verdun

On 8 December 1915, Falkenhayn decided to attack Verdun. Why he chose to attack the strongest fortress of France is a question that has interested historians ever since the war, not only because of the significance of his decision for the German conduct of operations in World War I, and because the name 'Verdun' is synonymous with the insanity of war in both Germany and France, but also because no evidence survives to shed light on Falkenhayn's decision-making process and his strategic approach for 1916. Due to the lack of sources, nearly all researchers after the war resorted to Falkenhayn's notes for a situation briefing of Wilhelm II shortly before Christmas 1915, which were published in 1919 in his memoirs.[9]

There has always been doubt that these notes, referred to as 'Weihnachtsdenkschrift' ('Christmas Memorandum'), actually date from the time of the briefing, or accurately represent Falkenhayn's reasoning at the time, but in the absence of any other sources they were until recently used as the basis for all descriptions of the OHL strategy in 1916. Even though Falkenhayn most likely never presented this entire 'memorandum' to Wilhelm II, it contains thoughts that he repeatedly stated in talks with staff and which formed the basis for his strategic considerations. There are many indications that aspects of the notes were 'contrived' by Falkenhayn as a justification after the war but the ideas laid out in the memorandum have, nevertheless, coined the picture of Falkenhayn as an attrition strategist and of the battle of Verdun as a 'blood mill' for nearly a century.

The notes begin with a strategic general overview. According to Falkenhayn, though Russia was not defeated by the successful offensive of the Central Powers its offensive power was broken. The Serbian army was destroyed, Italy successfully stopped and France was strained to near breaking point as regards its economy and military. The real opponent of the Central Powers – Great Britain – was weakened, too, but its will to break Germany was unbroken. Great Britain's goal was to exhaust Germany through its superior resources of personnel and equipment. Therefore, it was necessary was to take away Great Britain's confidence in its ability to achieve this goal. To attack the British on the Western Front would prove difficult. Due to the nature of the terrain, the conditions in Flanders were not favourable for an offensive. In Falkenhayn's view a breakthrough seemed tactically unfeasible. An opponent with intact morale and barely inferior numbers would quickly seal any gap. In addition, it was nearly impossible to command and control such a large-scale breakthrough attempt. And finally, the OHL did not have available the 30 divisions thought necessary to achieve a great operational breakthrough. A decisive breakthrough in the British front, Falkenhayn concluded, would thus not make sense, unless the opportunity for a counter-thrust opened up. Great Britain could only be attacked via its allies. But even if great successes arose out of that, there was no certainty of strategic victory. Thus all assets, even unlimited submarine warfare, had to be used to force Great Britain to its knees.

Falkenhayn then discussed which ally of Great Britain Germany should attack. Because of the geographical characteristics, he thought, like Schlieffen, that an offensive against Russia would be hopeless.

A victory over Italy would not have the desired effect, but if France could be convincingly weakened, the French population would no longer support the war, and Great Britain's main support would disappear. This would not require a mass breakthrough of the French lines, because directly behind the French front were targets which would achieve the desired success with limited means, because France would deploy every soldier it had to hold Belfort or Verdun. Such a regionally confined operation would not require the commitment of all German reserves. In addition, Allied relief attacks could be warded off as Germany was able to increase, reduce or cancel its offensive flexibly at any time. For geographical reasons, Falkenhayn opted to attack the fortress of Verdun. After the defeats in autumn 1915, it was thought that the French Army had low morale and would be tempted by a local invasion to perform a counter-attack. Artillery placed on the heights surrounding Verdun would gun down the French troops. Verdun would become the 'blood mill' of the French Army without the German troops suffering excessive losses.

There were sound tactical reasons for choosing to attack the fortress of Verdun: the outdated nature of much of its fortifications, the nature of the surrounding terrain, and its proximity to German lines all offered advantages to German attackers. In order to forestall a potential Allied offensive, the attack, codenamed *Gericht* (*Judgement*) was to be launched in spring. In early January 1916, the attack plan was prepared: aided by surprise and supported by heavy artillery, the attackers would swiftly take the eastern bank of the river. On 11 February, Falkenhayn explained his plans to the Chief of the General Staff for the Western Front to seize the fortress in a fast and focused attack. As Rupprecht's diary entries state: 'He wanted the decision in spring, but declared a breakthrough impossible – so how should the transition from trench warfare to mobile warfare be enforced differently'.[10] it is obvious that he, and probably many other high-ranking officers, did not understand Falkenhayn's strategy.

This was probably because Falkenhayn's true intentions were hidden by the secrecy he was employing to try to protect himself against his internal enemies. The result was that the officers each interpreted his words differently. Knobelsdorf, for example, was convinced that the objective of the attack was the fortress of Verdun. Other participants saw the plan as confirmation that Falkenhayn had no strategic concept. Others regarded the plan as an attrition strategy, a betrayal of the Empire's annihilation strategy.

Based on new source material,[11] historians now conclude that Falkenhayn had not categorically turned away from the German annihilation strategy – the attrition was only a means to the end by wearing down the opponent. Falkenhayn did not plan to 'bleed out' the opponent but aimed at a war-deciding breakthrough with subsequent mobile warfare which would open up the option to make peace. The initial breach would take place indirectly through exhausting the enemy in a counter-attack against a decisive German attack. Falkenhayn hoped that, in response to a precarious situation at Verdun, the British would launch a relief attack in the Artois with their under-trained formations. He planned to throw a German counter-attack into this and achieve the breach he thought would otherwise be impossible due to the strength of the defenders. If the British attack did not happen, he hoped that the French would throw everything they had into recapturing the high ground. Because of the terrain and the superior German artillery they would suffer very high losses, and the remaining, demoralized French soldiers would then be pursued and broken. Falkenhayn would hold back strong reserves, which would be ready to achieve a breakthrough in the course of the pursuit. If this succeeded against the British in the Artois north of the Somme River, the plan was to separate them from the French forces, press them against the Channel and drive them off the Continent. If the breakthrough at Verdun proved successful, the French front was to be cleared up towards the west.

On 21 February, after several hours of heavy barrage with 1,250 guns, a total of 140,000 soldiers in eight and a half divisions set out to attack Verdun. This started a battle which lasted until mid-December. In the first days, the attack went according to plan. On 24 February, Fort Douaumont fell. The way to capturing the eastern ridge of heights seemed open. Falkenhayn's strategic plan seemed to work, but soon further German attacks bogged down and the French front stabilized. The attack on the western bank, starting on 6 March, did not change this. The battle became more and more one of attrition.

In early June, the Imperial Headquarters displayed a hint of optimism. Although the offensive at Verdun had not brought the desired success, the Russian relief offensive at Lake Narach, which had started on 18 March following an urgent request by the French, had collapsed after heavy losses within a few days. Falkenhayn's considerations in the East seemed to work. In addition, the Austrians' Tyrol Offensive, launched on 13 May, had succeeded against all odds, and all signs pointed towards the British making preparations for a larger offensive. Would Falkenhayn's strategy be crowned by success despite all the difficulties at Verdun?

In truth, Falkenhayn knew that the apogee of the German offensive was almost past. Meanwhile, further cornerstones of his strategy had broken off. From a tactical perspective, the artillery had not been as disruptive as anticipated. The French at Verdun were far from being exhausted – on the contrary, the German divisions were in danger of being exhausted. The German reserves melted away in the 'blood mill' of Verdun. In addition, the French Commander-in-Chief, Général Joseph Joffre, had prevented the commander-in-chief of the British Expeditionary Force (BEF), General Sir Douglas Haig, from deploying his formations immediately at the start of the German offensive as a relief, thus avoiding Falkenhayn's trap.

Falkenhayn knew that his plans had failed. At the end of May, he told the Chief of the General Staff, Western Front, that there were disappointments and that the Verdun operation would not decide the war. But, and here his justification begins, the objective of containing the French Army and breaking its offensive capabilities had been achieved. Kuhl comments on Falkenhayn's explanations with the words: 'Above all, he does not seem to know what should happen next.'[12] Only marginally noticed by the OHL, the failure of the ocean-going fleet in the battle of the Skagerrak (the German name for the battle of Jutland) at the end of May meant a further strategically detrimental decision for Germany. Into this unstable situation, Russia launched the large-scale Brusilov Offensive on 4 June across a wide front. The offensive came as a complete surprise to the Central Powers, and disrupted large sections of the Anglo-Hungarian forces within a few days. Although the Austrians immediately stopped their Tyrol Offensive and moved troops to the

Eastern Front, they were unable to stop the Russian offensive. Only when Falkenhayn released the army reserve divisions could the Eastern Front be stabilized.

On the defensive

Only three weeks after the Brusilov Offensive had begun, the Anglo-French attack along the Somme River started with a massive artillery barrage on 24 June. The artillery fire continued over the next days with alternating intensity, until on 1 July, the Allied infantry launched their attack, with the British leading the offensive because of the French losses at Verdun. What Falkenhayn had hoped for – a British counter-attack near the Verdun battlefield – now became reality. Contrary to his expectation, however, the British had not rushed hastily into the attack but had deliberately completed their preparations, sought coordination with the Russians, and started their offensive supported by the French. Despite the enormous British losses suffered in the first days of the Somme Offensive, it was out of the question for the German forces to launch the planned counter-attack. Not only had the Germans suffered substantial losses at Verdun, but the Allied attack was relentless. Even though 1 July saw the largest casualty figures in one day for any British force in history, the Allies resolutely kept up the attack on German positions for weeks, because the Germans continued to attack Verdun until mid-July. Almost up until the launch of the Somme Offensive, Falkenhayn had continued to assume that the Allies would attack in the Artois region. He therefore assigned reserves to 2. Armee on the Somme River very late, nearly too late. Although he stopped the Verdun Offensive after the last unsuccessful attack on Verdun, holding the front at the Somme River was only possible with the greatest effort. Falkenhayn reacted to the Allied offensive with an extensive regrouping. All forces north of the Somme River were consolidated into 1. Armee, all forces south of the Somme into 2. Armee. Combined with 6. Armee, they formed Heeresgruppe Kronprinz Rupprecht (Army Group Crown Prince Rupprecht) with General Fritz von Loßberg, the leading German defence strategist appointed Chief of Staff of 1. Armee. Over the next weeks, the

German defenders suffered high losses and were gradually pushed back, although a breakthrough was not achieved by the Allies. Falkenhayn had to admit that the planned strategic counter-thrusts had to be postponed, justifying to himself that Verdun and the Somme River had illustrated the impossibility of a massive breakthrough.

At the end of July, the Central Powers, fighting along interior strategic lines, saw themselves exposed to heavy concentric attacks on exterior lines. The attack on Verdun, which had been launched with so much hope, had failed; at the Somme River, the army had mobilized all available forces to repel the Allied attacks and nevertheless suffered terrible losses; in early August, the Italians resumed their attack on the Isonzo River. Furthermore, the Brusilov Offensive threatened the cohesion of the Eastern Front. The culmination of the strategic crisis was approaching.

Just when the situation seemed to ease in late August, Romania entered the war on the Allies' side on 27 August. The Allied all-fronts attack reached its climax. Falkenhayn, who had not expected the Romanians to enter the war, was completely taken by surprise. The Kaiser, his nerves strained by the tense military situation, suffered a severe shock when told of the news during his evening card game. He wanted to request peace immediately. Overwhelmed by the situation, he finally acquiesced to the long-standing pleading of Falkenhayn's opponents and dismissed him. Although Romania's entry into the war was the occasion for Falkenhayn's dismissal, his position had become untenable because of Verdun and the lack of success in the West. On 29 August, Wilhelm II appointed Hindenburg as Chief of the General Staff and Ludendorff as Erster Generalquartiermeister (First Quartermaster General). In view of the precarious military situation and as a consequence of the Oberste Heeresleitung reshuffle, the Central Powers agreed on 6 September that the German Kaiser – and thus the German OHL – were to command the operations of the allied Central Powers. Although the Western Front situation was critical due to the continuing fighting at the Somme River, the new OHL leadership decided, based on plans of the old OHL, to form a distinct centre of gravity and to conduct an immediate offensive against Romania. Falkenhayn was put in command of the newly established 9. Armee. Within weeks, the Romanian Army had been defeated and the Central Powers were now able to exploit the Ploiesti oil fields and the Romanian food resources. Despite heavy losses, the Central Powers' victory had ultimately stabilized the situation at the Eastern Front at the end of 1916.

Hindenburg and Ludendorff: a new strategy?

One of the first official actions of the new OHL was to cease all attacks at Verdun and assume a defensive posture. At the Somme River, the Allied offensive continued despite the high losses and the minor successes. They fought for every inch of ground. The battle became one of pure attrition. Simultaneously, it became a proving ground for the development of modern mobile defence and assault force tactics.[13] The last British attack failed in mid-November. Over nearly five months, the British had pushed back the German front by only a few miles and had suffered dreadful losses. They shared the same fate as the Germans at Verdun. After heavy French counter-thrusts in October and December, the Germans had to abandon all captured areas and were back in their initial positions by the end of 1916.

Soon after taking control of the OHL and German strategy, Hindenburg and Ludendorff had to accept that the character of war had changed. Only two days after taking up office, they presented a comprehensive armament and economy programme. This Hindenburg programme was designed to make the German Reich survive the war of attrition. The annihilation concept temporarily faded into the background. But the aim remained to annihilate the enemy if possible in large offensive operations and thus bring about victory. Having understood the military reality facing the OHL, Hindenburg and Ludendorff did not move the strategic focus towards the East, as they themselves had always demanded, but instead stabilized the Western Front. Bearing the overall military responsibility, they had to accept the overall strategic situation and realize that, considering the operational-strategic general condition in the East, only political change could lead to a decision. This insight would lead to the German secret service organizing Lenin's railway passage through Germany in 1917, which eventually led to the October Revolution in Russia. In addition to the option of ending the war in the East politically through a revolution, the OHL wholeheartedly backed unlimited submarine warfare. A maritime war of attrition was to force Great Britain to its knees, therefore opening up the option of victorious peace. Falkenhayn and his successors both agreed in this matter. Ultimately, all three of them had no idea how Great Britain, protected behind the steel hulls of the Royal Navy, could be persuaded to make peace even after withdrawal from the Continent. This was a strategic problem which even Napoleon had not been able to solve and which in Germany had neither been contemplated by the political leadership nor the Admiralty or army General Staff.

Different strategic concepts

At the beginning of 1916, the strategic situation looked favourable for the Germans and their allies. Despite severe doubts, Falkenhayn hoped that he would be able to bring the war to an end in 1916 and, for the sake of preventing a war of attrition that Germany could not win, he planned for a decision in the West. In his view, this could only be achieved by delivering a decisive blow against Great Britain, Germany's main enemy. The German offensive at Verdun was only the first step in Falkenhayn's strategic plan for 1916. A hasty British offensive as the answer to the German offensive at Verdun would give the Germans the possibility to defeat the British forces in a mobile battle, then turn against the French and thus bring the war to a successful conclusion. This implies that the battle of the Somme fitted well into Falkenhayn's plan. So, why did it not result in the defeat of the Entente forces in the west? A number of factors contributed to this: firstly, the coordinated efforts of the Allies to crush the Central Powers by offensives on several fronts showed had the effect that the Germans did not have enough reserves to conduct the mobile defensive–offensive battle that Falkenhayn had envisaged. Secondly, Verdun had turned into the 'blood-mill at the Meuse' and used up more resources that initially planned. Finally the fact that the Somme offensive was not a hasty one, as hoped by Falkenhayn, but a meticulously planned offensive that could rely on logistical superiority, presented the Germans with a different situation than hoped.

With this ambitious plan for the conduct of war in 1916, Falkenhayn was reacting to the tactical change occurring in warfare, where massive artillery fire had gained significant importance over tactical movements, resulting in trench warfare and preceding the breakthrough with a phase of wearing down the opponent. To him, attrition was only a means to the end and not the centre of his operational-strategic thinking. The repeatedly voiced reproach that Falkenhayn had betrayed German operational thinking does not encompass enough facts. He envisaged the war decision in the West and not in the East. He wanted to avoid an unwinnable war of attrition. In pursuit of this aim and against the backdrop of trench warfare, Falkenhayn instead combined attrition and annihilation strategy into a new holistic strategy. Therefore, it was not a strategy of annihilation or attrition but of annihilation and exhaustion on which Falkenhayn's plan for 1916 was based.

Falkenhayn's strategy failed not least because his opponent Joffre knew the appropriate responses to his moves. It is an irony of history that the fast triumph over Romania, which was mainly an achievement of Falkenhayn's operational ability, brought about Joffre's dismissal. Romania, in the true sense of Clausewitz, was a friction which both parties had not consequently deliberated in their strategies. The turn of the year 1916/17 saw Joffre in retirement and Falkenhayn in a subordinate position on the Balkans. The row of graves at the *Chemin des Dames* and in Flanders demonstrates that Joffre's and Falkenhayn's successors would find no better operational-strategic solution to the problems that they had to deal with while they held the reigns in their hands.

CHAPTER 3

FRENCH STRATEGY IN 1916 AND THE BATTLE OF THE SOMME

Professor Georges-Henri Soutou

At the end of 1915, Allied and French strategy was in shambles: their offensives on the Western Front had been costly and had failed to break the German defensive lines; Italy had entered the war on their side in May, but without any decisive result; and Bulgaria had joined the Central Powers in October, allowing the defeat and occupation of Serbia and establishing a physical link between Germany, Austria, and Turkey. Anxious to compensate for the stalemate in the West, the Allies had tried the indirect approach: their navies tried to reach Istanbul through the Dardanelles Straits in February–March, but were unsuccessful. After the failure of the naval approach in the Dardanelles, the Allies widened their approach and carried out amphibious landings at Gallipoli in March. Again, these did not achieve the envisaged success and the Allies eventually had to admit defeat and withdraw from the peninsula. Troops were sent to Salonika in October to offer support to the Serbs but arrived too late to save them; the troops then remained in the region, organizing and fortifying themselves against a possible Bulgarian attack and in the face of a very hostile reception from the Greek government.[1]

Thus, the situation at the end of 1915 was grim: the direct approach had not worked against the continuous, entrenched fronts in the West, and the indirect approach had been tried and had failed. There was now a general understanding that the war would not, as generally forecast before 1914, be a violent but short affair. One result of this realization was an increased emphasis on starving Germany into submission by blockading its ports. The naval blockade had begun in earnest in 1915, but the Germans had been bypassing the blockade to a certain degree, transporting supplies through neutral countries.[2] On the Eastern Front, the Central Powers had conducted a number of successful offensives. Also, in 1915 the Central Powers had had much more success in encouraging the many non-Russian people of the Russian Empire to reject Russian domination, from Poland to the Caucasus, than the Allies had experienced in turning Slavic populations of Austria-Hungary against the German Reich.[3]

In October 1915 important changes took place in the French government and Aristide Briand replaced René Viviani as head of the government in Paris. He was a much more aggressive war-leader than his predecessor. In contrast to other nations, the French politicians were in overall command of the war effort throughout the duration of the conflict and as such they had influence not only over the strategic outline of the general direction that the country would take, but also the operational implications – as summed up by Georges Clemenceau, French Prime Minister 1917–20: 'War is too important to be left to the military'. As a consequence of Briand coming to power in the autumn of 1915, France abandoned its previous, fruitless strategy of quick, under-equipped frontal offensives and adopted a strategy of attrition and material superiority aiming at achieving a decisive offensive, but conducted in depth and lasting for months. This direct strategy was supplemented by a new round of the indirect approach, in particular with the entry of Romania into the war in August 1916 and the inception of total war, including economic measures beyond the traditional blockade. For all these strategies British support was crucial. As a consequence of the changed strategy and the horrendous casualties that France had suffered in 1914 and 1915, Great Britain became the main ally of France in 1916, supplanting Russia. The battle of the Somme, where for the first time on the Western Front the British effort was larger than the French, was evidence of that important shift.

Soon after taking power, Briand pleaded for the Allies to reach agreement on their aims and coordinate their actions, and was instrumental in setting up both an Allied military and an Allied political council meeting, in November and December 1915.[4] At the Allied military council meeting, which took place in Chantilly in December, it was decided to take the offensive simultaneously on all fronts. This would deny the Central Powers the advantage of their interior lines of communications. This time, they would not be able to move troops to the endangered parts of the Western or Eastern fronts, because all fronts would be under attack. Furthermore, Briand played an important role in persuading Romania to enter the war on 27 August 1916. With Romania's involvement there was a prospect of getting the Salonika front moving at last, thus compounding the pressure on the Central Powers.[5]

At the same time the French and British armament industries fully transitioned to a war footing, meaning that the Allies now had material superiority, which was in evidence for the first time on the Somme and which would become a characteristic of future Allied operations on the Western Front. Furthermore, the blockade of Germany became much more effective after the spring of 1916, increasing the gap in available *matériel* between the Central Powers and the Allies. Despite the fact that the Somme was less successful than the Allies had hoped, the results were such that the French and British then felt they could win the war in 1917 with a new decisive offensive. Accordingly the French started to plan in earnest for the future peace terms as early as August 1916.

In strategic terms, Verdun was a defensive battle, forced upon the French by the Germans. The Somme was a planned Franco-British offensive, meant to break the deadlock in the West and to achieve, if not a complete victory, at least a major success at the operational level, putting the Allies in good position to finish the war in 1917. There were however major differences among the French civilian and military leaders about the possible scope of the battle, especially after Verdun had upset the initial French plans.[6]

New strategies

The unsuccessful and costly offensives on the Western Front in 1915 had shown that new strategies, operational ideas and tactical methods were necessary. Hopes placed in Romania when it first entered the war were quickly crushed when its army was swiftly defeated by the Austrians and Germans. The only other hope that still existed in the Balkans was the tattered remnants of the Serbian army, which had escaped to Corfu. Rebuilding this force would, in the long run, provide the Allies with opportunities in this part of Europe, especially if the bridgehead at Salonika could be held and used as a starting point for a future offensive.[7] Alternative strategies had therefore to be devised, based upon the understanding that the war could only be won with a long-haul perspective, and that there were no shortcuts to victory. The French and the British believed that the only possible strategy in the context of trench warfare and fixed fronts was an attritional strategy, relying on superiority of firepower, in combination with a much more serious blockade of Germany. It was only after, and largely because of, the Somme experience that both sides began to devise new means to break the deadlock and return to mobile tactics; the Germans through a new organization of their infantry in small troops largely provided with machine guns and mobile heavy weapons (*Stoßtruppen*), the Franco-British through the extensive development of a new weapon, which the British first trialled at the Somme: the tank.

But in 1916 the Allies were unable to escape from the concept of attrition, after the failure of mobile warfare in 1914 and 1915. For the strategy of attrition the French high command finally realized the importance of heavy guns, which the French industry was now able to produce in great numbers, under the supervision of the new and effective

French 6e and 10e army gains, July to November 1916

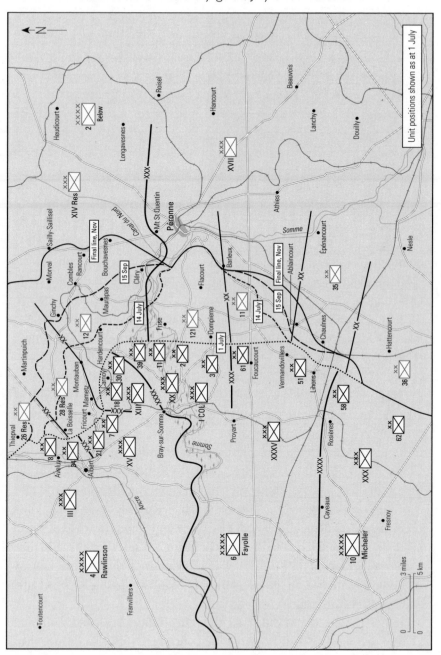

minister of armaments, Albert Thomas. The naval blockade was still incomplete in early 1916 and in any case it would take time for this kind of strategy to have a significant impact on the German population and economy.[8]

One way to achieve this impact and to make the German population suffer was a higher degree of cooperation among the Allies, including some pooling of military and material resources, in particular to ensure that the blockade would be more effective. As soon as he became prime minister in October 1915, Briand pushed for this increase in cooperation, in particular between Paris and London.[9]

During a meeting held in London on 20 January 1916, Briand persuaded Asquith to accept the formation of an Allied committee for allocating shipping. Philippe Berthelot, the principal diplomat under Briand, called this 'a pact of economic solidarity'.[10] A government member, Denys Cochin, was put in charge of matters pertaining to the blockade. The General Staff was increasingly convinced of the blockade's importance, and appointed an influential banker, François-Marsal, to organize the coordination of the numerous and ineffective services which had dealt previously with the strategy.[11] A new inter-Allied conference took place in Paris on 27 and 28 March 1916, and decided to form a permanent blockade committee, which would be in charge of coordinating the necessary worldwide measures to curtail the imports of the Central Powers. An Allied economic conference in Paris on 14–17 June extended those measures and proclaimed the economic solidarity of the Allies during and after the war, building on a previous agreement between Clémentel, trade minister in Paris, and Lord Runciman, chairman of the Board of Trade.[12] At about the same time the British introduced conscription and agreed to follow a much stricter blockade policy than previously. President of the Republic Raymond Poincaré could stress in his memoirs that Briand had achieved a major change: the Allies had now a common plan of action.[13] It was now realized that grand strategy in modern war relied on the integration of economy (including blockade) and industry into military strategy.

In one theatre, the Middle East, the Allies did not agree on a common plan of action. The British were more concerned with this theatre than the French. For France, the main enemy was Germany and Germany could only be beaten on the fields of France and Belgium. Nevertheless, plans for the future of the Middle East were summarized in the Sykes-Picot agreements of February 1916. As early as 1917 Great Britain had reneged on those agreements. France, with only one regiment in the whole theatre against 1 million British soldiers, was in no position to prevent this overall change to Allied strategy.

The Somme Offensive

Général Joseph Joffre had been against the landings at Gallipoli in the spring of 1915, and at Salonika in the autumn. He believed in the direct approach and thought that nothing should distract from the main front, the Franco-German one. In contrast to the British government, Joffre believed that the only positive result possible from a peripheral strategy was the withdrawal of German troops from the Western Front to strengthen the defence on other fronts. This would give the French and British forces a much-needed superiority on the Western Front which could then be exploited. But Joffre was very clear in his mind that the indirect approach would not create any grandiose outflanking strategic thrusts.[14]

At the Chantilly conference held on 6 December 1915, Joffre outlined his ideas for the conduct of war in the following year to the Allied chiefs. He thought that the Allies should have two objectives in 1916. The main one was a purely military objective: to destroy the German and Austrian armies. His secondary, more political objective was to thwart German plans of expansion in the East. His ideas were accepted and it was decided to go on the offensive as soon as possible in all the main theatres of the war: France, Russia, and Italy. Those offensives would not be coordinated in the full meaning of the word, but would be launched in the shortest possible time span, in order to prevent the enemy from moving his forces between the several fronts. For their part the Anglo-French would attack astride the Somme between 1 March at the earliest and 1 July at the latest.[15]

Initially, Foch, commanding the Groupe d'Armées du Nord (Northern Army Group) and in charge of planning the Somme Offensive, had conceived an attack on a 43-mile front, with the French astride the Somme River but mostly south of it, and the British to the north of the French. On their 26-mile sector of attack the French would commit three armies totalling 39 divisions, and 1,200 heavy guns. The British would throw into battle two armies with 25 divisions on a 17-mile front. The operational objective was the major German railway hub between Cambrai, Le Cateau and Maubeuge, 50 miles behind the German front line. If the Allies managed to occupy this hub and thus sever German communication lines, the Germans would be unable to maintain their hold in northern France. It was thus hoped that an operational success – breaking through the German defensive lines – would result in strategic victory. But there was a major ambiguity: while the plan called for a breakthrough, followed by a far-reaching phase of operational, or even strategic exploitation, it was known that the Germans had strongly reinforced their positions, so the breakthrough might not succeed – similar to the battles of 1915. In this case the Allies would try to draw and exhaust German reserves, thus reverting to an attrition strategy. This ambiguity, which influenced Allied thinking from the beginning, gives an indication why the Somme turned into such a tragedy for the Allies.[16]

The surprise German attack at Verdun on 21 February changed the game. The defence of Verdun became the priority of the French command and two thirds of the total number of French divisions were, at one time or another, committed to the battle.

As for the Somme Offensive, there was a major difference of opinion between the French commanders: Pétain, in charge of the defence of Verdun, was in favour of scrapping the Somme Offensive and concentrating all the resources at Verdun for a counteroffensive in his sector of the front line. He thought that the British and the French forces on the Somme should content themselves with deception and small attacks, in order to prevent the Germans throwing all their reserves at Verdun.

But Joffre stubbornly kept to the schedule agreed in Chantilly and the Somme Offensive began on 1 July – the last day of the time span originally agreed upon for the Allied offensive in the West. His decision was much disputed at the time, but concentrating on Verdun would not have much changed the situation: the Germans were forced to stop their attacks on Verdun on 3 September, because they had to move troops to the battlefield of the Somme. This gave the French the chance to go onto the offensive at Verdun and, between the end of October and mid-December, they regained most of the ground that they had lost since February. So the Somme Offensive did relieve Verdun. And, at the strategic level, Joffre's stubbornness, combined with the Russian Brusilov Offensive which lasted from June to September, probably helped save the Italian front. Despite his limitations, Joffre understood the strategic interdependence of the various fronts much better than Pétain.[17]

Another major issue at high command level was whether a decisive victory could be achieved through the Somme Offensive. Pétain was convinced such a victory was impossible, at least in 1916. Joffre wrote in his memoirs to the contrary: 'we could expect this offensive to enable us to achieve a breakthrough and final victory'.[18] This is not just *ex post facto*, but is confirmed by the very useful diary of Marie Émile Fayolle, who at the time was commanding one of the French armies on the Somme front and who met Joffre on several occasions. He stated that Joffre strove for a decisive victory and was convinced it was possible.[19]

At the operational level, things were less clear-cut, and the relationship and force allocation between the ongoing battle for Verdun and the planned Somme Offensive was much debated. On 12 April 1916 Général Edmond Buat was appointed first assistant to the Deputy Chief of Staff Général Maurice Pellé, with authority over the Second (Intelligence) and Third (Operations) departments of the General Staff. Buat understood the political game well, because he had belonged to Alexandre Millerand's office until he left the War Ministry in February, and he was very well connected in the army and in the political class. He was in charge of the detailed planning for the offensive. One of the best minds of the army (he later rose to become Chief of the General Staff after the war) his diaries are a major source.[20] From the beginning he was convinced that the Somme Offensive should be as strong and forceful as possible, and in that way it would be the most effective way to support Verdun.[21] A first study by the Third Department had foreseen 44 French divisions and 1,200 heavy guns (and 30 British divisions). Buat understood immediately that it would be difficult to achieve that number, because a jittery high command feared for Verdun and other parts of the front. But in order to release as many divisions as possible for the offensive, he arranged that Pétain, now in command of the Groupe d'Armées du Centre (Central Army Group), would be able to use the 52 divisions under his command as he wished for the defence of Verdun, rotating them into the battle, but would no longer ask for reserves from the two other army groups. Thus Buat could theoretically count on 40 divisions for the Somme, and initial planning was made accordingly. The divisions available were deemed sufficient to launch two attacks, one astride the Somme synchronized with the British to the north, and a second one towards Roye to the south, with a third possible attack from the centre if the other two strikes were successful.

But Castelnau, deputy to Joffre, was a cautious man and did not want to commit so many troops, fearing the Germans could renew their offensive in Verdun or even launch another attack elsewhere. Buat could not convince him that the offensive on the Somme would prevent the Germans from advancing anywhere else and that the best way to relieve Verdun was to attack on the Somme, so the number of divisions was reduced to 30. In addition, the preparations for the offensive – the establishment of railheads, the preparation of deployment areas etc – were slowed down, because material and manpower was not made available in the necessary numbers.[22]

Finally, when the offensive started on 1 July, they attacked on a 20-mile front instead of the planned 43 miles, and with only 26 French divisions and 840 heavy guns. The offensive was now mostly a British effort. The French divided their efforts, launching two new offensives at Verdun, in October and December, with eight divisions and 400 heavy guns. The offensives in Verdun delivered what they had promised and resulted in the reconquering of the ground that had been lost to the German attacks since February. This was a huge political and psychological boost for the French, but, despite this, it was without strategic importance.

At the tactical level the battle on the Somme was further hampered on the French side by strong disagreement among the commanding officers. Foch, commanding the Groupe d'Armées du Nord, wanted the main French effort to take place north of the Somme, in order to support the

British offensive which was now the main effort. But Fayolle, in charge of 6e Armée, preferred to attack south of the Somme, in order to protect his left flank behind the river. Tactically, Fayolle's views may have been sound – he was very prudent and disapproved of the offensive mindset of the General Staff. But at the strategic level Foch was right: it was necessary, in a coalition war, to support the British fully, as they were providing the main effort.[23] But Fayolle was very distrustful of the British, suspecting them of wanting a long war in order to be better able to divide the Europeans and retain their control of the seas and world trade.[24] That view was not an isolated one, and it explains a lot of French history during and after World War I.

After initial gains, and a breakthrough near Péronne which was not exploited because the French infantry was now completely dependent on heavy preliminary artillery preparation, the offensive, with two diverging thrusts north and south of the Somme, progressed very slowly and was bogged down around mid-November. The Franco-British had gained 6–10 miles, at the cost of 400,000 British and 350,000 French casualties. The Germans had lost 'only' 500,000 men. Undaunted, Joffre wanted to resume the offensive in February 1917, on a wider front, but in December 1916 he was replaced by Nivelle, who in October had led a successful counteroffensive at Verdun, with comparatively few losses.

The Somme Offensive did not achieve anything of strategic value. Nevertheless, after the defensive victory around Verdun in June, and the promising beginning of the Somme Offensive in July 1916, French diplomats in neutral countries all noted the onset of a real political 'disarray' in Germany.[25] In Berlin the political leadership took the situation quite seriously, and so did the new military leaders Hindenburg and Ludendorff (Falkenhayn had been demoted in August, because of the initial failure on the Somme).[26] The big steelmakers recognized, during a meeting of their association, that for the first time they had trouble delivering arms and ammunition in sufficient quantities to the front.[27] Germany was struggling to cope.

That is why Berlin and Vienna, under the impression of the failure on the Somme, used the opportunity of their victory over Romania and of the entry of their troops in Bucharest on 3 December to issue their peace note of 12 December.[28] It has been hotly disputed whether the note was only a manoeuvre to divide the Allies, or whether it was sent in earnest. Everything we now know proves that it was meant seriously: Berlin still hoped to extract the best deal, but they were for the first time ready to negotiate at a general conference, and not just looking for an opportunity to conclude a separate peace with one or the other of the Allies. While still ambitious in their aims for an agreement, the Germans were prepared to compromise more than the Allies realized at the time. For the first time a belligerent was willing to revert to multilateral, Concert of Europe-style diplomacy. It was a telling consequence of the Somme Offensive.[29]

The Somme Offensive and French plans for peace

The Germans' willingness to discuss peace was to some extent recognized in Paris, but not everyone drew the same conclusions. For the majority of the French leaders, it was an opportunity to define French war aims. For a minority, it was time to try a return to secret diplomacy, in view of a negotiated peace.[30]

At the beginning of the Somme Offensive, when a breakthrough seemed possible, French leaders were more sanguine. Some of them became more cautious as it became clear that the Somme victory would be both limited and costly. It is not surprising that, soon after the beginning of the battle, with the perspective of hopefully decisive strategic developments, the war aims question, which had been until now discussed at government level only in the most general terms, came to the fore. On 12 August President Poincaré asked Joffre to prepare terms for an eventual armistice. This launched a process which went much further and embraced all war aims. Those studies at government and General Staff level led to a very important meeting of the principal ministers with Poincaré on 7 October 1916, and French war aims were put in writing, with approval of the Cabinet, in a letter to the French ambassador in London, Paul Cambon, on 12 January 1917.[31]

During those discussions, it was agreed Alsace-Lorraine would of course be recovered, but within its borders of 1790, not 1815, thus including a large part of the Saar province. Within the government there were different views as to what was to become of the Rhineland – and thus no final decision was made on this subject. Three possible solutions were discussed by the government: outright annexation of the Rhineland; a permanent military occupation (but the region remaining part of the Reich); and the establishment of one or two independent states closely linked to France, similar to the Rheinbund of the 19th century). Paris would demand from the Allies full freedom to choose at the end of the war. Some leaders wanted to go further: one discussed with the Russians the opportunity of signing the peace treaty with all German states rather than with the federal government, thus disposing of the unitary Reich. On top of that Austria-Hungary might be dissolved, and many German territories might be annexed by its neighbours, but these last points were not unanimously accepted and provoked a lot of debate.

Meanwhile Luxembourg drew more and more attention, and extensive economic war aims were devised, including customs unions with Belgium and Italy and an inter-Allied control system for major raw materials after the war, to the detriment of German economy and to the benefit of the French one. With a steel capacity increased three-fold due to the recovery of Lorraine and the annexation or control of the Saar region and Luxembourg, France would become a major industrial power in Europe.[32]

Exactly in the same time span (October 1916–January 1917) the General Staff (under Joffre and after 17 December under Nivelle) prepared, in full agreement with the political leadership, what was to be known in April 1917 as the 'Nivelle Offensive'. It was explicitly stated that, after the blow delivered to Germany by the battle of the Somme, the next offensive would 'seal the ruin of the Central Powers'.[33] Nothing less than complete victory was contemplated. Several meetings of Joffre with the principal ministers and Poincaré ensured that all the necessary preparations were fully coordinated.[34] Even at the operational and tactical levels differences existed between Joffre and Nivelle: Joffre had argued for a follow-on attack as early as February 1917 along more or less the same axis as the Somme Offensive, while the Nivelle Offensive took place in

April at a different part of the front and with other tactics. However, the two generals did agree on the general strategic outline: the German Army had to be broken by a major offensive on French soil.

The French General Staff issued a memorandum on 12 November 1916, which was sent to Poincaré and Briand, outlining the French strategic view for 1917. The message was reinforced at an Allied staff conference in Chantilly three days later: the year 1917 and the French (and Allied) operation would be 'decisive'.[35] Joffre's successor, Nivelle, retained the projected offensive and its extensive aims: not only the liberation of territories occupied by the Germans, but also the 'control of enemy territories, possession of which is necessary to negotiate peace and achieve favourable terms'.[36]

Despite the optimism of Joffre, and later Nivelle, the political class was not monolithic in its resolve, and the lobbies of the Parliament were abuzz with despondent conversations and intrigues, far from the official line. The country was exhausted, the Somme Offensive had jolted the Germans but had been inconclusive, Romania's entry into the war in August, on which the Allies had put so much hope, had ended in disaster and the Germans and Austrians had occupied Bucharest on 6 December.

The Prime Minister himself, Aristide Briand, was evidently having second thoughts. Since August 1916 he had been fully involved in the discussions of war aims at government level, but the initiative of those discussions always came from Poincaré: Briand was constantly opposed to those who wanted to communicate the French war aims to the Allies as soon as possible, as if he did not want to tie his hands. That is why they were sent to London as late as 12 January 1917, and even then Briand's hand had been forced by his colleagues. But he had had the envisaged terms toned down in the letter to Paul Cambon: there was no longer any question of destroying the Austrian-Hungarian and the German empires.

At the same time, in December 1916, Briand tried to open a secret line of communication with Berlin through Professor Haguenin, who was in charge of the so-called 'Bureau de Presse' of the French embassy in Bern (actually an intelligence organization under shallow cover). Since September Professor Haguenin had been in contact with Count Harry Kessler, a well-known German publicist and arts specialist who was one of the foremost socialites of his generation and very well connected all over Europe. As such he enjoyed the best connections in Berlin, including the Kaiser and Chancellor Bethmann. Their long conversations from December until March 1917 touched on very sensitive issues: a possible autonomy for Alsace-Lorraine, a return of part of it to France and a condominium for the rest, in exchange for which Paris would grant the Germans free access to the iron ore of Lorraine and an economic pact. France would also guarantee that it would not build an anti-German block with Great Britain. Briand's fall from power in March 1917 put an end to those contacts, but they were very serious: Briand wanted to explore other options before the launching of the Nivelle Offensive in April, about which he was apprehensive, and which, to the contrary, Poincaré supported most energetically. Briand had led the war most forcefully since October 1915: evidently, after the Somme, he had doubts.[37]

The strategic legacy of the battle of the Somme

The Somme Offensive certainly made sense at the strategic level, because the several fronts were interconnected and it was useful to deprive the Central Powers, as much as possible, of the advantage of being able to shuttle their forces along interior lines from one front to another. It made sense at the operative level because it was the best way to relieve Verdun and because the conquest of the railway lines running behind the German front would have forced the German Army to fall back far behind its original lines. The concept of a major effort on the Somme should have been more forcefully implemented respective to the rest of the front: the counteroffensive at Verdun certainly provided a psychological boost to the French, but it was a meaningless sideshow which deprived the Somme of much-needed forces. At the tactical level, the offensive was nevertheless ill-conceived, despite the considerable effort put into its preparation and the Allies' material superiority. The result was the failure to exploit two breakthroughs, which resulted in it being remembered by the fighting men as a senseless slaughter, a battle fought in vain.

If for the British the Somme Offensive sums up their experience of World War I, it is less the case for the French – the Somme is still overshadowed by Verdun. Nevertheless, the battle had many important consequences. Briand, under pressure from parliament, had to dispose of Joffre on 17 December 1916 and change the whole high command. Joffre felt this politically motivated change deprived him of the victory he expected to win with the prompt re-launching of the offensive he was planning on the Somme, where he was convinced the Germans were at the end of their tether.[38] But public opinion, many politicians, and even many high commanders were now convinced that the conduct of war had to be changed and that the experience of the Somme should not be repeated. Not that they all followed the extreme views of Pétain, who was in favour of a strictly defensive strategy until new armaments (tanks and aircraft) arrived which, together with the United States' entry into the war, would allow the Allies to resume the offensive.

The decisive and final offensive planned for as soon as possible in 1917, was to be launched changed tactics – to avoid the mistakes of the Somme. The Somme Offensive had been launched on a relative narrow front and with huge preparatory artillery barrages (up to six days), in order to avoid the mistakes of 1915: insufficiently prepared offensives on too large a front. But at the Somme the reversed tactics had not been successful either: the very long artillery preparation gave the Germans time to bring up reserves; the infantry was dependent on the artillery and did not exploit two opportunities to advance in open country after having broken through the German lines; and anyway the ground was so churned up by the artillery that any advance on foot was very difficult. It was therefore decided that for the Nivelle Offensive the attack would be carried out on a wide front and the artillery preparation would be shortened to a few hours, in order to maintain the element of surprise. But the Nivelle Offensive was a costly failure; one of the reasons was that the Germans had moved their line considerably backwards shortly before the offensive, thus nullifying much of the elaborate preparations made by the French. Verdun and the Somme had taught the Germans a lesson: it was more important to drain the enemy while preserving one's own forces than to hold ground at any cost.[39]

Another consequence of the Somme was that the French, initially optimistic and rightly sensing that for the first time Germany was reaching its limits, embarked on a journey of demanding extended war aims. This played its part in precluding any negotiated settlement. At the same time some French leaders realized, as did some British ones, that the (relative) victory of the Somme was a good opportunity to try to negotiate an end to the war, with reduced aims. That is why 1917 witnessed the only peace-feelers the French extended during the whole war. The impression of the Somme was, of course, reinforced by the disaster of the Nivelle Offensive. The Germans were ready to consider those peace-feelers, also because of the Somme. Far-reaching consequences indeed, even if largely overlooked today, and even if, as we know, the course of events was not fundamentally altered by the battle of the Somme.

CHAPTER 4

AIR WAR OVER THE SOMME

The evolution of British and German
air operations

Dr James S. Corum

The air battles over the Somme campaign in 1916 represent a turning point in the evolution of aerial warfare. During the intense battle from July to November 1916, both the Royal Flying Corps (RFC) and the Fliegertruppen des Deutschen Kaiserreiches (German Imperial Air Service) were pushed to make major changes to their organization, doctrine, and technology in the struggle to gain the upper hand in the desperate battle to gain air superiority over the front.

Between the start of the war – when the RFC had been able to field only 60 aircraft to support the BEF when it landed in France – and 1916, the role of airpower had changed dramatically. Initially the mission of the German, French, and British air services in France had been providing operational reconnaissance for the ground armies. In this role the air services performed admirably in their ability to observe enemy movements and positions well beyond the front lines and to provide accurate reports quickly to the high command. The Germans credited their great victory at Tannenberg in August 1914 to the accurate air reconnaissance carried out by their air service.[1] After the battle General von Hindenburg, commander of 8. Armee, noted, 'Without the airplane, there is no Tannenberg.'[2] At the same time, in the West it was the British and French reconnaissance fliers who spotted the gap between the German armies advancing on Paris that enabled the successful British and French counter-attack that drove the Germans back and stabilized the Western Front. With such dramatic evidence of the usefulness of air units in hand, the senior German and Allied commanders urgently called for more aircraft and insisted that their national governments mobilize the aircraft and engine industries to create large air forces. From being an auxiliary support arm in the autumn of 1914, the combatant air forces soon became major military forces in their own right and undertook new missions.

In the autumn of 1914, both the Allies and Germans pushed their aviation industries to develop larger and more powerful aircraft that would be able to bomb vital targets well beyond the front lines. At the same time, both sides began to mount radios in aircraft to enable them to serve as aerial observers for the artillery. As artillery was the main killing weapon of World War I – it is estimated that more than 80 per cent of all casualties were inflicted by artillery fire – using aircraft to enable accurate massed fire on the battlefield became key to operational success. Aerial photography also became a major mission for all the air forces. Photos taken above enemy lines became a major component of intelligence analysis, enabling commanders to monitor the enemy lines and to identify and map enemy strongpoints, logistics movements, and force build-ups behind the front. Winning air superiority over the front in order to carry out these missions became the objective of both sides. Air superiority offered the enormous advantage of observing the enemy's movements and undertaking aerial spotting for the artillery while denying these advantages to the enemy. To achieve the goal of air superiority in 1915 the Germans introduced the first purpose-built fighter plane, the

Fokker E-1 monoplane. It was designed with one purpose – to find and destroy enemy aircraft.

The Fokker, in many respects a mediocre aircraft when introduced, had the great advantage of being able to fire a machine gun directly through the propeller thanks to an interrupter gear developed in 1915. Instead of bringing down an enemy by firing the observer's machine gun, normally mounted in the rear of the standard two-seater reconnaissance planes used by both sides – and requiring a difficult bit of marksmanship for even the best observer/gunner – the pilot of the light and nimble single-seater had only to aim his plane directly at the target. In the autumn of 1915, before the British and French fielded their own version of the interrupter gear, the Germans were able to inflict heavy losses on Allied aircraft and protect their own observation planes with their flights of Fokkers. By being just one step ahead of their opponents the Germans were able to claim air superiority in early 1916.[3]

The first major campaign that featured air superiority as a key element of the battle plan was the German offensive at Verdun, which began in February 1916. The German plan was to use their Fokkers, organized into special flights of six to eight aircraft, to establish an air barrier over the front lines and enable the German air observers to support the 2,200 guns deployed to attrit the French Army.[4] The Germans moved to mass their forces in a quiet sector and deployed 168 aircraft, 14 balloons and four Zeppelins to Verdun, an impressive concentration of airpower at that time. The French had few aircraft in the Verdun sector and failed to spot the German build-up, so the Germans achieved initial surprise and advanced to take key ground. But the French soon recovered from their surprise and reacted effectively. German fighter patrols could not mount an effective barrier once the French massed their aircraft to punch through the German fighters.

The French air service, the Aéronautique Militaire, had created its own fighter arm early in the war and by 1915 it was out-producing the Germans, and fielding superior fighter planes such as the new Nieuport biplanes that were much faster and more manoeuvrable than the Fokkers. The French had overcome the teething problems of the early interrupter gear by mounting a light machine gun on the top wing of their fighters that fired above the propeller arc. At Verdun the French were able to turn the tables on the Germans and gain air superiority over Verdun, which inhibited the German artillery-spotting aircraft considerably.[5] The Verdun campaign featured large numbers of aircraft on both sides and by the end of the campaign both sides had learned a great deal about coordinating large-scale air and ground operations.[6]

For the RFC, commanded in France by Major-General Hugh Trenchard, the Verdun battle provided important lessons. To prepare for the upcoming battle at the Somme, in which the New Army of the British Empire would be put to its great test, Trenchard proposed to mass as many aircraft as possible and throw them over the front in a relentless offensive to control the air over the battlefield. Verdun provided some important lessons to the British in terms of operational doctrine. Until the spring of 1916 the RFC support squadrons were general-purpose units containing two or three models of aircraft – two-seaters for observation and bombing, and nimble armed planes such as the DH 2 Vickers 'Gunbus' used to fight enemy planes and escort the observers and bombers. For the less intense air war of 1915 this system might have worked, but for the large-scale air operations that the Somme required, larger and specialized squadrons would be needed. So in late April the fighters were taken from the corps support squadrons and concentrated into the army support wings.[7] As the air war grew in scale in March 1916 the strength of RFC squadrons was increased from 12 to 18 aircraft.[8]

British squadrons of two-seater observation planes were also tasked with carrying out extensive bombing operations against German transport, supply depots and troops concentrations in a zone up to 30 miles behind the front lines. The intent was not only to support the army by observation and artillery spotting, but to cripple and harass the German logistics and troop movements. General Haig, who had taken over command of the British armies on the Western Front in 1915, strongly endorsed Trenchard's concept of air operations and pushed the government in London to provide more aircraft to support the planned offensive at the Somme. As the Somme was the main focus of the British effort in the West, air squadrons were pulled from every other section of the front to support the main effort.

Opposing aircraft and technologies

In June 1916 the RFC had massed more than 400 aircraft to support the British army, most of them two-seater observation planes.[9] At the start of the war each of the major armies flew as their primary aircraft a two-seater biplane carrying a pilot and observer. The two-seater observation plane would remain the main aircraft of every air force of World War I as it could effectively carry out the primary missions of the air arm such as reconnaissance, artillery spotting, and bombing. The British BE 2 biplanes, and the Aviatiks and LFG biplanes that equipped many of the German air detachments in 1914 and 1915, had small engines, usually under 100 horsepower, and had top speeds of 70–90 mph. While both sides used their observation aircraft as light bombers, the very limited engine power of these planes meant that bomb loads were very small, with the observer able to drop only a few 20lb bombs. However, as the war progressed, the Germans and British and French fielded better versions of their two-seaters. In 1915 and 1916 these were often just improved models of the aircraft of 1914, with larger engines and slightly higher speed and more bomb-carrying capability.

In 1916, the purpose-built fighter planes of the Germans and British were still the first generation of fighter aircraft developed in the war.[10] In the summer of 1916 the RFC fighter force included Martinsyde Scouts, the FE 2, the B, C, and D models, DH 2s, and some Bristol Scouts. Many of the British aircraft, such as the Vickers Gunbus with the engine mounted at the back, were already obsolescent and being replaced by the faster FE 2 pusher biplanes. While fairly manoeuvrable and able to hold their own against the first generation of German fighters (the Fokker E-1s), the pusher-engine planes had some poor handling characteristics and were highly vulnerable to an attack from the rear due to their poor rear visibility.[11]

One of the important advantages held by the Allies at the Somme was the efficiency of French aircraft design and production. By 1916 the French had effectively mobilized their engine production for their air force and were also turning out a surplus of very capable fighter aircraft. Throughout the war the British (as well as the Americans,

Russians, and Italians) would use thousands of French aircraft engines in their own production planes, and some of the better fighters of the RFC were supplied by France. These included the Morane biplane, the Morane Type N monoplane and a few Nieuport Scouts.[12] The Morane monoplane fighters were a rough match for the Fokker E-1s, and the Nieuport 11 and 17 biplanes, fighters of the second generation, were far superior to the German Fokker E1 planes in every respect (engine power, speed, climb, and manoeuvrability). In addition, some good British aircraft designs were appearing that could outclass the German planes. The Sopwith 1½ Stutter, a two-seat fighter which was the first British aircraft to be armed with a machine gun able to fire through the propeller as well as a rear machine gun, was highly manoeuvrable and, with a top speed of 100mph, was considerably faster than the Fokker Eindecker. The Nieuports and Sopwiths then coming on line signalled a big improvement in aircraft design. In short, the Germans would face a qualitative as well as quantitative disadvantage at the start of the Somme campaign.

In 1915 the Germans had developed and fielded an effective purpose-built bomber. The first production bomber was the AEG K I, a two-engine biplane powered by 100-hp Mercedes engines. The next version, the AEG G II, soon followed. Powered by two 150-hp engines, it was able to carry a 200kg bomb load a considerable distance.[13] However, only a few squadrons had been fielded by 1916. Although the Germans had heavy bomber squadrons of this type on the Western Front they considered the risk of British fighters too great to use their very capable bombers on the Somme. So, German bombers flew missions against French targets south of the Somme. The British at this point were still relying on small single-engine aircraft as bombers, although all the powers were racing to build multi-engine aircraft able to carry heavier bomb loads.

The other key technology for the Somme Offensive was the aircraft radio. This was one of Britain's strongest advantages. Early radios were very heavy and awkward to mount in two- seaters with small engines and limited carrying capability. Still, the British were experimenting with radios in aircraft before the end of 1914, knowing that radio-equipped aircraft would transform the effectiveness of the artillery. Rapid advances in radio technology meant that in 1916 the British had small and effective radios mounted in their reconnaissance aircraft and had already acquired considerable experience in using radios to support the artillery. During the Somme campaign the RFC fielded 306 aircraft mounted with radios, communicating with 542 ground stations. Indeed, the number of aircraft equipped with radios as well as ground-based signals personnel increased during the campaign.[14] Radio-equipped planes could communicate directly with the artillery batteries. Both the Germans and British used a grid system for the radio-equipped artillery planes, enabling the observers, using Morse code, to tap out two to three letter signals that provided the grid square reference. Another few letters provided information about the target and allowed the guns to adjust their fire.

The opposing air forces brought their strengths and weaknesses to the campaign of 1916. Through much of the war the Germans held advantages in aircraft design and the Germans were pioneers in the effective use of plywood construction over steel-tube airframes, which made their aircraft sturdy but light. However, the Germans lagged behind the Allies in aircraft engine manufacture and design. The French led the world in engine design and production before World War I and continued to hold their edge during the war with 88,000 aircraft engines produced to Germany's 43,486.[15] Moreover, the French were able to manufacture more powerful engines which usually gave their aircraft a speed advantage. However, the French advantage in engine power was offset to some degree by the superior reliability and durability of the Daimler, Benz, and BMW in-line engines that powered most of the German aircraft.[16]

Training in the air services

While the British held some significant advantages in 1916, especially in using radio communication for artillery spotting and contact patrols, the RFC had major weaknesses, of which the system of training was the most significant. After very basic pilot training in the UK, British pilots in 1916 were sent to the front units without advanced training in the type of aircraft they were to fly. The pilots of the corps support squadrons assigned to fly the escort fighters had no special preparation, nor was there a special selection process to identify and assign the pilots who would be most suited to fighter operations. In the middle of the campaign, pilots assigned to fly fighters would arrive at the squadron, be assigned an aircraft that he had never flown, then told to check it out as he was expected to fly on operations the next day.[17]

Arthur Harris, later air marshal and chief of the Royal Air Force (RAF) Bomber Command in World War II, flew in the Somme battle and his experience illustrates the approach to selection and training in the RFC in 1915–16. After brief service as an infantry private in the Southwest African campaign of 1914–15, Harris managed to get himself to England in late 1915 where an uncle in the War Office arranged for his entry into the RFC. Harris had a few hours of dual flight instruction and an hour and a half of solo flying and was duly commissioned a second lieutenant in the RFC Special Reserve. He then progressed to Upavon, the RFC's central flying school, where he attended a two-month training course which consisted of mostly theory and about ten hours' flying time in BE trainers and Martinsyde biplanes. With that, and less than 20 hours' total flight time, Harris became a fully qualified RFC pilot in January 1916.[18]

Harris was first sent to a home defence squadron where, without any prior night flying training, he was expected to fly a BE 2 at night and find and destroy the Zeppelin airships then raiding England. As his squadron comrades were getting killed flying in poor weather and at night, Harris developed on his own initiative a night-flying training programme and took part in anti-Zeppelin missions in early 1916 without any success.[19] Harris' competence as a pilot was noticed and he was sent to the Somme front in September 1916 to serve as a flight commander in No. 70 Squadron, which was just being equipped with the Sopwith 1½ Strutters. The Sopwiths were a big step forward for the RFC, its first plane to be equipped with an effective interrupter gear that allowed its machine gun to fire directly through the propeller. Harris, who arrived at the Somme as a relatively experienced pilot, did not last long. On 1 October he crashed his plane and injured his arm and was sent back to England with one confirmed kill and two probables. Given the constant overclaims by both sides, it is unlikely that he shot down more than one aircraft above the Somme.[20]

Most British pilots had much less flying time than Harris when they were posting into front-line combat. Throughout 1916 and 1917, the pilots of the RFC commonly entered combat with no more than 17 total flying hours, only a few of them solo.[21] This informal and haphazard approach to training by the RFC killed far more British pilots than the Germans – the biggest cause of death for British airmen in World War I was training accidents. A total of 8,000 British aircrew were killed while training in the UK – a record of casualties per training hours that exceeded that of the Germans, French, and Americans by several times.[22] It was not until the latter half of 1917 that the RFC moved to improve the standard of flight training.

The German flight training curriculum of 1915–16 provides a distinct contrast to the British. The German Imperial Air Service required several months of training for the observer pilots who formed the majority of the air service flying personnel. German observer pilots had a fairly rigorous curriculum for the era that required several cross-country flights and some night flying, and required the pilots to demonstrate their ability to land under various conditions. The German pilot training included both short-range and long-range flying, night flying, day and night landings. In 1916, by the time a German pilot earned his wings, he had approximately 65 flight hours.

That amount of training did not, however, qualify a pilot for fighter pilot duties. In contrast to the informal British system of recruitment and assignment, the Germans had a rigorous pilot application and selection process. Pilots applying to serve in fighter units were men already qualified as observer pilots and many already had extensive experience in flying over the front. They had to show pilot leaders such as Oswald Boelcke that they had the right combination of skill and aggressiveness to fly a single-seat fighter. In 1916 the Germans established a special training centre at Valenciennes in occupied France. There, the aspiring fighter pilots were given an intensive, one-month course in combat techniques, taught by airmen who had just completed tours of several months flying above the front lines.[23] The course included learning the new fighter tactics created by leutnants Max Immelmann and Boelcke, and flying in tactical formations. Despite having inferior aircraft for much of the

Somme battle, and being outnumbered, the Germans at least had the kind of flying experience and training that would help them to fly and survive in combat. The training that was provided to the German pilots gave them an edge on the battlefield that, to some extent, compensated for the British superiority in numbers.

Preparing the RFC

To prepare for the Somme attack the RFC massed the greater part of its total force on the Somme front. This meant that other operations that promised significant results were shut down or reduced to support the big battle. In Flanders the Royal Navy Air Service (RNAS) was building and training a bomber wing of 60 aircraft with the mission of striking targets deep within German lines. By June 1916 they had planned to have 60 operational aircraft to begin a major bomber offensive against the German rear. But as the Somme took precedence, aircraft for the Royal Navy's bomber units were diverted to the units supporting the Somme and by mid-summer the RNAS bomber wing had only ten aircraft.

The work of assembling hundreds of aircraft, preparing dozens of airfields, and establishing a reserve of aircraft and parts to deal with the expected high wastage rates, was a major logistical feat carried out by the RFC headquarters located at St Andre-aux-Bois. For the Somme front at the beginning of the offensive the RFC was organized into four air brigades, each with two wings. One wing, called the 'corps wing', commanded the observation squadrons for army support, which also had the mission of bombing the Germans. The second of the brigade wings, called the 'army wing', each had two fighter squadrons assigned. Finally, the RFC headquarters had an additional two fighter squadrons under its command (No 27 and 60 squadrons). The British fighter squadrons had 13 to 18 aircraft assigned.[24] This gave the RFC at the Somme a total of ten fighter squadrons with 167 operational fighters. The corps support units contained more than 200 aircraft. However, the process of reorganizing the fighter forces was not complete. A few units contained aircraft of one type, but most fighter squadrons had a mix of aircraft types, causing nightmares for the unit maintenance personnel.

To oppose this aerial mass the opposing German 2. Armee had only 104 operational aircraft and of these only 16 were fighter planes assigned to the two fighter flights. The German Imperial Air Service had proven itself a highly capable organization. Like the British, the primary German aircraft were sturdy two-seaters, at this time derivatives of pre-war designs, such as the Aviatik C 1 and the DFW B 2 reconnaissance planes. In 1916 the German Imperial Air Service was able to field much improved versions of the Aviatik and the DFW, providing the Aviatik with a 160-horsepower Mercedes engine that boosted its speed from a sluggish 88 to 99mph. The DFW went from a 100-hp engine to a 150-hp engine in 1916. Another improved aircraft model was the LVG C 5, which had a top speed of 103mph and an impressive maximum flight time of 3½ hours. Armed with two machine guns, the German two-seaters were tough to shoot down.[25] Again, like the British, the Germans routinely used their two-seater observation planes as light bombers. Unfortunately for the Germans, their fighter escorts were now obsolete and the RFC numbers were so overwhelming that for the first part of the campaign the Germans could only rarely conduct effective artillery spotting and photo reconnaissance flights.

First phase of the battle

The Germans could hardly fail to notice the upcoming British offensive. Air activity of all types increased dramatically on the Somme front in June and the British were busy conducting aerial reconnaissance of the front and German rear, and also directing massive artillery barrages on all known German strongpoints and along the entire German front-line trenches. Haig's concept of operations was to simply crush the entire German front lines with firepower, enabling the British Fourth Army to break through the centre of the Western Front.

On 1 July, after two weeks of massive artillery barrages, the 27 divisions of the British Fourth Army attacked in the Somme sector. The RFC had been given six clear tasks in the campaign plan: aerial reconnaissance, aerial photography, observing for the artillery, bombing, contact patrols to support the infantry, and air combat with the German

Imperial Air Service to obtain air superiority. When the air offensive began, the Germans were simply overwhelmed, which had been the intention of Trenchard's plan.

The British airmen were highly successful in carrying out the objectives Haig had set the RFC. With overwhelming air superiority in the first weeks of the battle the RFC was able to fulfil its reconnaissance and artillery observation duties as well as providing vital information on the situation on the front lines via contact patrols. The RFC's artillery spotters were active through all phases of the campaign and helped the British artillery deliver highly accurate fire on German positions. Although the British did identify and bring counter-battery fire on German artillery positions, especially those near the front lines, the main priority target was the German defences. This decision to target the front lines rather than prioritize the German heavier guns to the rear was one of the biggest British mistakes of the campaign. While the British guns inflicted heavy damage on the Germans, the artillery fire, much of it lighter shrapnel rounds, failed to cut the German wire. Moreover, the Germans had had a long time to prepare the Somme defences and had built deep concrete bunkers to protect their troops in the second and third trench lines. When the barrage finally ended and the British infantry attacked, enough German forward strongpoints and machine guns had survived to decimate the British battalions, who in many cases had to advance half a mile or more over open ground with little cover.

Although some ground was won on the first day of the Somme, it was the single bloodiest day in British military history and did not achieve the expected decisive breakthrough. The British attacks continued into mid-July when the BEF's decimated units had to pause to reinforce and reorganize.

The battle from July to September

The British control of the air and the ability to bring artillery fire on the Germans whenever they massed for a counter-attack not only inflicted heavy casualties among the Germans, but had a serious effect on German morale. Captured German letters and prisoner interrogations showed that the German infantry felt helpless as the British flew freely overhead and directed artillery fire on them while other planes strafed the trenches.[26] German General Fritz von Below, commanding 1. Armee, reported to the high command and referred to the 'complete inferiority of our own air forces', and noted that the relentless bombing was causing morale problems.[27]

After the initial attacks in July the campaign became a series of major corps-level battles designed to take key terrain. Delville Wood and Pozières Ridge became the scene of heavy fighting from July to September. In addition, 6e Armée Française to the south and the British Third Army to the north carried out major supporting attacks to tie down the Germans. While the RFC carried out its support tasks on every clear day, the downside of the relentless offensive also meant heavy losses for the airmen. Although the British controlled the air the Germans fought back with their small fighter force and British planes operating over the Germans lines also faced heavy ground fire. Still, all through July and into August the RFC dominated the skies over the Somme, enabling the British corps squadrons to go about their vital work of observation and artillery spotting. Aerial superiority allowed the corps squadrons to quickly spot German troop concentrations or counter-attacks and call in heavy artillery fire. While German losses did not equal the disastrous first day of the British offensive, the Germans nonetheless took massive losses as well – largely due to the air-directed artillery fire. Divisions were quickly rotated into the Somme to hold the line and replace German divisions decimated in battle.

One important feature of the Somme campaign was a series of regular bombing missions carried out by the British two-seaters. Trenchard sent his observation planes, armed with light bombs and escorted by his fighter squadrons, into the German rear to attack troop concentrations, artillery positions, and supply points. In the first four days of the battle alone the RFC dropped 13,000 bombs (most of them quite small). Through the campaign the RFC would bomb 298 German targets.[28] The most important targets were the German railways and major junctions upon which German logistics depended. Despite a major British effort these bombing raids were the only one of the tasks assigned to the RFC which failed to achieve real success. Post-war German analysis noted that of the dozens of bombing missions against the German railways behind the Somme front lines from July to September 1916 three quarters of the raids did no real damage. Twenty-one per cent of the attacks resulted in moderate damage, and only 5.5 per cent of the raids resulted in serious damage that restricted or temporarily shut down the railway lines.[29] The key factor in the Somme battle was the small carrying capacity of the RFC aircraft, such as the obsolescent BE 2Cs which were still used in large numbers. Another problem was the small size of the bombs as well as the small number of aircraft involved in each attack. As the war progressed, both sides learned that only large formations carrying heavy bombs had any real chance of inflicting serious damage upon rear installations. The bombing in the Somme campaign was a worthy attempt by the RFC, but the damage inflicted was not worth the cost of lost aircraft and personnel.

September to November – later phases and the tide turns

By the mid-point of the Somme battle it was no longer a battle to achieve a breakthrough, but an attrition battle like Verdun. Both sides heavily reinforced their air units as the air battle progressed. No. 40 Squadron arrived in August, followed by No. 41 Squadron in October. That month the RFC received a welcome reinforcement from the RNAS's 8th Squadron with 18 fighters. The RNAS Nieuports, Sopwith 1½ Strutters and Sopwith Pups were especially important as some of the few planes available that could meet the new Albatrosses and Pfalzs of the German *Jastas* on anything like equal terms. The RFC began the battle in July with 27 squadrons, and ended the campaign in November with 35 squadrons on the Somme front.[30]

The Germans also increased their air units on the Somme front in August and September, although they would not come close to the British in aircraft numbers. The effectiveness of British air superiority was a major shock to the Germans and pushed the German high command to reorganize the air service and to build up the German fighter arm. In August 1916 the Germans reorganized their fighter force from flights of six to eight planes into fighter squadrons of 14 planes – now called *Jagdstaffels (Jastas)*. The Germans sent two of their new fighter squadrons to the Somme front to challenge the British air supremacy. The German units had been specially recruited and trained by Leutnant Oswald Boelcke, who developed a system of tactics for close combat.

In September the Germans introduced a new fighter plane, the Albatros D I, into combat over the skies of the Somme. The Albatros D I and Pfalz D I aircraft represented an entirely new generation of fighter planes and a new stage in aviation technology. The new German fighter had a beautifully streamlined plywood fuselage, so they were fast and sleek as well as structurally strong. The Albatros D I with its 160hp Mercedes engine had a top speed of 110mph, faster than the Allied fighters. Moreover, the D I was the first plane to mount two forward-firing machine guns with no loss in speed. With two 7.9mm machine guns (each with 500 rounds), the nimble D I fighters not only had a speed advantage, but a big advantage in firepower in any dogfight.[31] The new fighter alarmed the British as the British pusher biplanes like the DH 2s, which could handle a Fokker E-1, were little more than live targets for the D Is. The RFC found it needed to provide even heavier escorts for the artillery spotters. It was a similar case to the advent of the Fokker E-1 in 1915 when General Trenchard ordered that each reconnaissance plane be escorted by three British fighters.[32]

Poor weather put an end to the Somme campaign in early November 1917. In general, one cannot describe the Somme as anyone's victory or defeat. The war in the air had been extremely bloody for both sides in terms of the numbers of planes and airmen lost. The RFC lost 982 aircraft destroyed or missing from all causes during the campaign. Of these less than half were shot down by the Germans and the others lost to accidents. The RFC lost 499 pilots and observers to combat (with more lost to non-combat operations).[33] The Germans lost 300 planes in combat with an unknown number (but certainly a high one) to accidental losses. Simply replacing the lost and obsolete aircraft and replacing aircrew losses required a vastly increased air support infrastructure, a challenge that both sides met.

Changes in aerial warfare in 1916

The sheer size of the Somme operations represented a major change in aerial warfare. The large ground infrastructure that had evolved to support the air forces and the need to coordinate the efforts of hundreds of planes on several fronts forced the Germans to make major organizational changes and in October 1916 the newly named Luftstreitkräfte (German Air Service) was granted its own commander-in-chief, its own general headquarters, its own general staff, and effective centralized control of most aviation assets of the German Army. The principle of centralized control meant that all aspects of aviation – aircraft production, training, the disposition of air logistics, civil air defence, and flak units – now came under the single direction of the air service.[34] The Luftstreitkräfte headquarters had staff sections for operations, weather, flak, home air defence, and medical services as well as the logistics and administrative sections. Each army air commander had a staff with communications, operations, intelligence, airfield engineer, transport, and equipment sections. While the Luftstreitkräfte operated under the command and direction of the army high command, its senior air officers operated at the direction of the air service commander. Units attached to an army reported to the air commander for that army, and squadron commanders were no longer subordinate to lower-echelon ground commanders. By the end of 1916, the air service had complete control of its own weather service, communications network, flak units, and the full infrastructure necessary for a modern air force.

In October 1916, General der Kavallerie Ernst von Hoeppner was appointed chief of the German Air Service. Though not an airman, Hoeppner was a highly experienced general staff officer who had proven himself as a division commander, and was a long-time advocate of a strong air arm. With a central headquarters and an air general staff in 1916, the Luftstreitkräfte had a means to evaluate and create air doctrine. By early 1917 new manuals provided the air service with guidelines for an operational doctrine that centred around large-scale air operations and emphasized the air superiority campaign as well as effective support of the ground forces. The new organization allowed improved doctrine and tactics to be quickly disseminated throughout the Luftstreitkräfte.

More than anything, the Somme changed the dynamics of the fighter forces of both sides from escort planes mixed into the observation squadrons into a concentrated force specializing in the air superiority mission. It was over the Somme in September 1916 that a new German fighter pilot, Manfred von Richthofen, shot down his first enemy aircraft in the new Albatros D I. Soon the gifted Richthofen was given his own fighter squadron and would meet the RFC again over Arras in April 1917, a disastrous month for the RFC. German squadron commanders like Richthofen provided the air service commander with critical reports detailing the state of German equipment and tactics, and offering some accurate and practical evaluations of Allied technology and tactics.

Five clear generations of fighter planes evolved between 1914 and 1918.[35] The first fighters of 1915 began as slight modifications of pre-war designs and by 1918 all-metal fighters had appeared. Through the war, as illustrated at the Somme, small jumps in aircraft technology, such as the interrupter gear, could change the state of the air superiority battle overnight. Aircraft became obsolete in about one year. The Albatros D I that inflicted devastating losses on the RFC over Arras in April 1917 would be completely outclassed in the summer of that year over Flanders when the British fielded the SE 5as and Bristol fighters – both more manoeuvrable and faster than the Albatros. At the same time the French fielded the Spad VII, another plane clearly superior to the Albatros.

CHAPTER 5

THE BRITISH ARMY'S OPERATIONS ON THE SOMME

Dr Stuart Mitchell

The battle of the Somme was the furnace within which the war-winning BEF was forged. From the disastrous opening day, through highs like the battle of Bazentin Ridge on 14 July 1916 and lows such as the attritional slogs over places like High Wood, Delville Wood and Guillemont in late July and August 1916, the British Army on the Western Front was transformed from a mass of partially trained men into an organized modern army equipped to stand toe to toe with a determined, skilled, Continental opponent. This chapter will not only explore the operational problems that hamstrung British efforts during the battle of the Somme; but also highlight the developments that improved the operational capabilities of the British. Ultimately it was the experience accrued by soldier and general alike that would prove invaluable as the war dragged on.

The Somme was the largest battle in British military history up to that point by nearly any metric of measurement: numbers of men involved, casualties, and munitions expended. Although precise figures are difficult to ascertain, some 53 divisions (of 10,000–12,000 men each) were involved to varying extents (many multiple times) in the fighting across three British armies (Third, Fourth, and Reserve).[1] The British casualties alone amounted to 419,654 – of which 127,751 died – and over 19 million shells were fired between 24 June and 20 November 1916. The BEF was in uncharted territory. The French and German armies had greater experience in conducting large-scale battles: Artois, Champagne and Verdun were already scorched into the national psyches of those two nations. In many respects they were further along their respective learning curves than the British. Indeed, many of the techniques that would become central to the way all three armies fought had been conceived of during 1915 yet it was on the Somme that many of these ideas matured to become integral components of the BEF's set-piece battle.

The outcome of World War I was the product of a series of races: which society could mobilize the resources of the state most efficiently and quickly? Which side could endure the losses and hardships incurred? And perhaps most importantly, which side could adjust their fighting methods in response to their enemy's actions swiftly enough that they might not be countered? If 4 August 1914 was the day the starter's gun was fired for the British then the battle of the Somme was the moment they joined the leading runners. It would take another two years of hard slog before the Germans were worn down enough for the British and French to pull ahead sufficiently to bring the war to a close. For the British those years owed much to the improvements made during the battle of the Somme.

Politics and context

By the start of 1916 the British Empire found itself in a strategic quagmire. During 1915 the strategic focus swung between different fronts as political and military divisions exerted themselves as to how best to defeat Germany. Thus, relatively small-scale efforts on the Western Front at Neuve Chapelle, Aubers Ridge and Festubert were followed up by the larger Dardanelles expedition to Turkey, before swinging back to the Western Front in September to support the French. The Dardanelles expedition revealed a fracture in British strategic thinking. This has often been simplistically depicted as the 'Easterners vs Westerners' debate. However, there was much common ground between the two sides: they both saw the ultimate defeat of Germany as the primary end to be achieved. The crucial difference was that individuals such as David Lloyd George, Winston Churchill and Arthur Balfour saw the unleashing of the vast manpower of the Russian Empire as the best means of achieving this.[2] By focusing on 'knocking Germany's props', in Lloyd George's words, the Entente Powers could attract neutral support in critical regions such as the Balkans, they could serve their own imperial ambitions in the Middle East and unlock the potential of the sleeping Russian giant.[3] In principle this was a sound strategy, but it overlooked the necessities of a global total war. The idea of softer fronts in an age of industrial warfare was misguided and attitudes tinged with racist undertones towards the Turkish soldiers led to folly on the beaches and hills of Gallipoli. By 1916, the political class reluctantly accepted the need to focus on the Western Front that year. Although many on the War Committee continued to harbour significant reservations, they could offer little argument against the increasing French demands for support.[4] The grand strategic direction of the British efforts was a difficult compromise between well-intentioned politicians seeking a quick and easy alternative to the long casualty lists created by a continental approach and military strategists more familiar with the difficulties of expeditionary operations. Ultimately it was recognised that if victory was to be achieved it would only be as a result of defeating the Germans in France and Flanders. Coalition pressures and the difficulties of campaigning in far-flung theatres removed any possibility of the war concluding victoriously after a campaign fought elsewhere.

It was into this environment that the battle of the Somme was forged. The ultimate strategic aim in Westminster was to bring the war closer to a conclusion, and increasingly, to aid their French coalition partners.

Strategic vision for the assault

The battle of the Somme had its genesis at the second inter-Allied conference held at Chantilly between 6 and 8 December 1915. In this grand château 24 miles north-east of Paris, representatives of the Entente

Powers–France, Britain, Russia, Italy, Serbia, and Belgium–came together to decide the unified strategy for defeating Germany in 1916. Shortly after 0915hrs on 6 December 1915 Général Maurice Pellé, Chief of Staff to Général Joseph Joffre, the French Commander-in-Chief, explained to gathered delegates the French plan for the coming year. Joffre's strategy aimed at 'the destruction of the German and Austrian armies' by way of a 'simultaneous and combined offensive.'5 The enemy would be worn down through a series of concurrent attritional blows to be followed up by a decisive offensive to end the war. After a year of almost universal failure the gathered delegates were receptive.

In recent times attrition has taken on a number of negative connotations and is largely seen as the last resort of the unimaginative commander, yet the inescapable truth is that when the resources of major states clash it is often a necessary precursor to victory. Attrition, or the erosion of the enemy's capacity to fight chiefly but not solely through the destruction of their armed forces, occurs in all wars to differing degrees and, as the Dardanelles had exposed in the summer of 1915, there was no front where it could be easily avoided. At Chantilly General Alexieff, the Russian army's Chief of Staff, offered the only alternative plan: the Entente Powers would focus on the destruction of Austro-Hungarian forces in the Balkans. Although superficially appealing to British politicians mindful of the cost of war on the Western Front, the plan was unpalatable for the French who would still have to liberate their occupied territory even if it was successful. At the conclusion of the conference the French had secured ageneral agreement for the main powers to conduct a simultaneous combined offensive. The finer details remained undecided.

On 19 December 1915, shortly after the Chantilly conference, General Sir Douglas Haig was made Commander-in-Chief of the BEF replacing Field Marshal Sir John French. There was change in London too; General Sir Archibald Murray, the 'stop-gap' Chief of the Imperial General Staff (CIGS), was replaced by the popular, gruff-speaking General Sir William Robertson. Both Haig and Robertson were committed to the strategy of seeking a decision on the Western Front and in the months following Chantilly advanced the plans in tandem with their French equivalents. The result was agreement on a combined Anglo-French offensive in the Somme region where the two armies met. In these discussions lay the seeds of confusion that would shape Haig's concept of operations for the battle. A major point of departure between Haig and Joffre occurred when they met once again at Chantilly on 29 December 1915. Joffre pushed for the British to take the lead in the 'wearing out' battle, attacks made in April or May to draw the German reserves behind the Western Front and wear them down. Haig thought that this burden should be shared between both allies and wanted the attacks to directly precede the decisive blow. Both Joffre and Haig had to be mindful of domestic politics: Joffre, aware that French manpower was running low, was under pressure to ensure the British did their bit; while Haig was still mindful of the reservations of politicians in London. Haig's first choice was for a preliminary offensive in the Somme sector with the major effort taking place in the Ypres sector where the channel ports might be freed from German occupation. Both sides initially agreed to this proposal when they met in St Omer at the British General Headquarters (GHQ) on 20 January 1916. Yet this compromise was rapidly changed as domestic politics and mutual suspicions of each other began to emerge. Further meetings took place and the plan was slowly altered. By the time Haig and Joffre met on 14 February the preliminary 'wearing out' battle had been completely jettisoned. The attack would now be one large offensive with the British committing 25 divisions and the French 40 astride the Somme River.

Events overtook the Valentine's Day plan. On 21 February 1916 the German Army launched a major offensive on the symbolic French town of Verdun. After initial German success the French stabilized their front but reserves that had been earmarked for the major Anglo-French offensive were rapidly eroded. By May the French commitment of 40 divisions had fallen to 22. Alternative ideas of a British offensive in Flanders re-emerged but these were soon quashed by Joffre. Haig remained uncertain of French intentions and the extent of their involvement until the matter was finally settled on 31 May 1916. The French commitment was confirmed, although vagaries over its precise size persisted. For Joffre and the French the battle was now about easing the pressure being exerted upon them at Verdun. The British would take the primary role. For Haig its precise strategic function was uncertain. He knew he had to act but possibilities remained for greater things to be achieved. From its nascent inception at Chantilly in early December 1915, the strategic aims of the battle of the Somme had radically changed. The French-led plan to strike a decisive blow after subsidiary attacks gave way to a British-led offensive to relieve Verdun. The ambiguities that persisted at British GHQ would have disastrous ramifications for many of the men of the Fourth Army who went over the top on 1 July.

Haig and Rawlinson divided: breakthrough or bite-and-hold?

Differences of opinion over what could be achieved in the forthcoming offensive would hamstring the coordination of British operations on the Somme. Haig was inclined towards optimistic hopes of breakthrough shaped by his experiences in 1915. His attitudes were sculpted by the fleeting, missed opportunities at Neuve Chapelle, Loos, and for the Germans at the second battle of Ypres. Rawlinson had reached a more pessimistic view. He developed an operational approach known as 'bite-and-hold' whereby the British forces would mass artillery along a narrow frontage, capture the enemy's line at an important tactical position, consolidate, and defeat the inevitable German counterstroke. It was limited in its aims and was, in principle, less costly in lives in the short term, yet even Rawlinson recognized it could not deliver a decisive victory. Furthermore, it inclined the commander towards caution and on the Somme this would lead to missed opportunities and friction between the army commander and his commander-in-chief. Both concepts were understandable given the conflicting lessons of the various battles of 1915, but the failure to reconcile these two contradictory operational approaches led to missed opportunities and tragic failures.

In some respects the operational conduct of the battle of the Somme for the British can be defined by the conflict between Haig and Rawlinson's competing ideas of what was possible and achievable at any given time. History has largely favoured Rawlinson's more limited conceptions, but this is to overlook missed opportunities for greater territorial gains that a commander with a more dynamic approach might have exploited, and the inconsistency with which both commanders held to their ideas. To be sure, Haig's adherence to the possibility of a breakthrough at least until early August, only to subside and re-emerge again in mid-September in time for the battle of Flers-Courcelette, was costly for the infantry expected to push on to objectives well beyond their capacity to reach. But it was not completely devoid of merit nor was it based on an ignorant understanding of the front-line conditions. Perhaps the more egregious error was that Haig failed to fully impart his way of thinking to his subordinate while Rawlinson proved obstinate and reluctant to accept his superior's approach. While similar disagreements occurred between Général Ferdinand Foch and Joffre, the different circumstances, inter-personal relations and the greater experience of the French Army ensured it never proved quite as disastrous as it did for their British counterparts.

The operational planning for the battle of the Somme began in late March for the British, despite the enduring lack of clarity at the highest level over precisely what purpose the battle would fulfil and what resources would be committed. The first plan of attack was largely the work of Rawlinson's Chief of Staff, Major-General A. A. Montgomery and was submitted to British GHQ on 3 April 1916. It called for a methodical assault on the first-line positions with a pause of two weeks to bring the guns up before assaulting the German second line. This limited approach was appealing to Haig in its potential for attrition of German manpower but was unsuited to the more ambitious French plans as they then stood at that time.[6] As the circumstances at Verdun gradually diluted French hopes of what could be achieved, the ambitions of Foch and Fayolle became more limited; objectives were scaled down in accordance to what could be achieved before re-orientating to meet the British aims after the 31 May agreement. No such process occurred for the British. Haig's ambitions gradually expanded, fuelled by the ambiguities of Joffre's contradictory proclamations on what could be realistically gained and the freedom of action imparted by the decision to make it a British-led battle.[7] Rawlinson's subsequent plans in April had accepted the need to make swift progress along a wider and deeper front. Rather than simply capturing the German first line, the second-line position would also be assaulted. This had the catastrophic consequence of diluting the density of artillery to below the levels deployed at the battle of Neuve Chapelle, fought over a year earlier. To attempt to mitigate this Rawlinson advocated a move away from an intense hurricane bombardment to a prolonged, methodical one. Although resistant at first, Haig eventually yielded to his subordinate. Yet it would not be enough, as events of 1 July were to prove. The cavalry was given a role too. As the only arm of exploitation available to the armies fighting at this time the decision to assign regiments of cavalry to the army corps to be used in small numbers to seize and hold vital ground was a sound one. Rather than the hide-bound, horse-obsessed general depicted in popular culture, Haig was acutely aware of the cavalry's role on the battlefield. Had he not planned to take advantage of any success achieved he would have been abrogating his duties as a commander.

British intelligence had indicated that the Germans had only 32 battalions on the Fourth Army's front and a reserve of 65 which could be pulled into the battle inside the first week. This information led Haig to conclude that the 'wearing out' battle that had been taking place at Verdun was reaching its tipping point and the Germans could be decisively defeated. So in the third week of June Haig set distant objectives for the cavalry to exploit in the event of a complete collapse in resistance. He also placed Gough's Reserve Army, now a mounted formation tasked with exploitation, under Rawlinson's command so that they were ready: 'once a break is effected, a Commander and Staff is necessary to take command on the spot.' This principle was militarily sound, but it empowered Rawlinson to marginalize Haig's contingencies in the event of success.[8] This was borne out by the commander of Fourth Army's lukewarm delivery of the changes when briefing his corps commanders. Rawlinson prefaced Haig's extended objectives with the qualification that: '…it may not be possible to break the enemy's line and push the cavalry through at the first rush.' He went on to acknowledge that a situation may later develop but that it was impossible to predict the exact moment when the horsemen might be committed to the battle.[9] This was hardly a ringing endorsement and belies Rawlinson's scepticism of what was possible. Some historians have been uncharitable towards Haig's ambitious adjustments.[10] Certainly the decision to extend

British attack at Bazentin Ridge, 14 July 1916

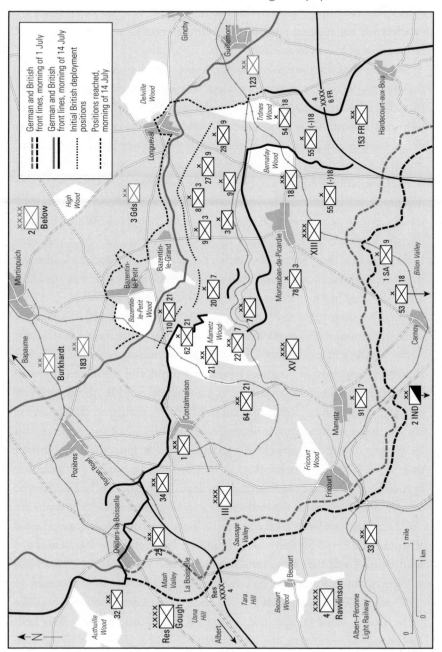

the objectives for the infantry to the German second line had disastrous consequences, but even his critics would agree that he should not be condemned for creating contingencies in the event of success.[11] Moreover opportunities for exploitation did arise.

At 0730hrs the intense bombardment pouring onto the German trenches, wire and strongpoints ceased. The infantry, employing a variety of tactical formations, pushed forward from their positions; some were jumping off from their own trenches, others had stalked forward into no man's land to await the start of the attack. In the north the diversionary attack at Gommecourt by two divisions – the 46th (North Midland) and 56th (London) divisions – was a failure. The initial success of the Londoners quickly faded as German barrage and enfilade fire isolated the attackers, while German counter-attacks gradually forced them back. When the 46th (North Midland) Division, operating on the far left of the line, arose from their trenches they found uncut wire and were exposed to withering machine-gun fire. Some penetration into the German line was made by 139th Brigade but further attacks were called off as a waste of lives. Major-General Montague Stuart-Wortley paid for this decision with his job and was sent home on 5 July 1916. Things were not much better for Fourth Army, a mile to the south of VII Corps at Gommecourt. VIII Corps was facing the formidable German defences around the fortified villages of Serre and Beaumont Hamel. The attack was preceded by the detonation of a 40,000lb high-explosive mine at 0720hrs. Not only did this signal the British intent to attack but it necessitated the early lift of the medium and heavy guns from the first line providing vital respite for the German defenders. When zero hour struck, the 31st Division made little headway against Serre; the Pals battalions, largely drawn from the northern industrial towns, and who formed the bulk of the attacking waves, paid a heavy price. To their right the 4th Division broke into and captured Quadrilateral Redoubt, a formidable German strongpoint between Serre and Beaumont Hamel. Yet the failure of the 31st Division to their left and the 29th Division to their right meant the gain had to be relinquished the following morning.

Operating on the right of VIII Corps, X Corps made some impressive gains; most notably the Ulstermen of the 36th (Ulster) Division reaching and capturing the Schwaben Redoubt. But as was the case with the 4th Division, the failure of the neighbouring 29th Division and 32nd Division exposed the Ulstermen to withering flanking fire. The position fell to German counter-attacks before the day's end. The 32nd Division facing the 'hardest nut to crack in the whole line' in Thiepval village managed to make minor gains in the adjacent Leipzig Redoubt but failed to capture the village.[12] On III Corps' front, the 8th and 34th divisions faced the formidable obstacle of Ovillers and La Boisselle villages. Moreover, the 8th Division had to cross 750 yards of no man's land, exposed to flanking fire from the Leipzig spur on the left, La Boisselle to the right and Ovillers in front. Despite this, elements of all three brigades committed to the attack managed to get into the German front line. Yet once again, as the German defensive fire created an impassable wall and the defenders regrouped, the British troops were driven back, captured or killed. A similar fate befell the 34th Division. The failure of the British artillery to adequately subdue the German defenders was felt acutely on III Corps' front. The lifts proved to be much too quick leaving the infantry exposed and unable to make further progress. In the months to come the British infantry would prove more adept at using their own firepower to push forward but these changes were still some time away.

It was south of the Albert–Bapaume road, on XV and XIII Corps' fronts, that the real opportunity for exploitation presented itself. With more limited objectives, a higher density of artillery and the use in places of a creeping barrage of shells fired ahead of the infantry to force the Germans into cover as the British advanced, the German resistance fell apart between Fricourt and Assevillers. The 21st Division and the 7th Division successfully flanked Fricourt village prompting a withdrawal, while Mametz was captured by the latter. Perhaps the most notable successes came on the front of Lieutenant-General Sir Walter Congreve's XIII Corps: the 18th (Eastern) Division and the 30th Division captured Pommiers and Glatz redoubts while the village of Montauban also fell into British hands. The artillery preparations here were more sophisticated, with both divisions of XIII Corps using a creeping rather than a lifting barrage. Moreover the German defensive arrangement south of the Albert–Bapaume road was weaker with less depth. The more experienced French to their south, using a greater weight of heavy artillery and dedicating more resources to counter-battery work ensured that the gains could be reinforced.[13] Indeed the two French corps of Fayolle's 6e Armée achieved all their objectives on 1 July, taking over 4,000 German prisoners in the process. Both north and south of the Somme the French pushed towards the German second-line positions. The only thing that held them back was the lack of progress by the British on their left flank.

Despite this success, at midday Rawlinson stood down Gough's Reserve Army at precisely the moment it might have been of most use. Rawlinson's motives remain obscure but from the evidence available it seems likely that he simply did not believe greater success was possible. On 2 and 3 July the situation remained critical for the Germans, a counter-attack by the 12th Reserve Division floundered upon the British defences at Montauban.[14] Meanwhile Mametz Wood, Bernafay Wood, Trones Wood would all be bitterly fought over in the coming days and weeks. Bolder action may have taken them on the first day. While a breakthrough of the proportions Haig hoped for on 22 June was always highly unlikely, with greater vigour Rawlinson might have been able to turn a catastrophic defeat into a qualified victory, albeit at the cost of validating Haig's operational conception.

The importance of Rawlinson's and Haig's fundamentally different views of operations would flare up again in the battle of Bazentin Ridge, 14 July 1916 and once more at Flers-Courcelette, 15 September 1916. Haig's wise insistence on exploiting the success gained in the south rather than attempting to reinforce failure in the north left Rawlinson with the task of organizing an attack on Bazentin Ridge. This would be conducted along a 6,000-yard frontage to a depth of 12,000 yards. Crucially the attack would employ 1,000 artillery pieces, of which a third were medium or heavy calibres. This increased the strength and density of and in doing so addressed one of the critical failures of 1 July.[15] Rawlinson's plan also called for the distance between the British and German lines to be closed by an advance conducted at night before launching the attack at dawn. Haig had reservations, which he aired to his army commander on 11 July. He explained how he thought the plan overly complex and required the capture of Mametz Wood and Contalmaison.[16] Rawlinson assented to redeveloping the plan but quickly performed a *volte face* the following day. Discussions with his staff led Haig to approve the original plan with only minor adjustments.

The battle went well. Haig described it as 'the best day we have had this war'.[17] The superior weight of artillery allowed the British infantry to rapidly secure most of the German second-line positions by midday. In the planning stage Rawlinson had made provisions for the utilization of cavalry. Unfortunately for the British the plan placed the cavalry at the disposal of XIII Corps, yet once the battle had begun it was clear they were most needed on XV Corps' front. Despite two regiments of the Secunderabad Brigade reaching the front lines by 0700hrs it would be 1800hrs before authority switched between the corps commands. The cavalry that went into action managed to occupy a portion of High Wood and inflicted losses upon the Germans. The cavalry by this point was not simply an arm for chasing down a broken and routing enemy, but a force well-trained in dismounted combat. The speed allowed them to swiftly advance and hold key tactical positions until the infantry could advance to support them. Had the command structures been in place on 14 July to facilitate the swift deployment of the mounted assets it is not unreasonable to suggest that the key position of High Wood, a scene of vicious fighting throughout mid-July and August, might have fallen. The relationship between Haig and Rawlinson was not a static one. Leading up to 1 July Haig's more ambitious, strategic outlook contrasted with Rawlinson's more limited, tactically rooted concept of operations. By 14 July it was Haig who concerned himself with the potential damage Rawlinson's innovative plan might incur. The roles would once again reverse by 15 September.

The battle of Flers-Courcelette is best remembered for the first use of tanks, but it was the coordination of the artillery, infantry and tanks that decided the outcome. By early September the British had bludgeoned their way through to a line encompassing Ginchy, Delville Wood, Longueval, the southern corner of High Wood and Pozières. The Germans, however, had responded by developing the defences around Flers, Gueudecourt, Lesboeufs, Morval, and Courcelette.[18] The development of the British plan of attack took on a familiar pattern. Rawlinson favoured a limited assault on the German first-line positions while Haig, buoyed by intelligence of crumbling German morale, felt that more could be achieved. Haig's position was again, not wholly without merit. In early September there was an increasing sense of desperation amongst some of the German soldiers and higher leadership feared they were losing the *Materialschlacht* (war of *matériel*).[19] Yet for Haig to extrapolate from this that the Germans were close to complete collapse was reading too much into the evidence. Once again similar problems arose between Haig and Rawlinson. Haig's hopes of a breakthrough had dwindled in August after the success of 14 July, but by September the pressure exerted upon the Germans led him to conclude that it was once again possible. The Cavalry Corps was placed in reserve for the battle of Flers-Courcelette. Both Fourth and Reserve armies would take part, although the latter in a much more limited capacity on the left flank. In total five cavalry divisions were allocated to the battle. Despite this large allocation, Rawlinson manoeuvred to limit their possible use. He stipulated that the cavalry would only be used once the advance had progressed 2.5 miles and that roads should be kept clear to bring the guns forward.[20] Haig's conceptions went far beyond the Somme – he hoped that the attack might provide opportunities for First and Third armies to seize key positions in their sectors. Second Army was to do what it could to draw the attention of the Germans.[21] In his understanding of how close the Germans were to defeat it is enough to say that he was simply wrong. Nonetheless, Rawlinson's active subversion of his commander's intent proved problematic once more.

Unlike 1 July, 15 September was a limited success, albeit one which fell far short of Haig's expectations. The British advanced 2,500 yards and further in some areas. High Wood was finally captured and Reserve Army's Canadian Corps occupied Courcelette. The introduction of tanks had created a number of tactical dilemmas for Fourth Army. How could these heavy, lumbering machines cross the shell-cratered ground? The solution proffered was to leave lanes in the preliminary bombardment of the German front line. Had the tanks been mechanically reliable this may have been a reasonable decision; in the end it simply exposed many of the leading infantry battalions to fire from the unsuppressed German defenders. That the infantry were largely able to fight through was a testament to their determination and increasing tactical sophistication. For example, when attacking High Wood, 47th Division utilized a hurricane bombardment of trench mortars, firing 750 rounds in 15 minutes to subdue the Germans occupying the remainder of the wood.[22] That a disaster was avoided was predominantly down to the maintenance of the density of the bombardment, which was largely confined to the German first- and second-line positions.[23] Neither Haig nor Rawlinson emerge from Flers-Courcelette with much credit. Haig's optimistic assessment of German morale led him to reach grandiose conclusions which overestimated a temporary decline in the mood of the German units they were facing. Rawlinson, through his marginalization of the cavalry, undermined his commander-in-chief and disregarded one potential means of expanding gains where they were achieved.

The Somme would drag on for another two months, but Haig's hopes of a breakthrough were extinguished at Flers-Courcelette. There would be greater successes still to come and further bloody failures. The battle had at least achieved its immediate aim of relieving pressure at Verdun and in the process accelerated the downfall of the Chief of Staff of the German Army, General Erich von Falkenhayn, who was removed in August 1916. The strategic initiative now firmly lay with the Entente Powers – a point recognized by Falkenhayn's successors Generalfeldmarschall Paul von Hindenburg and his Erster Generalquartiermeister General Erich Ludendorff when they began to prepare for the evacuation of the Bapaume salient in spring 1917 by building a new formidable defensive line, the Siegfriedstellung, or 'Hindenburg Line'. Work began on this in September 1916. Despite these strategic successes Haig's grander aims had not been fulfilled and the victory still seemed a distant prospect. However, the British were still learning at all levels, from the private soldier to commander-in-chief. Perhaps Haig summed it up best in a conversation with Major-General Sir Oliver Nugent, commander of the 36th (Ulster) Division: 'Well, we were all learning.'[24]

The operational legacy of the Somme

While Haig and Rawlinson's different operational concepts created problems during the planning phase of major battles, the BEF was, at least, much more successful at drawing lessons from their experiences. Artillery techniques improved, a new infantry organization and doctrine evolved, personnel were better able to apply existing doctrinal principles and logistics were overhauled.

After the bloodletting of 1 July the search for improvements began in earnest. Divisions sought answers for their failures and reasons for their successes. The 8th Division's Brigadier-General H. D. Tuson, commanding 23rd Brigade, argued that the failure of his formation could be attributed to casualties incurred and the artillery losing touch with the infantry. Major-General William Rycroft, commanding the 32nd Division, reached similar conclusions annotating a memorandum dissecting the reasons for French success with: 'Our lifts were as experience shows much too quick'.[25] The result of this interrogation, which occurred in the divisional headquarters up and down the line, was a widespread recognition of the need to improve artillery techniques. The value of the creeping barrage was proven on XIII Corps' front and would become *de rigueur* for the set-piece attack for the rest of the war. The creeping barrage was not a new technique, the idea of a curtain of shells predated World War I, and each side groped their way towards it. The French experimented with it at the second battle of Artois in the spring of 1915 with some success.[26] There is some uncertainty over the first use by the British. The bombardment used by the 15th Division at the battle of Loos in September 1915 was at the very least an important step towards it. Yet it was during the battle of the Somme that the creeping barrage came of age, shifting from a 'novelty' to an integral part of the set-piece battle.[27] One report from a division returning to the Somme in late October after a period rebuilding after 1 July recognized just how important the creeping barrage had become: 'All ranks must be made to understand clearly that the considerable success which has been achieved in recent operations is almost entirely due to the infantry following close behind a rolling barrage.'[28] The technique steadily increased in complexity as the war progressed. On the Somme, 'Chinese' barrages were incorporated to attempt to deceive the Germans as to the exact start time of the operation; heavy barrages were fired at depth and rolled back towards the British lines to break up counter-attacks; and sophisticated fire plans were developed with varying speeds tailored to the terrain being assaulted. By October the German III. Königlich Bayerisches Armee-Korps and XXVI. Reserve-Korps were moved to remark on the technical ability and coordination of the British artillery and infantry and when the Germans formed up for counter-attacks: 'magnificently directed artillery fire would inflict appalling and almost instantaneous losses upon them.'[29] The creeping barrage was no panacea for victory. It was costly in munitions, took time to prepare and placed a heavy burden on supply. With such intensive use gun barrels wore down and careful staff work was required to avoid laying down a barrage in the wrong place. Yet as the gunners gained experience these processes became more efficient, the infantry became more confident in their gunners' abilities and, when planned well, it could provide them with the vital seconds required to beat the Germans in the 'race to the parapet'.

The enduring image of the Somme in popular culture is that of the heavily laden soldier walking in line towards their death at the hands of the German gunners. Yet even on the most disastrous day of the campaign this was far from the reality. True enough, some formations chose to maintain cohesion among their infantry by attacking in waves at a walking pace, but there was great variety up and down the line. Lightly armed assault troops with Lewis gunners and snipers were used in VIII Corps' front. Both divisions in X Corps advanced their leading infantry into no man's land before zero hour to 'hug' the barrage. Sectional rushes, fire and movement, and trench mortars were used at varying times to aid the infantry in getting forward.[30] On that first day infantry tactics alone would not prove sufficient. The problem was not a lack of innovation or knowledge but the coordination and application with other arms. If the artillery and infantry failed, the latter would rarely have enough cohesion or firepower to advance under their own steam. Over the course of the Somme, battalions experimented with different tactical dispositions. This sort of bottom-up learning would filter into doctrine and the product would be a new standardized, specialized infantry platoon organization outlined in *SS 143: Instructions for the Training of Platoons for Offensive Action*. Published in February 1917, this manual formed the bedrock of British infantry methods for the next two years. The specialization of infantry sections increased the firepower available to the infantry and aided in the standardization of training. Each platoon would now contain a section of bombers, riflemen, Lewis gunners and rifle grenadiers. This effectively gave the infantry greater organic firepower and made them less reliant upon the success of the artillery.

The Somme also provided an opportunity for middle- and lower-ranking tactical commanders to gain valuable experience. The pre-war doctrine of delegating authority to the 'man-on-the-spot' relied upon leaders, from corps command and below, to be able to decide the best course of action. This was not always the case. Brigadier-General Yatman's interventions during the 32nd Division's assault on Thiepval confined the re-bombardment of the village to strongpoints in the south and east with disastrous results for those men of 96th Brigade tasked with mounting a subsequent attack.[31] The fundamental principle of decentralized command was not at fault during the Somme, but the execution was. It has been persuasively argued that this had been refined by September 1916, within II Corps and the 18th (Eastern) Division at least.[32] The delegation of command authority of command would address some of the difficulties in command and control within the relatively rigid confines of the set-piece battle.

The operational legacy of the Somme extended beyond infantry and artillery. A new arm made its debut; logistics were gradually improved under the guidance of the civilian transport expert and rail magnate Sir Eric Geddes; munitions were developed including the phased introduction of the 106 fuse, or 'graze' fuse, which dramatically reduced the chances of high-explosive shells burying themselves into the mud before exploding. The organization of staff at corps level was formalized and the discrepancies of seniority and rank ironed out. Moreover, a staff officer dedicated to counter-battery work was created in a move that would see the BEF lead the way in scientific counter-battery techniques for the rest of the war. But perhaps the most important development during the Somme was a fundamental willingness to experiment and share new ideas. Haig and Rawlinson certainly had their differences and operational flaws were often exposed by a dynamic enemy adjusting its own methods to counter Allied developments, but they both should be given credit for fostering an environment in which subordinates were given the freedom to innovate. Through the shock of battle, the BEF improved in nearly every respect, but more importantly they built up a bank of experience and enshrined it in doctrine. It is not appropriate to categorize a battle of such mixed fortunes and staggering human cost as a 'victory', but the experience of the Somme was of critical importance in pushing the BEF along its path towards defeat of the Central Powers.

CHAPTER 6

TRIAL AND ERROR

The Dominion forces on the Somme in 1916

Lieutenant Colonel (Ret'd) Christopher Pugsley ONZM

The Dominion forces of the British Empire that took part in the battles on the Somme between 1 July and November 1916 included contributions from Newfoundland, South Africa, the Australian Imperial Force (AIF), the Canadian Expeditionary Force (CEF), and the New Zealand Expeditionary Force (NZEF). This involved four Australian divisions of Lieutenant-General Sir William Birdwood's 1st Australian and New Zealand Army Corps (I ANZAC), which from the time of the arrival of Lieutenant-General Sir Alexander Godley's II ANZAC in France in June 1916 became the de facto Australian Corps, the three Canadian divisions of Lieutenant-General Sir Julian Byng's Canadian Corps, with the 4th Canadian Division that replaced them in the final phase of the battle. There was also the New Zealand Division commanded by Major-General Sir Andrew Russell, which usually formed part of Godley's II ANZAC, but fought as part of XV Corps in General Sir Henry Rawlinson's Fourth Army on the Somme. It was the New Zealanders' fate to fight as part of a British corps again on the Somme in 1918, this time as part of Lieutenant-General Harper's IV Corps in Byng's Third Army. In this its experience on the Western Front made it more typical of a British division, which was sent from army corps to army corps according to the operational need.

Dominion involvement in the battle of the Somme in 1916 is a topic steeped in national mythology and emotion. The impact that this has can be glimpsed in a visit to Newfoundland Memorial Park at Beaumont Hamel, perhaps the most visited location on the Somme battlefield. This is the site of the near annihilation of the Newfoundland Regiment, then one of the units of 88th Brigade of the 29th Division, on 1 July. Walking these now grassed trenches, perhaps the only place where one can get a sense of what the front line of the Somme looked like 100 years ago, and the overwhelming impression is one of the cost of war and its futility. A national army of regimental size from a small British colony that suffered 604 casualties or 70 per cent of its strength through attacking from the support trenches after the initial attacks had failed, with many of the casualties occurring before the leading elements reached no man's land.[1] There was no question of them learning from this mistake – as a single battalion the Newfoundlanders' fate was determined by decisions at brigade, division, and corps level. Here its commanding officer simply obeyed orders and the regiment was destroyed.[2]

The next Dominion force to fight on the Somme was the South African Brigade, which formed part of the 9th (Scottish) Division. Today the South African Memorial in Delville Wood commemorates the destruction of the brigade in attempting to take the wood over five days of fighting, 15–20 July 1916, at a cost of 2,300 casualties. This memorial of truly epic architectural proportions was initially a tribute to Afrikaans effort in World War I when it was opened in October 1926. Today it commemorates not only the 10,000 South African dead of World War I, but other major conflicts as well including World War II and Korea. Its focus has shifted to reflect the realities of South Africa today.[3]

This holds true for any examination of Australian, Canadian, and New Zealand achievement in World War I – one has to strip back what we believe now of the iconic images of the Australian and New Zealand 'Diggers' and the 'Canucks' of the Canadian Corps that have shaped the perceptions of national identity in each country to see what they were and how they functioned in 1916.

Bill Rawling in *Surviving Trench Warfare*, his seminal study of the Canadian Corps, made a statement that was applicable to every Dominion force on the Somme in 1916. 'Compared to their regular army predecessors, the soldiers arriving at the front in 1915 and 1916 were ill-trained novices with poor fighting and survival skills.'[4] This was true for three of the four Australian divisions of I ANZAC and for two of the four Canadian divisions. It was certainly true of the New Zealand Division that had been raised in Egypt in February 1916, like its 4th and 5th Australian division counterparts, and had arrived in France in late April–early May 1916.

The Newfoundlanders and the South African Brigade's fates were determined by their size far more than their level of skill. How effectively they were committed to battle was dependent on a divisional plan into which that they had little or no input. It was when and where they were committed to the battle that determined their fate. Being committed early in July meant that they had no opportunity to learn from the mistakes made in the first days – their experiences provided the lessons for others to benefit from.

Of the Australians, New Zealanders and Canadians, only the latter could be termed to be experienced in fighting on the Western Front, having been there since early 1915. The Canadians were also fortunate as they and the New Zealand Division were not committed to the Somme until September 1916. Both forces had some time to digest the lessons emerging from the Somme and benefited from the training days available en route to the third battle of the Somme, which started on 15 September 1916. All three Dominion forces had their successes during the Somme fighting, but such was the nature of the fighting that the import of this was lost in the overall impression that we have today of almost stationary armies drowning in a sea of mud and blood as the battle dragged on into the winter of 1916. Each learned from this experience but as we will see, where they went after the Somme and whose army they were part of, also determined how quickly they benefited from it.

I ANZAC on the Somme

The Australian divisions of the AIF were split between the two ANZAC corps; the 5th Australian Division was the least experienced and was assessed to be not yet ready to go to the Somme. Ironically, this unfitness was confirmed when it was committed in the tragically flawed and disastrous attack at Fromelles on 19 July 1916. Like its British New Army counterparts it consisted of a superb standard of volunteers of enormous potential, most of whom had never seen the front line before being committed to this battle. A flawed plan and inexperienced command at every level showed that potential and quality of manpower counts for nothing without careful planning matched by training and rehearsals. Fromelles destroyed the 5th Australian Division and although rebuilt with reinforcements it would play only a minor role at the end of the Somme Offensive.[5]

The most experienced Australian divisions were drawn upon first. On 2 July 1916, the day after the battle opened, Headquarters I ANZAC and the 1st and 2nd Australian Divisions were placed under orders to be prepared to move south at 24 hours' notice. Major-General Sir Harold 'Hooky' Walker, a British regular officer, commanded the 1st Australian Division, which was the first to move. It was a veteran division that had served throughout the Gallipoli campaign, and which had split its battalions to form cadres for the 4th and 5th divisions that were raised in Egypt in early 1916. Major-General James Gordon Legge's 2nd Australian Division had also seen Gallipoli service, arriving on the peninsula towards the end of the August offensive in 1915. Its units were not used to bolster the expansion of the AIF because its veteran status was not matched by any experience at formation level. It had never trained by brigades or as a division, and the Somme was its first divisional-level operation. It was veteran in name only and, unlike Walker's seasoned staff at 1st Australian Division, Legge's staff were as inexperienced as any of the British New Army and Territorial Force divisions that attacked on 1 July 1916.[6]

Birdwood's I ANZAC came under command of Lieutenant-General Sir Hubert Gough's Reserve Army (later Fifth Army) on the left or northern flank of the Somme Offensive. The attacks of 1 July had seen no success at all on the left or northern flank against the Thiepval–Pozières Ridge but some success in the south; at a cost of almost 60,000 casualties. The south became the focus of General Sir Douglas Haig's attention and Rawlinson's Fourth Army mounted a series of nibbling attacks that culminated in the night attack of 14 July which seized the German second defensive line from Longueval to just south of Pozières. Haig reorganized the battle front and directed Gough's Reserve Army to assume responsibility for the northern flank against Thiepval–Pozières with Rawlinson's Fourth Army responsible for the south. The Australians, and the Canadians who followed them, were to rue coming under Gough's command.

Instead of waiting for Birdwood's Corps Headquarters to be established, Walker's 1st Australian Division received orders on 18 July 1916 that placed it directly under the command of the Reserve Army for special operations. Gough was impatient to capture the highest point of the Thiepval–Pozières Ridge astride the axis of the Albert–Bapaume road around the shattered village of Pozières, and so outflank and turn the Germans out of Thiepval.

Pozières had been the 8th Division's objective on 1 July but its attack, and four later British attempts to seize it in the middle of that month, failed. Gough wanted Walker to attack immediately, 'I want you to go into the line and attack Pozières tomorrow night!'[7] Walker had been in these situations before, having planned and executed the assault on Lone Pine during the August 1915 offensive on Gallipoli. He would not be rushed by an impatient army commander before he had assessed the problem, and a problem it was. His division relieved the 34th Division in the period 20–23 July in the battered trenches before Pozières and Walker insisted on time to strengthen the position and construct new trenches as an assembly area for the proposed attack, which he planned to mount from the south-east. Walker's Australians had little time to train since marching in stages down from Armentières to the Somme, but had sought advice from divisions that had fought on the Somme as to what had worked and what had not.

The General Staff circulars detailing lessons from the Somme were circulated and became the basis for Walker's planning and preparation.[8]

The experiences of the 7th and 19th divisions provided guidelines on soldiers' individual loads, with soldiers expected to each carry two primed grenades, 120 rounds of small-arms ammunition in their pouches and two further 50-round bandoliers, plus two sandbags to consolidate the captured trench. Identification and control measures were discussed and drinking water points provided on the way to the front line so that each soldier's water bottle would be untouched before the attack.

Clearly defined objectives in Pozières were selected, with phases allocated as stepping stones to each objective, and each phase being covered by an artillery barrage. Attack procedures were also examined. Under cover of darkness a jumping-off trench was dug 200 yards from the first phase objective to get infantry close enough. Within each battalion the rifle companies attacked on a platoon frontage with a proportion of the battalion's Lewis guns or light machine guns, with the second platoon in the second line and with each man following up in the third and fourth platoons carrying a pick or a shovel in order to hold ground won by digging in as quickly as possible.

The need to clear enemy dugouts was emphasized, as was the effectiveness of 'P' smoke or phosphorus grenades. 'If the enemy occupants did not come out very quickly, they were burnt to death.'[9]

The 1st Australian Division's attack on Pozières on night 23 July justified the care Walker had taken with his planning. A line up to the Albert–Bapaume road was captured. Only on the eastern flank along the line of the old German trenches, known as OG1 and OG2, were the divisional objectives not gained. Walker noted that his men moved to within 50 yards of the protective artillery barrage and that up to 30 per cent of his infantry strength was needed to bring supplies forward to defend and hold the ground won.[10] Further attacks saw Pozières taken by 25 July. It was critical ground and the German response saw intense artillery fire and constant counter-attacks which enabled the German defenders to hold onto the actual crest in the OG lines. By the time Walker's division was replaced by Legge's 2nd Division it had suffered 5,285 casualties. Birdwood congratulated his British divisional commander on the performance of his men and said that while he wished he could award many more VCs to them, all he could promise Walker was more of the same.[11]

Canadian Corps' attack on Thiepval Ridge, 26 September 1916

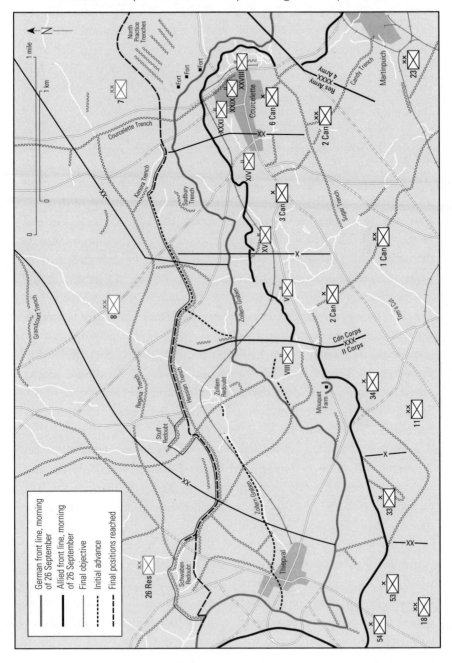

Birdwood's Headquarters I ANZAC took command of the 1st Australian Division on 23 July and the fight for Pozières became a corps battle. Both Birdwood at corps and Legge commanding the 2nd Australian Division proved less willing to stand up to Gough's demands for speedy progress. The 2nd Australian Division's attack on 28/29 July lacked Walker's care and preparation and failed. Heavy shelling fell throughout and the division's casualties were estimated at 96 officers and 3,041 other ranks.[12] By the time the small bridgehead around the village had been expanded and the 2nd Australian Division relieved by the 4th Australian Division, its casualties numbered 4,649.[13]

The conduct of this phase of I ANZAC's battle drew Haig's criticism of Legge ('not much good'), his division ('ignorant') and of Birdwood's staff, whom Brudenell White, Birdwood's Brigadier-General General Staff, stoutly defended.[14] Both the attacks on Pozières, and then Gough's demands that I ANZAC secure Mouquet Farm in order to cut off Thiepval, offered little scope for innovation involving, as they did, attack after attack on a narrow front under constant German artillery fire, matched by an equally determined German defence, which ate through the strength of the Australian divisions.

Gough, as always, drove his army on, demanding that 'Relentless pressure must be exercised everywhere and always'.[15] Australian attacks seized then lost fiercely defended scraps of ground where any trace of the former village had been pulverized beyond recognition. Walker's 1st Australians were committed again on 16 August, as were the 2nd Australians on 26 August with the 4th Australians replacing them on 29 August, all attempted to seize Mouquet Farm and failed. By the end of August, when I ANZAC was withdrawn to the Ypres salient, Australian casualties numbered 23,000 in six weeks, the same number as in the eight months of the Gallipoli campaign.[16]

Once again it had been proved that the superb material of the Australian divisions only counted if they were effectively used and knew what they were doing. Lieutenant-Colonel Iven G. Mackay, one of the outstanding battalion commanders in the 1st Australian Division, noted that the AIF battalions he relieved with his battalion at Mouquet Farm withdrew leaving a number of wounded men, as well as two Lewis guns, behind in the trenches. Driven beyond what the human spirit could endure, all they were concerned with was getting out of the hell-hole. The conditions they had endured had cracked even the strongest of the men and the care for one's mates, seen as central to the Australian 'digger ethos', was gone. Mackay knew that the only way forward for his battalion after the Somme was not 'mateship' but professionalism and he wrote: 'In an army formed quickly from citizens there is a great tendency to treat troops kindly and let them train without too much exertion. This is no kindness to the troops. The real kindness is to make them hard – if possible harder than the enemy.'[17]

Contrary to what we believe and Australians preach – discipline and training were the principal lessons that emerged from the Australian experience on the Somme. Soaring sickness rates and cases of drunkenness and absenteeism in the Australian divisions indicated formations that had been strained to the point of collapse. The Fifth Army lists 184 convictions for desertion in December 1916, 171 of which came from the Australian divisions.[18] Between August 1916 and April 1917, 54 death sentences were awarded by Australian courts-martial in the firm determination by Australian commanders that this was necessary to arrest the rot. When it was pointed out to them by Haig's Judge Advocate General that a provision in the 1903 Australian Defence Act did not allow the confirmation of the death penalty without reference to the Australian Governor General, the Australian divisional commanders' petitioned Birdwood and Haig to recommend that the AIF come under the provisions of the Army Act when deployed overseas.[19]

I ANZAC, now consisting of the 1st, 2nd, 4th and 5th divisions, returned to the Somme at the end of October into a battlefield that had been reduced by rain and mud into an impassable morass. They were committed into the area once occupied by the New Zealand Division near Gueudecourt in a series of small nibbling attacks that failed with heavy loss among men worn down by their previous acquaintance with the Somme. By 31 December 1916 Australian casualties on the Somme numbered 1,115 officers and 31,085 other ranks killed wounded and missing.[20]

The mud became their winter home. There was little time to evaluate their experience and all efforts were concentrated on making the best they could of the atrocious conditions.[21] Circumstance determined that Birdwood's Australians were the last to benefit from the tactical lessons on the Somme. However, the realities of trying to maintain an all-volunteer force were striking home. Lieutenant-Colonel Mackay of the 4th Battalion was critical both of the 'merest trickle' of reinforcements that the under-strength battalions were receiving and of their poor standard of training.

Sustaining an army at an effective fighting standard is the most difficult problem faced on operations, and Australia was now paying for its enthusiasm in basing its strength on the numbers of recruits that came to the recruiting halls in 1914 and 1915 without considering how they would be replaced. Prime Minister Billy Hughes' attempts to introduce conscription, without splitting his Labor administration, by means of a national referendum, failed. Today Australia takes pride in its all-volunteer 1st AIF of World War I, yet the reality was that the dwindling supply of trained recruits crippled its effectiveness as a fighting force by 1918 and placed an unwarranted burden on the soldiers at the front.[22] The impact of inadequate replacements was already being felt in France in late 1916. Surviving the winter on the Somme meant that there was no opportunity to reflect on the lessons of the campaign so far, and the battles before Bullecourt showed that the Australians lagged behind the Canadians and indeed the New Zealand Division, not to mention the newly arrived 3rd Australian Division of Godley's II ANZAC. It would take a change of army for Birdwood's I ANZAC to improve.

The Canadian Corps on the Somme

Gough's Reserve Army role for the renewal of the offensive on 15 September 1916 was carried out by the 2nd and 3rd Canadian divisions of Byng's Canadian Corps astride the axis of the Albert–Bapaume road. Mouquet Farm was captured on 3 September but the major success was the seizing of the village of Courcelette by Major-

General R. E. W. Turner's 2nd Canadians as part of the major offensive on 15 September. The allotted tanks were unable to keep up with the infantry but one, named 'Crème de Menthe', assisted tied-down Canadian infantry in the capture of the sugar factory on the outskirts of the village, using its 6-pounders to destroy German machine-gun posts. The success at Courcelette was the combination of what had been learned since July: the use of an artillery creeping barrage, infantry hugging the barrage, and changes to the infantry formations to reduce the effect of German counter-bombardment. Nevertheless by 22 September casualties in the two attacking Canadian divisions numbered 7,230.[23]

Canadians had more opportunities than the Australians to train for their role on the Somme and like the Australians drew on the General Staff circulars for the latest tactical doctrine. Battalions attacked in the recommended disposition of four waves following closely behind the creeping artillery barrage on the principle that 'a single line of men has usually failed, two lines have generally failed, but sometimes succeeded, three lines have generally succeeded but sometimes failed, and four or more lines have generally succeeded.'[24]

The Canadian Corps was once again heavily committed in the Reserve Army's attack on Thiepval ridge, first attacking north of Courcelette on 26 September which led to the capture of Thiepval and of the Schwaben Redoubt by Major-General Maxse's 18th (Eastern) Division, and then mounting a series of attacks against the Regina Trench between Courcelette and Grandcourt on 1 and 8 October in a series of attacks on a narrow front with little gain for heavy losses. Regina Trench was finally captured by the newly arrived 4th Canadian Division commanded by Major-General David Watson fighting as part of II Corps on 21 October.[25] By now commanders insisted on rehearsals before each battle and Major-General Arthur Currie, commanding the 1st Canadian Division, blamed the failure of the attack on the Transloy Ridge on 8 October on the battalion commander's failure to rehearse his troops.

The habit of practice became standard in Canadian units with the attacking waves walking behind a creeping barrage represented by mounted officers carrying flags, while attention was paid to the individual skills of bombing and using the Lewis light machine gun.[26] It was the artillery's effectiveness that was the key to success. Infantry could advance behind the creeping barrage into the German trenches if the protecting wire barricades had been cut through and destroyed. Uncut wire stopped the infantry advance, giving German machine gunners time to bring their guns into action and for German artillery to turn no man's land into a death zone. By the end of the Somme Offensive Canadian losses numbered 24,029, one quarter of the corps' original strength shared among the three divisions, 4,407 infantrymen per division or a third of their infantry strength.[27]

Central to the growing professionalism of the Canadian Corps was its corps commander, Lieutenant-General Hon Sir Julian Byng. In July 1916 he directed the establishment of a Canadian Corps Officers' School to improve the professional knowledge of his officers in drill, tactics, field engineering, interior economy, and duties in the field. A Canadian Corps Training School was established in November 1916 for the training of junior officers and non-commissioned officers or NCOs in general duties (A Wing) and specialist instructors in weapons such as the Lewis light machine gun, grenade and gas drills, etc (B Wing). Divisional schools were also established.[28]

After the Somme the Canadians were redeployed to the Vimy sector north of Arras. Lessons developed from engagement to engagement and were debated in detail after the offensive. Infantry loads and formations, organization of the Lewis gun team and its position in the attack, use of bombs, training in the use of German bombs that were usually captured in great numbers, use of the Stokes mortar and discussions on how to keep it supplied with ammunition, the efficacy of tanks and an appreciation that they were at this time confined to an infantry support role were all topics discussed.[29]

Byng and his commanders dissected the Somme experience and decided that the key to breaking the trench deadlock was to improve the organization and efficiency of the infantry platoon so that it could develop the 'maximum offensive firepower bestowed by the weapons with which it is now armed'. Byng believed that infantry fire and movement was the key to allowing an advance to work its way forward through the German defences:

The largest unit that, under modern conditions can be directly controlled and manoeuvred under fire by one man is the Platoon. The Platoon Commander is therefore in most cases, the only man who can personally influence the local situation. In fact, it is not too much to say that this is the Platoon Commander's war. Realizing this, it becomes the duty of the Company Commander to see that each Platoon is trained by its leader to act either with independence or as a component of the Company. In each case the fullest development of all the various Infantry weapons should be the object to be achieved.[30]

What was important was 'to develop to the utmost the manoeuvring and attacking power of the platoon' this meant that special efforts were needed to:

Train the Platoon Commander in handling his Platoon, not only in a set piece previously rehearsed, but in dealing with unforeseen situations such as must occur both in attack and defence.'
Train every man in the platoon to act in case of necessity as a specialist, ie., as a bomber, rifle grenadier, or Lewis gunner.[31]

Byng took the initiative and reorganized his battalions so that each battalion consisted of four companies, each of four platoons with four sections. The sections were organized on the basis of a Lewis gun section to provide the suppressive fire, a rifle grenadier section to provide immediate overhead fire support by targeting trenches out of reach of those thrown by hand, a hand-grenade section and an assault section of riflemen; with every individual being trained in all platoon weapons. In February 1917, Haig's GHQ laid down that a battalion would consist of a battalion headquarters and four companies consisting of four platoons of four sections. Byng acknowledged the instruction and said that while there was some variation, the principles were already being followed.[32]

The Canadian Corps attack on Vimy as part of the battle of Arras in April 1917 showed how much the Canadians had progressed since the

Somme. Byng summed up what he saw as the reasons for his corps' success to Headquarters First Army:

> In the Canadian Corps we adopted a form of platoon training early in December before any instructions were issued and our experience on the SOMME, and with a few hints from the French a system was inaugurated. It was the perpetual interest and enthusiasm displayed by all Commanders in training their platoon leaders to act quickly and intelligently under various circumstances that brought about the success achieved.
>
> The whole of the Winter training had for its end the attack and capture of an enemy's heavily entrenched position and Corps, Divisional, Brigade and Regimental Commanders and Staffs were invariably present to see and adapt new ideas.
>
> How far we were right, in view of the future when the Company Commander will and must be the trainer of his platoon leaders, it is impossible to say and that is a point which must not be overlooked, but under present conditions, when so many Senior Officers in Battalions are still inexperienced, the interference even of Corps and Divisional Commanders in the training of the Platoon was beneficial.[33]

The New Zealand Division on the Somme

The New Zealand Division was committed at the same time as the Canadian Corps on 15 September 1916. It attacked north of Longueval as part of XV Corps with its objectives sandwiched between High Wood and Flers. This suggests that, as a comparatively new division, it was positioned between two divisions who had far more difficult objectives and that its success was dependent on the 47th Division's ability to clear High Wood and the 41st Division's clearing of the village of Flers. However, Russell, the New Zealand commander, was a veteran of the Gallipoli campaign where he had been promoted to command the New Zealand and Australian Division and commanded the rearguard during the final evacuation. Like Walker, he and his division had taken every opportunity to learn from the Somme and, after being relieved from the line at Armentières on 13 August, there were three valuable weeks devoted to intensive training. The New Zealand divisional history records:

> By night as well as day, all over the meadowlands and the stubble of harvest fields, battalions in fighting kit incessantly practised the advance of assault waves in extended formation, the avoidance of crowding, the progress of small columns of supporting troops in rear, and the methods of communicating with co-operating aeroplanes.
>
> The different objectives were represented by different coloured flags and the lifts of creeping barrages by lines of men waving branches to indicate the fall of shrapnel, or by horsemen galloping forward in successive 'bounds' in accordance with a prearranged timetable.[34]

Russell watched and critiqued each rehearsal and invited comments from his officers. It would become his way before every operation. He and his officers studied *Preliminary Notes of the Tactical Lessons of Recent Operations* issued by GHQ and each of the recommendations became New Zealand practice.[35] Great care was taken to explain to all ranks the changes in the German defensive doctrine in what was now called 'semi-trench' warfare. As a result standing barrages and creeping barrages were now employed to ensure that parties of Germans between the known trench lines were dealt with.[36] All of this was practised and rehearsed. Russell was happy with his division's task. After the XV Corps conference on 5 September he noted in his diary, 'a good one, and quite to my liking. We are lucky so far.' After reconnoitring the ground and discussing it with his brigade commanders he noted on 13 September: 'Everything I think is on a sound footing.' The attack on 15 September saw the New Zealand Division take three of its four objectives and placed it north of Flers, where it assisted both divisions on its flank. The final objective was taken the next day. Russell wrote in his diary on 17 September: 'Very fair – the Division took all objectives allotted. A weak counter-attack easily driven back.'[37] For 23 days the New Zealand Division remained in this sector, enlarging the ground held in small narrow, expensive attacks against stiffening German defence during which New Zealand casualties accumulated in conditions made worse by the mud and rain. When they were relieved on 3 October they had suffered some 7,000 casualties, including 1,560 dead. The New Zealand artillery remained to spend 52 consecutive days on the Somme before being relieved on 25/26 October 1916 at a cost of some 500 casualties, having fired 500,000 rounds.[38]

There was no room for complacency in Russell's after-action reports. He and his staff dissected the tactical lessons and drew similar conclusions to that of the Canadians. One thing stood out. He and his officers at every level had to become more professional in everything that they did, particularly the administration of the men, who he recognised as his most valuable asset. Russell's aim in wintering on the Lys in northern France was to absorb the lessons of the Somme in the training of his division and to improve its administration: '21 [October] Divisional Conference – Outlined policy – Men's comfort and safety first, the rest nowhere.' He expanded on this in a letter to the Minister of Defence:

> ... and [I] have told Brigadiers and Commanding Officers to forget all about the Germans for a few days and devote their minds and energies towards establishing a good system of interior economy, and improving the discipline of their Units. It is no reflection on the men when I say we are weak in these matters. I certainly confess that personally I have thought a good deal more about fighting than about administration, and I believe most officers would say the same of themselves, but when one sees the waste and unnecessary friction which is set up by want of administrative experience and knowledge, one realizes it plays just as important a part in the success of the war as the actual fighting.[39]

The Somme was a salutary reminder to the British armies that they were the amateurs and the Germans were the professionals and that this war would only be won when the citizen armies of the British Empire matched their opponent in tactical and operational skills.[40] That learning process was well in train as the Somme progressed and how it was put into practice in 1917 depended on circumstance.[41] We can see that the Canadians under Byng and then Currie flourished in Horne's First Army as did the New Zealanders and Australians of II ANZAC who grew in confidence and skill under Plumer's Second Army. Birdwood's Australians in I ANZAC had a less happy time in Gough's Fifth Army. The actions at Bullecourt in April and May 1917 saw the Australians lagging behind the Canadian Corps and the New Zealanders and Australians in Godley's II ANZAC in their offensive tactical doctrine, with poor planning, inadequate preparation and coordination, and equally faulty tactical skills.[42] It was at Vimy and Messines that the lessons of the Somme were first applied to effect by Dominion forces, but it would not be until the battles of Menin Road and Polygon Wood during the third battle of Ypres that Birdwood's I ANZAC showed the same progress. The Dominion forces were part of an evolving professional expertise that was shared by the armies of the BEF on the Western Front in 1917 and came to fruition in 1918.

CHAPTER 7

FRENCH GENERALSHIP ON THE SOMME

Professor Michael S. Neiberg

We can only understand French generalship on the Somme as it relates to the titanic battle of attrition that raged simultaneously 155 miles to the southeast at Verdun. The German Army launched a massive assault on the French at Verdun in February, reducing the French contribution to the planned coalition assault on the Somme from 40 divisions to about half that number. Consequently, the French part of the attack on the Somme went from being the primary effort to a secondary effort designed to support the British Army's attack to the north of the Somme River.

Conventional wisdom and even some scholarly histories of Verdun treat it as the primary (or even the only) battle for the French Army in 1916. Until quite recently, the Somme had all but disappeared from academic and popular treatments of the French Army in that year.[1] The oversight is understandable, given the importance of Verdun to subsequent French memory and the raw numbers of Frenchmen killed and wounded at the 'mill on the Meuse'.[2] Verdun undoubtedly limited the resources that France could dedicate to the Somme Offensive and led to serious concerns about the impact of attrition on the French Army.

Still, Verdun did not initially force French leaders to abandon the idea of the Somme Offensive being their decisive engagement for 1916. The American military attaché to France, Colonel Spencer Cosby, noted in late May that the senior French generals 'now seem to be pretty well agreed that the present objective of the Germans, whatever it may have been originally, is to wear out and weaken the French Army, their "principal adversary", [so] that it will not be able to take an effective part in the long anticipated combined Allied offensive set for this spring.' The French, Cosby reported, were confident that they knew both the goals and the methods of the German attacks at Verdun.[3] Having contained most of the damage, the French could return to a focus on the Somme, even if circumstances at Verdun would perforce limit the overall French contribution to the coalition's combined effort.

French Army Chief of Staff Général Joseph Joffre agreed with Cosby's assessment. Although the war had thus far not gone as he had predicted and although several French politicians had begun to weary of his dictatorial ways, 'Papa' Joffre still had the charisma and the presence to dominate Allied strategy. At the same time that Cosby was making his assessments of the French, Joffre still thought that the attack on the Somme would be the main effort for France in 1916. Future Prime Minister Georges Clemenceau, then the president of the Senate Army Commission, grew sufficiently concerned about Joffre's continued ambitions for the Somme to schedule a meeting with British General Sir Douglas Haig. At that meeting, Clemenceau took the highly unusual step of asking Haig to 'exercise a restraining hand' on Joffre's ambitions for the coming offensive.[4]

Some of Joffre's senior lieutenants were also thinking in terms of restraints. At the Chantilly conference of December 1915 French generals had concluded, based on their bloody experiences in Champagne and Artois earlier that year, that victory would come not from a single rupture of the enemy line, but from a series of engagements 'at intervals as brief as possible'. They had decided to abandon the operational model of 1915, namely the idea of finding a critical point on the enemy line, massing force against it, then creating exposed flanks and, finally, a breakthrough. Experience in the war thus far had shown the futility of such an approach as well as the speed with which the enemy could mass reinforcements into threatened sectors.[5]

Instead, the French sought to fight on an extended front to prevent the enemy from concentrating its reserves and artillery. This extension of the front ran somewhat counter to the new 'scientific' methods of war at the tactical level, which placed the main burden of the attack on heavy artillery, guided and supported by aircraft.[6] 'One does not fight *matériel* with men' and 'the artillery conquers, the infantry occupies' had become doctrinal buzzwords since the Champagne and Artois offensives.[7] Still, the more the French extended the front, the more they risked diluting the power of their own artillery.

Managing a modern battlefield

French generals had learned through painful experience how to manage a modern, combined arms campaign whose emphasis had shifted from infantry to artillery. Under this system, brigade commanders had the responsibility for directing the infantry onto fixed objectives. Division commanders were responsible for ensuring the proper coordination of artillery, infantry, and aviation, 'putting everything in place to remove (enemy) resistance'. Higher still, corps commanders would determine where the attack was experiencing successes worth reinforcing with the reserves they commanded. The army commander was to keep his guiding hand on the entire campaign, stopping attacks unlikely to achieve strategic success and reinforcing ones that showed promise.[8]

The initial German attacks on a narrow front at Verdun only seemed to confirm the wisdom of the broad-front approach to the French. Colonel Cosby noted that French generals at Verdun had seen the narrow German attack front as a mistake, allowing the French to respond and then contain the German assault.[9] The Germans, too, seemed to have learned that lesson, expanding their attack on Verdun to both banks of the Meuse River a few weeks into the campaign.

But if Verdun had confirmed in the minds of French leaders the wisdom of a broad-front approach, the realities of Verdun made it harder for them to execute one on the Somme. By 30 June, 65 of France's 96 infantry divisions had fought at Verdun, leaving just 18 infantry divisions and four cavalry divisions for the Somme. This represented a reduction of half of the original plan's call for 40 French divisions. The diminution of French resources, men as well as the heavy guns on which the new scientific system depended, forced a narrower approach and also changed the upcoming campaign from a predominantly French-led one to a British-led one.

French generals understood that the change in preponderance of force from the experienced French to the novice British would likely lead to a narrow-front battle. Such battles were easier to manage and did not demand as much coordination from division, corps, and army commanders. After the war, the French official history argued that as the British took over more of the front, Joffre faced 'a developing trend, (namely) keeping the battle going for as long as possible along narrow fronts'. Continuing on in a slightly condescending way, it noted that the trend 'may perhaps follow British temperament but it does not fit into the intentions of the Coalition'.[10] For 'Coalition', one may read 'Joffre', who clearly saw the narrowing of fronts as a danger to the success of the campaign.

Despite the changes forced upon him by Verdun and the fundamental change in France's role, Joffre persisted in seeing the Somme as the decisive Anglo-French action of 1916. In May, Joffre argued that Verdun was not an isolated battle, but part of a larger ploy to denude Germany of reserves while striking where the Allies could bring maximum force to bear. Thus did he hope to hold, or even attrit, the Germans at Verdun while his original Chantilly plan took effect on the Somme. In his view, the Anglo-French attack would still go ahead (if in altered form), while the Italians engaged the Austro-Hungarians and the Russians launched a potentially decisive offensive of their own in the East.[11]

The basic strategic vision of the Chantilly conference therefore remained in place. The Somme Offensive, even if now largely British and perforce on a smaller front than Joffre had initially envisioned, would still be part of a Continental vice that would crush the Central Powers on multiple fronts more or less simultaneously. The Somme was therefore more than an isolated battle along the muddy banks of an otherwise insignificant French stream. Rather, it was a critical piece of a Continental strategy for bringing France's enemies to their knees and turning the Central Powers' interior lines of communications from an advantage to a disadvantage by preventing them from moving men and *matériel* from front to front.

Joffre and the senior French generals sometimes spoke of the Somme in terms of a continental policy of attrition (*usure*) pursued simultaneously with the Russians. In March and April, Fayolle noted that Joffre and Foch sought *usure* as the primary goal of the Somme, although he also hints that Foch spoke of *usure* as a goal for the campaign only if the French could not pierce the German lines.[12] It seems clear that French generals saw a rupture of the enemy lines as the key to a successful operation and attrition as the next best achievement if they could not break through – and if the Russians succeeded in the East.

On the Somme itself the French planned not attrition but to break the heavily guarded lateral (i.e. parallel to the Western Front) line of German railway communications that ran from Bapaume to Péronne to Ham. That line supplied and fed hundreds of thousands of German soldiers. Without it, the Germans could not hope to remain in their trenches. Destroying or interdicting this line would require the Germans to retreat to the next lateral line of communications and abandon their sophisticated field defences. The ideal outcome was that the Germans would then be retreating through areas without fixed field defences, and pursuing Allied troops could bring their artillery and air assets to full use.

The French Army could no longer seize that line on its own, however; the bulk of the work would now have to fall on the British. Just weeks before the Somme Offensive began, Joffre set the line Ham–Maurepas– Flaucourt as the French goal. This line protected the German-held railway running through Péronne. Taking the line would not only give the French the advantage of high ground, it would also establish a launching pad for an attack on the railway juncture of Péronne itself, and support British operations to the north.[13]

Général Foch and French ideas for the Somme

The commander of the Groupe d'Armées du Nord, Ferdinand Foch, did not much care for either the plan or the choice of ground. Aggressive, energetic, and absolutely confident of final victory, Foch nevertheless thought the ground around the Somme unsuited to the offensive. He especially worried about the lack of good roads on the French side of the lines and a conical-shaped piece of ground north of the river that he feared would draw in and trap French forces like a cul de sac. Foch, who had a deeper understanding of the strategic level of war than Joffre, disliked any offensive that did not promise some decisive result larger than the capture of relatively unimportant ground. He had written 'To what end?' on his original assessment of Joffre's plan for the Somme. He later confided to his Chief of Staff, Maxime Weygand, that 'to aim so large with the means given to us will be to condemn us to great and useless sacrifices.'[14]

In late May, Joffre announced that Foch's Groupe d'Armées du Nord would have just 26 divisions. Foch was thus planning a campaign while at the same time watching the means at his disposal evaporate. Knowing that such reductions rendered a broad-front attack impossible, Foch wrote, 'We are a long way from that wide, powerful offensive which has in view an attainable objective and which can keep going. And yet these are the sole conditions which permit an attack to reach a strategic result and not fade away into helplessness.' Foch thus reduced the goal of the offensive even further, to the area between Maricourt and Péronne.[15]

However mistrustful he may have been about the chances of success, Foch knew that the emergency at Verdun required the French to make every effort to try to turn the tide of the war. At a meeting with French President Raymond Poincaré, Foch suggested waiting until 1917 to launch an attack, although he also confessed in that same meeting that a large-scale attack in 1916 had become necessary given the urgency on the Meuse. Foch supported the Somme plan in public, keeping his doubts hidden, even from his most important subordinates. He retained faith, at least, in the capabilities of French soldiers and the prospects for the new scientific method of waging war.

General Sir Douglas Haig became commander-in-chief of the BEF in December 1915. (Getty Images)

Lieutenant-General Sir Henry Seymour Rawlinson, commander of the Fourth Army on the Somme, standing on the steps outside his headquarters, Château Querrieu near Amiens, in July 1916. (IWM Q 4032)

Lieutenant-General Sir Hubert Gough, who commanded the British Reserve Army (later renamed the Fifth Army) during the battle. (IWM Q 35825D)

General Sir Hugh Montague Trenchard (1873–1956), c. 1929. He was commander of the Royal Flying Corps on the Western Front during the battle of the Somme, and is known as 'the father of the RAF'. (Photo by Hulton Archive/Getty Images)

French Commander-in-Chief Général Joseph Joffre (1852–1931), *c.* 1914. (Photo by Hulton Archive/ Getty Images)

Général Ferdinand Foch (1851–1929), commander of the Groupe d'Armées du Nord. This portrait was taken during World War I. (Photo by Haeckel Collection/Ullstein Bild via Getty Images)

Portrait of Général Marie Émile Fayolle (1852–1928), commander of the 6e Armée, in 1918. (Photo by Photo12/UIG/Getty Images)

The French President Poincaré confers the Légion d'honneur on Général Joseph Micheler, the commander of the 10e Armée and the great winner of the battle of the Somme, in 1916. (Photo by Photo12/UIG/Getty Images)

General Erich von Falkenhayn (1861–1922), Chief of the German General Staff, at the beginning of the battle of the Somme, c. 1905. (Photo by Hulton Archive/Getty Images)

General Max von Gallwitz (1852–1937), commander of the German 2. Armee. The photo was probably taken during World War I. (Photo by Haeckel Collection/Ullstein Bild via Getty Images)

General Fritz von Below (1853–1918), commander of the 1. Armee. The photograph was probably taken in 1914. (Photo by Ullstein Bild/Ullstein Bild via Getty Images)

Crown Prince Rupprecht of Bavaria (1869–1955) c. 1910. In July 1916 he was promoted to Generalfeldmarschall and on 28 August assumed command of Heeresgruppe Kronprinz Rupprecht, consisting of 1., 2., 6., and 7. Armee. (Photo by Estate of Emil Bieber/Klaus Niermann/Getty Images)

Generalfeldmarschall Paul von Hindenburg, Kaiser Wilhelm and General Erich Ludendorff look at a map at German General Headquarters during World War I. (Photo by Time Life Pictures/German Official Photo/War Dept./Natl. Archives/The LIFE Picture Collection/Getty Images)

General Ernst von Hoeppner (1860–1922), Commanding General of the Luftstreitkräfte in World War I (right) photographed with German aviator Manfred von Richthofen (centre), 1917. (Photo by Ullstein Bild/Ullstein Bild via Getty Images)

French troops advancing across the Somme battlefield. Low oblique photograph taken from an aeroplane. (IWM Q 69585)

French soldier walking in a trench in devastated terrain of the Somme. (IWM Q 69695)

A French colonial soldier wearing a gas mask in the Somme area, 1916. (IWM Q 61058)

The French fighter plane Nieuport II Bébé, photographed in 1915. (Photo by Roger Viollet/Getty Images)

French gunners in the process of loading a 400mm railway gun in a sunken position at Harbonnières, 30 June 1916. The French used a greater number of guns than the British in the bombardment. (IWM Q 70524)

French donkeys carrying soup to the front line at Maurepas, 17 October 1916. (IWM Q 79006)

French gunners preparing to load a 370mm mortar in the Baraquette Ravine, west of Foucaucourt, 16 September 1916. (Q 78094)

A French gunner of the 53e Régiment d'Infanterie (10e Armée) with his Chauchat machine gun in the Somme area, 25 August 1916. (Q 55032)

Vertical aerial reconnaissance showing German trenches north of Thiepval. The firing-line, and supporting trenches, are at lower left, connected by four communications trenches ('Fiennes Street', unnamed, 'Price Street' and 'Market Trench') to the third-line trench and the Schwaben Redoubt at upper right. (IWM HU 91107)

Captured German trench and sandbagged dugout entrance in the ruined village of La Boisselle, July 1916. The entrance is relatively undamaged and the barbed wire on the Spanish Rider obstacles has not been much disturbed despite the bombardment.

German trenches after continuous barrage, summer/autumn 1916. (Photo by Ullstein Bild/Ullstein Bild via Getty Images)

Albatros D I single-seat scout biplane with Mercedes engine. The D I Scout ended the brief period of Allied air superiority over the Western Front in 1916 with its outstanding performance and twin synchronized machine guns. Flown by pilots such as Manfred von Richthofen, the D I and the later D III and D V dominated the Western Front in 1917. (IWM Q 66823)

German field telephonist at the Somme, 1916. Photograph from *Der Grosse Krieg in Bildern*. (Photo by Art Media/Print Collector/Getty Images)

Battle of the Ancre. A German colonel, major and adjutant captured near Beaumont Hamel, 13 November 1916. (IWM Q 4503)

Captured German heavy guns near Albert, September 1916. (IWM Q 1153)

Mark I 'Male' Tank of C Company that broke down crossing a British trench on its way to attack Thiepval on 25 September 1916 during the battle of the Somme. (Photo by Lt E Brooks/ IWM via Getty Images)

Men of the Border Regiment resting in shallow dugouts near Thiepval Wood during the battle of the Somme in August 1916. (IWM/Getty Images)

Sopwith 1 1/2 Strutter two-seat fighter reconnaissance aircraft. (IWM Q68151)

Three 8-inch howitzers of 39th Siege Battery, Royal Garrison Artillery, firing from the Fricourt–Mametz Valley during the battle of the Somme, August 1916. (IWM/Getty Images)

A British field dressing station on the battlefield at the Somme, France, 1916. (Photo by Paul Popper/Popperfoto/Getty Images)

Indian cavalry after their charge, at the Somme, 14 July 1916 (*c.* 1920). Illustration from *The Illustrated War Record of the Most Notable Episodes in the Great European War 1914–1918*, seventh edition (The Swarthmore Press Ltd, London, *c.* 1920). (Photo by The Print Collector/Print Collector/Getty Images)

Eight ANZAC soldiers wearing sheepskin jackets, and a mixture of slouch hats and steel helmets, resting on their way up to the trenches. (IWM E(AUS) 19)

Royal Australian Battery of 9.2-inch Howitzers Mark IV in action at Fricourt, August, 1916. (Photo by Robert Hunt Library/Windmill Books/UIG via Getty images)

Canadian troops leaving their trenches for a raid on the enemy trenches. Somme area, October 1916. (Photo by Robert Hunt Library/Windmill Books/UIG via Getty images)

Foch's subordinates included Marie Émile Fayolle, commander of the 6e Armée, which would attack astride both banks of the Somme itself and therefore directly into the cone that had so worried Foch. Fayolle had a reputation as a cautious, meticulous commander unwilling to risk French lives unless the potential gains outweighed the inevitable sacrifices. Although Fayolle, as much as anyone, would have the responsibility for making the French part of the offensive succeed, he harboured doubts about both the prospects for success and his own commanding officer. 'Foch came to show us his plan,' Fayolle wrote in his diary just a few weeks before the battle began. 'He has no intention of manoeuvring. The battle he dreams of has no goal.'[16] Fayolle was right about the first part: Foch envisioned the offensive as helping the French position at Verdun and supporting the British. He did not believe in the likelihood of French forces opening enough of a hole in the German lines to manoeuvre.

Other senior French leaders expressed doubts as well. Henri-Philippe Pétain, soon to be directing the French efforts at Verdun, saw little in the Somme plan to convince him of its merits. He saw instead a replay of the failures at Artois. French operations, he argued, should not aim for rupture of the enemy line as Joffre and Haig desired. Such ruptures rarely occurred and, even when they did, they were prohibitively costly and usually contained by the defender's reserves. He argued instead for the British and French to conduct smaller offensives all along the Western Front in order to force the Germans to expend their energy trying to meet a variety of contingencies.[17] This plan sacrificed the military principle of concentration of effort, but, in Pétain's view, it offered the best chance at success, if not in 1916, then in 1917. Pressed at Verdun and holding to his original strategic vision, Joffre pushed ahead despite these concerns. Even Pétain had come to agree that the attack on the Somme held out the best hope of relieving the unbearable pressure on Verdun.

Foch therefore gave his final orders for the attack, taking care to warn his subordinates of the limits of what they might achieve. On 20 June, just one week before the French artillery began its preparatory attacks on German lines, Foch wrote of French infantry that 'It is of primary importance to employ it with the strictest economy, not to ask of it efforts of which it is not capable.' This assessment reflected an awareness of the failures of Champagne and Artois in 1915. It also acknowledged the grim reality that France would need to husband its forces for a campaign in 1917, as Pétain, Fayolle, and Foch all recognized had become inevitable.

'Beaming' with success

In contrast to the historically bloody first day of the Somme on British lines, Joffre was 'beaming' with the success of the French on 1 July.[18] French forces took most of their territorial goals and captured 8,000 German prisoners of war in the first 72 hours. The French credited their scientific methods, especially their more accurate use of artillery, and their refusal to send in infantry in dense packets, the latter a lesson learned at Verdun. Foch had amassed an advantage in heavy guns (greater than 100mm calibre) of 500 to 184.[19] Experienced French gunners had targeted German strongpoints with devastating accuracy; as William Philpott noted in his extensive study of the campaign: 'The artillery had done their job so well that the assaulting infantry encountered little resistance in the enemy's front system: deep dugouts had been closed by well-directed fire, trenches had been flattened and machine gun nests destroyed, and enemy artillery batteries all but silenced.'[20]

The artillery having paved the way, French infantry could advance on remaining German positions with the fire and movement tactics that the French had learned the hard way in Artois, Champagne, and at Verdun. By 1230hrs on the first day, the French had captured the first line of German trenches opposite them. Divisional commanders pushed Fayolle to order further attacks, but, fearful of what lay ahead and aware that the British had to succeed or French achievements would amount to little, he hesitated.

Still, initial French successes were cause for celebration, especially given the contrast to the British experience further north. By 12 July, French forces had captured 12,000 German prisoners of war and 70 artillery pieces. By the standards of Champagne and Artois, these numbers suggested nothing short of a major triumph. But repeating a well-planned and meticulously organized initial attack proved difficult. Thereafter, French operations would depend on improvisation as much as planning. 'The Boche front is broken open for eight kilometres, and we cannot exploit it,' Fayolle complained. He, more than any other French general, appreciated how much staff work and preparation had to precede any major success.[21]

In part, the French could not exploit their gains because of the failures of the British further north, although the comparison was not altogether fair. French methods differed greatly from those of the British, which Fayolle belittled as 'infantile'.[22] Joffre later wrote that British troops lacked the tactical ability to mop up German positions before moving on, leaving dugouts and other German strongholds intact and therefore capable of inflicting avoidable casualties. French generals surely knew that British units mostly contained inexperienced soldiers, incapable of fighting the sophisticated scientific type of battle that the French generals saw themselves fighting. Joffre also recognized that the Germans had more heavily fortified their positions opposite the British, believing that the French would not launch an offensive of their own as long as the battle continued to rage at Verdun.[23] Whatever the reason, the French believed they were succeeding in their initial attacks while the British were not. Foch told Fayolle that French offensives 'are developing in an extremely happy manner'.[24]

Two problems nevertheless presented themselves. First, the British attack had to be the main Allied attack, given the distribution of resources and the original plan. Success in the French sector therefore meant comparatively little to the overall strategic success or failure of the coalition's operation. As Joffre wrote to Foch at the end of July, 'The fundamental intention of the Somme Offensive must continue to be supporting the British attack in the north; our offensive in the south must remain secondary or subordinate to the results obtained in the north.'[25]

Second, the same daunting challenges from 1915 presented themselves again in 1916. Even when the French could achieve a temporary break of the enemy line, they could not achieve a wider breakthrough no matter how much artillery and infantry they concentrated. The diminishing returns of smaller French offensives in the direction of Flaucourt on 6 and 7 July reinforced the point. The Germans found ways to concentrate artillery and infantry into threatened areas and thereby limited French gains.

The front stalemates

By mid-July, the French sector began to look too much like Artois and Champagne for Foch and Fayolle's comfort.[26] They also lacked confidence that the British could achieve a decisive result in their own sector. Seemingly losing sight of the strategic plan for the campaign that placed the French in support of the British, Foch and Fayolle narrowed their front again and tried for decisive results. They took satisfaction from the 20 July attacks toward Flaucourt that captured 1,200 prisoners and put French troops in a stronger tactical position. Even the generally optimistic French official history, however, took care to offer a restrained evaluation of French success. Writing of the attack of 20 July, the official history noted that 'It was a success. Undoubtedly, the results obtained were not those expected, but the infantry found itself on the second position of the enemy and in an excellent place from which to attack on the 23rd.'[27] It is not too difficult to read between the lines and see how far the French had reduced their definition of success from a breakthrough to merely establishing better positions for the next attack.

Still, it was enough to convince Foch, who asked Joffre to give him another corps to exploit the limited successes achieved thus far. But poor weather slowed the preparations Fayolle thought essential for success and the British focus on Delville Wood meant that French operations near Flaucourt would be too far away to provide any direct support. The French settled for an attack on 30 July designed not to break through but to support the British. They failed, with the French losing 3,500 men who 'paid dearly for a few insignificant gains of terrain'.[28] Joffre blamed the setback on the decision to advance on a narrow front and the perpetual problem of the lack of coordination between the French forces north and south of the river.

A more sober analysis showed that the Somme had indeed become an offensive all too similar to those of 1915. By early August the French had managed to find 29 divisions to fight at the Somme, engaging 30 German divisions. Thus it was costing the French roughly one division to tie down a German division, a calculus that offered little in the way of long-term success, even if the French believed that they were inflicting more damage on the Germans than they were taking. The defence still had the advantage, especially given the power of German artillery to survive all French attempts to destroy it. As the French observed in early August, 'Even if the German Army is wearing out as we have seen in the crucible of this new battle, it is not achieving less tangible results. It has still managed to halt the Allied advance on both the north and south banks of the river.'[29]

The cautious and meticulous Fayolle saw the diminishing returns and argued for a pause until at least September in order to regroup, reinforce, and plan. He knew that his men were tired and that French artillery badly needed new tubes and more ammunition. As he complained to French politician (and Joffre nemesis) Abel Ferry, his units had now undertaken three offensives on the Somme. 'After three attacks,' Ferry recalled him saying, 'leaders and specialists are dead and a division can only attack along two kilometres of front.' For the broad-front attack that Joffre and his political ally André Tardieu were then advocating, Fayolle calculated that France would need to use as many as 150 divisions, far more than was possible to raise. Speaking to Ferry 'with a shocking freedom', Fayolle criticized the French high command, especially Joffre and Foch, for their abiding optimism and daunting ambitions.[30]

And well he might have offered those criticisms, given the strength of German lines and the unrelenting power of German artillery. Nevertheless, Joffre and Foch wanted to keep up the pressure. Joffre was still counting on the Somme to be a large part of his grand vision as articulated at Chantilly. French success in turning the tide at Verdun and the start of the Russian offensive under Alexei Brusilov gave Joffre reasons for hope.

Foch still hoped for a breakthrough that could both change the face of battle and provide immediate help to the British. France then had four field armies in the Somme sector, and Foch envisioned them attacking almost independently of one another. This method would increase the tempo of operations and put additional pressure on the Germans to defend against attacks coming from multiple directions. Wearing down the Germans everywhere should lead to a breakthrough somewhere. The September attack that Foch and Général Joseph Alfred Micheler, commander of the 10e Armée, envisioned would, for the first time in the campaign, involve roughly equal numbers of French and British soldiers. This time, the French would take the lead and the British would attack in support.[31]

Micheler was competent, if less inspiring than Foch and less insightful than Fayolle. He could be optimistic about the chances for success in his sector south of the Somme River, but he could also become despondent and indecisive. He knew the challenges ahead of him and he also knew that most of his units were tired formations that had recently been engaged at Verdun. He and his staff studied the methods used by Fayolle's 6e Armée and aimed for a breakthrough, but from 3 to 6 September all Micheler could point to as evidence of victory was another batch of German prisoners and a favourable balance sheet of casualties. The long-hoped-for breakthrough remained as elusive as ever.

A change of methods

Scholars generally agree that, notwithstanding repeated failures to break through, in September Foch and Joffre remained optimistic that such a breakthrough could still occur if the French and British could only refine their operational methods and continue to wear the Germans down. They also generally agree that Fayolle no longer shared their faith, if indeed he ever had. Thereafter, scholars tend to disagree. Robert Doughty argues that the shift to Micheler's sector south of the river indicates that 'Foch and Fayolle had lost sight of the original purpose' of the offensive, namely to support the British, yet they continued to attack out of both frustration and the hope of achieving big results to justify their losses.[32]

William Philpott contends that the French had begun to see attrition as a critical rationale for the campaign. They came to argue that their attacks were having a greater impact on the defending Germans than on the attacking French. By this rationale, even if they could not achieve a breakthrough, they could still use their scientific methods of warfare to pursue a decisive result.[33]

While they certainly hoped to wear down the Germans opposite them, the French senior leadership still largely thought in terms of a breakthrough. They did not debate this fundamental point as much as they debated the means to achieve it. Joffre argued for a broad-front approach, with French movements carefully coordinated with those of the British. He saw reasons for optimism in the British attacks of mid-July, which seemed to show that the British were learning the lessons of modern war and would therefore soon become capable of the kinds of sophisticated use of artillery and infantry that his own army used.

The French official history does however make reference to attrition as a strategy. Reflecting on the results of the July and August battles, it argues that:

> Without doubt the Anglo-French armies did not break the enemy line; but it seems that they definitively forced the attrition of the effectives charged with defending the line. Thrown from the hell of Verdun into that of the Somme, German units found themselves forced into a moment perfectly well chosen for a great [Allied] attack (*un grand coup*).[34]

Nevertheless, the official history provides no direct evidence to support this assertion, not even in its voluminous supporting documents. It therefore seems to be as much a post facto justification for the failure to break through as an actual strategy.

In any event, Fayolle did not envision the mid-September attacks that Foch ordered as a grand coup or as part of a strategy of attrition. Fayolle wanted to win by manoeuvre, which, in his view, meant moving to a small front operation and largely abandoning the wider operational goal of supporting the British offensives. The offensive of 3–6 September largely failed to produce the results Foch had wanted, and the British attack on Guillemont at the same time also yielded unsatisfactory results.[35]

Poor weather and Anglo-French disagreements on the exact timing of the next phase of the campaign only contributed to the atmosphere of growing acrimony and confusion. On 15 September Foch and Fayolle had a contentious meeting, with Foch insisting that Fayolle attack in order to support the British movement near Flers, where the British planned to introduce their first tanks. Fayolle, who wanted more men and artillery, pushed back. Foch ordered the attack anyway, leading Fayolle to complain of a 'wasted day' filled with 'useless casualties'.[36]

Fayolle continued to argue that no geographic place on the Somme front was any longer worth the casualties it would require to capture. Joffre wanted to keep up the pressure at both the Somme and Verdun as long as the weather permitted. Attacks in late September and early October faltered as the fatigue of French troops, the lack of heavy artillery ammunition, and the poorer weather all favoured the defenders. The Germans had also been busy building new lines of defence and reorganizing both their infantry and their artillery. These efforts proved their value as the Germans kept the French from breaking through their lines. The Germans even launched a number of counter-attacks in September and October that threw the French off balance and recaptured some of the land that they had lost.

Foch turned to Micheler, hoping that he could achieve south of the river what Fayolle no longer could do north of it. In October, Foch ordered Micheler to capture the butte de Fresnes and the village of Ablaincourt. After what the official history called 'an active exchange' between the two generals, Micheler succeeded in convincing Foch that he had too few resources to achieve the mission. Foch and Joffre took comfort from mounting evidence that the Germans were weakening, but Fayolle and Micheler could see that the French, too, were weakening. They argued for a strategy of *grignotage continuel*, or a series of nibbling attacks to keep the Germans off balance and capture small pieces of ground from which to build a base for operations in 1917.[37]

On both the British and French fronts of the Somme, the troops were obviously learning the new scientific methods of war. They were successful in smaller operations aimed at seizing particularly valuable plots of ground on the tactical level. But Fayolle had been right all along: none of this land was decisive on the operational or the strategic level, and it was costing France far too many of its sons to justify the efforts. Despite the abiding faith that Joffre and Foch had in an ultimate breakthrough, Joffre's Chief of Staff, Général Noël de Castelnau had it right when he said: 'offensives with limited objectives were offensives which would certainly succeed, but yield no return'.[38] Except perhaps on the questionable calculus of attrition, the Somme Offensive had yielded few results worth the cost.

Legacies for the French Army

The Somme alone is not responsible for the changes in leadership that the French made at the end of 1916, but it certainly contributed to them. On 13 December, a new French government gave Joffre a fancy-sounding job description of *général en chef des armées françaises, comme conseiller technique du gouvernement* (general-in-chief of the French armies, technical adviser to the government, consultative member of the War Committee). He also received the Third Republic's first marshal's baton. Nevertheless, the government stripped him of any real power and replaced him with one of the heroes of Verdun, Robert Nivelle. Foch, too, found himself reassigned and in disgrace. Citing the rather dubious claim of his ill health, the government gave him a series of smaller jobs designed to keep him occupied with relatively unimportant matters and, not coincidentally, far from Paris.[39] Foch would eventually return and find success, but in a much different role.[40]

Only Fayolle emerged from the Somme with his reputation not only intact, but enhanced. He became known throughout the French Army as a commander who would not waste the lives of his men needlessly and a man unafraid to speak his mind to his superiors. He even appears in Sébastien Japrisot's acclaimed 1993 novel, *A Very Long Engagement*, as a hero of one of the main characters. Fayolle, says this veteran, 'was the best of a bad bunch' of French generals, '... and I'm glad those crummy politicians gave him his field marshal's baton [after the war]'.[41]

The generals of the Somme therefore largely avoided involvement in the disaster that became the Nivelle Offensive. Only Micheler, then in command of an army group, got drawn into that debacle. He had criticized Nivelle's overly ambitious plan for an offensive on the Chemin des Dames in April 1917. Perhaps he was influenced by his own experiences on the much better terrain of the Somme. He must have seen how the odds against Nivelle were even greater than those that Joffre and Foch had faced a year earlier. He predicted, correctly, that French forces might capture the first and second German lines on the Chemin des Dames, but they could not hope to achieve the breakthrough that Nivelle had so confidently promised.[42] The lessons of the Somme had had their impact, even if the generals of Verdun for the time being led the armies of France.

CHAPTER 8

THE ROAD TO MODERN COMBINED ARMS WARFARE

German land warfare tactics in the battles of *matériel* on the Western Front in 1916

Oberstleutnant Dr Christian Stachelbeck

In 1914, the guiding concept in the operational thinking of German army officers was to envelop the enemy on the battlefield in a war of movement, conducting rapid offensive manoeuvres and finally inflicting an annihilating defeat. The aim was to keep wars as short as possible on account of the Reich's unfavourable strategic position and lack of resources. This 'strategy of annihilation' was the foundation of the memorandum, later known as the Schlieffen Plan, written by the Chief of the Prusso-German Great General Staff in late 1905 entitled *Krieg gegen Frankreich* (*War against France*). The German military elite believed that this plan would enable them to rapidly bring about a decision in the main theatre of war against its western neighbour. They hoped to be able to make up for the enemy's superiority in numbers with their supposedly superior command and control, 'indomitable will' and, not least, higher-quality troops. After all, the German Army was considered to be the most powerful military machine in Europe. However, the German attack launched in early August 1914 was halted at the Marne, with the Germans forced to retreat by early September. The desired war of movement eventually ended in the vain efforts to outflank the enemy in Flanders. Artillery and automatic weapons had inflicted horrendous losses among the advancing infantry. The German Army on the Western Front sustained more losses in proportion to its size in the first three months of the war than at any other time during it.

The battles of Verdun and the Somme in 1916

The battle of Verdun was the only major offensive launched by the German Army on the Western Front between the transition to trench warfare in the autumn of 1914 and the major offensives in the spring of 1918. In Germany, the battle of *matériel* is still associated with the bloody struggle for the fortress of Verdun, which lasted almost the whole of 1916. It was not the fighting on the Somme, in which even heavier losses were incurred and where more use was made of artillery, but the 'Verdun blood mill' that later became an integral part of the collective memory of World War I. Most German officers remembered it as the worst defeat of the war and a static trench warfare nightmare.[1]

General der Infanterie Erich von Falkenhayn's planning began with the tactical and operational lessons learned in the West in 1915: Allied breakthrough attempts made without first destroying the enemy's reserves led to high losses in men and *matériel* on the attacker's side and had not achieved strategic or even operational victory. Falkenhayn's plan relied on the proven effect of the heavy German artillery. His initial intent was to seize the high ground on the east bank of the Meuse with a rapid thrust while maintaining a strong army reserve. Falkenhayn believed that it would be sufficient to employ nine infantry divisions with the 5. Armee in order to provoke the French into launching costly counter-attacks at Verdun and the British into mounting a relief offensive at Artois. According to the people around him at the Great Headquarters in April 1916, Falkenhayn was 'anything but an adventurer ... just the opposite, he's very cautious and spares as many men as possible. At Verdun the artillery does everything. Only one or two companies attack.'[2] Falkenhayn initially rejected demands from Armeeoberkommando 5 (Headquarters of 5. Armee, AOK 5), which was tasked with the attack, for significantly more forces and an expansion of the offensive to the west bank of the Meuse. Falkenhayn wanted to retain control of the army reserves in order to keep his options open during the offensive.[3] Regardless of all the operational differences between Falkenhayn and the AOK 5, the latter developed an accelerated attack technique for seizing the fortress: exploiting the element of surprise, the massive use of artillery, and the careful interaction of all the arms and services before and during battle. For the first time, aircraft and airships formed a significant part of operation planning, undertaking reconnaissance missions, preventing enemy reconnaissance, and providing close air support for ground forces.[4]

In order to improve the protection of the infantry during the assault, the 5. Armee resorted to what was later called a rolling barrage – a thick hail of shells delivered immediately before an infantry assault. As a continuation of the lessons learned at Gorlice-Tarnów, the breakthrough achieved on the Eastern Front in 1915, the barrage was regulated even more precisely by the clock at Verdun. An exact timetable supplemented the hitherto customary technique by which the infantry transmitted the progress of the attack to the artillery behind it by issuing agreed visual signals – a system which often failed when visibility was poor. The decentralization of the command of the artillery from the army to the divisional level remained a controversial issue among German commanders. Taking heed of the initial lessons learned, Falkenhayn fundamentally advocated the exercise of unified command by an artillery commander of the *Generalkommando* (headquarters of an army corps). Even so, mixed heavy and field artillery battle groups were to be assigned to the divisions in order to engage enemy infantry. The infantry commanders and artillery group commanders were to interact closely. The German artillery already used poison gas shells at the beginning of the battle. The front-line forces varied considerably, however, in their assessment of the impact this had on the enemy. Nevertheless, green-cross (phosgene) munitions, which had been fired over large areas for the first time in the summer of 1916, were considered an effective means of neutralizing enemy artillery, at least temporarily.[5]

At Verdun, stormtroop tactics became increasingly important for improving infantry mobility in trench warfare. This was probably the most important and forward-looking innovation at the elementary tactical level (section to company). Initially, units on the Western Front had starting evolving such a concept as early as the autumn of 1914. From the spring of 1915 onwards, special elite test forces were tasked with refining the new tactics. From mid-1916 onwards these units were called *Sturmbataillone* (assault battalions). These elite units were also ordered into battle at Verdun. Furthermore, a directive issued by the 5. Armee in February 1916 pointed towards a change of tactics even in the line infantry: 'Each company in the front line will set up a *Stoßtrupp* [stormtroop].'[6] The intent was to form smaller combat teams with greater mobility and more effective weapons and to disperse them according to the terrain. Engineers supported the advance of the infantry. An increased use of team weapons like flamethrowers and mine launchers, and later light machine guns, led to an increase in the fighting power of the smaller combat units. With the concept of combined arms combat being transferred to the elementary tactical level, non-commissioned officers and junior officers were employed as autonomous junior leaders and became considerably more important – gradually becoming the backbone of front-line warfare. General der Infanterie Erich Ludendorff, First Quartermaster General and the key figure of the OHL later termed this process the individualization of tactics.[7]

At Verdun, the first lessons-learned reports emphasized the effectiveness of *Stoßtruppen* in trench warfare: They 'advance without regard for the neighbouring detachment ... circumvent pillboxes, flanking facilities, conduct flanking attacks, if possible from the rear and support each other.' The OHL disseminated these reports to all armies along with general papers about stormtroop tactics.[8] The enemy's tactics and capabilities were also studied in the German Army. For instance, the translation of the *Studie über den Angriff* (*Study on the Attack*) by Captain André Laffargue of the French infantry that had been captured by German soldiers was circulated among the German troops as an 'example of the high morale' of the enemy forces.[9]

In early July 1916, the Anglo-French attack at the Somme forced the OHL to gradually give up the large-scale attack of 5. Armee at Verdun and to go onto the defensive. By the time the new OHL officially aborted the attack in early September, 48 German divisions had fought at Verdun; by late November, 95 divisions had fought at the Somme; and when their repeated employment is counted, a total of 146 divisions fought in the latter battle. What the German General Staff had aimed to avoid since Schlieffen had finally become reality: the protracted war of attrition against a superior enemy coalition. Although the Western Allies incurred immense losses during the battle on the Somme and managed to gain only a few miles of ground, the Germans had in the end suffered a strategic defeat: the offensive at the Somme had relieved the French front at Verdun, contributed to Romania entering the war on the side of the Allies, and finally exhausted the forces of the German Army in terms of manpower and morale to an alarming degree.[10]

At the tactical level, the battle of the Somme fitted in seamlessly with the experiences at Verdun, although the German Army was forced to engage in the 'unloved' pure defensive battle from the very beginning. Many tactical innovations, such as the formation of mixed artillery battle groups or the application of stormtroop tactics by the infantry, were implemented in the defensive battle on the Somme in a similar manner to the offensive battle at Verdun.[11] The responsibility for the conduct of combined arms combat was transferred down from the corps commands to the division level. All these developments took place in close correlation with addressing the issues surrounding the use of defence in depth, which had been a topic of controversy in the German Army for some time. When trench warfare began, the infantry had defended only one line. The effect of the artillery in the Allied offensives of 1915 forced Falkenhayn to rethink. Contrary to the opinion of several army commands, he enforced more depth by ordering the creation of more rear positions and bases. The combat power of the front line was to be based on the heavy machine guns used there, while stronger infantry forces were to be assembled in rear positions. Their task was to attack and recapture lost terrain before the enemy was able to establish a foothold. Falkenhayn thought it was futile and too costly to expel an entrenched enemy solely by making massive use of the infantry. The parallel to the attack at Verdun is obvious. He believed that once an enemy had conquered and then strengthened the German positions, a counter-attack would only be successful if it was well-planned and supported by a heavy preparatory artillery bombardment. Falkenhayn's recommendation to his commanders was that 'consideration must be given to whether the tactical success will be worth the inevitable cost in casualties and munitions'. In view of what was experienced at Verdun, he emphasized in May 1916 that the manning of the front line should be even thinner and that the echeloned use of machine guns was also possible.[12]

Everything was guided by Falkenhayn's principle that not an inch of ground of enemy territory should be surrendered. Any withdrawal from the enemy was considered an unacceptable moral defeat. The Germans therefore fought the defensive battle at the Somme with the tactical and operational objective of holding their ground at all cost. An order issued by General Fritz von Below, Commander-in-Chief of 2. Armee (1. Armee after 19 July 1916) endorsed Falkenhayn's prohibition on withdrawal and stated categorically: 'I forbid the voluntary withdrawal from positions. ... The enemy must only be allowed to find his way forward over our dead bodies.' The originator of the order was Oberst Fritz von Loßberg, Below's chief of staff and Falkenhayn's top expert on defence. Falkenhayn had ousted Loßberg's predecessor immediately after the beginning of the battle because he had issued an order regarding the possibility of surrendering ground to the enemy. Loßberg long remained one of the most vehement advocates of the principle of holding positions at all cost and felt vindicated in the battle of the Somme.[13]

Due to Falkenhayn's stipulations, the defence at the Somme was organized as a deeply echeloned defence, although the majority of troops continued to fight persistently for and in the most forward position:

Machine guns and light, medium and heavy mine launchers were installed in and between the 1st and 2nd trenches to provide flanking and frontal fire against no man's land ...; and the first supporting troops lay in this second and further rear trenches, also in deep dugouts; in the event of an attack they were to hasten forward in order to hold the most forward trench, as was demanded then of each German force as a matter of honour.[14]

The dispersal of men and *matériel* on the battlefield was also influenced by the Allies' use of massive and prolonged barrages. By late July 1916, the previously well-prepared trench system with its deep dugouts had already been turned into shell-hole positions. More and more troops proceeded to form the 'thinly manned' front line as Falkenhayn recommended, while the infantry positioned itself behind this line in echelons and sections making better use of reverse slope positions. This dispersal made it more difficult for the superior Allied artillery to engage targets and also offered protection from air reconnaissance. Within the division, infantry regiments now deployed one battalion forward (*Kampfbataillon*), an immediate reserve force behind the former (*Bereitschaftsbataillon*) and another reserve force that rested further to the rear (*Ruhebataillon*); at least some of the reserves were to remain out of range of the enemy artillery fire. The heavy machine guns became the main weapon in the defence. In order to increase the impact of the machine guns, and particularly to preserve them to repel enemy infantry attacks, they were now deployed in depth. This made it more likely that they would survive the enemy artillery shelling and could then be used as strongholds during a fight against advancing enemy infantry. Deploying them in depth also made it more difficult for the enemy to detect them; this, once again, increased their chances of survival and it also meant that the enemy infantry would be taken by surprise at the sudden opening of fire by the machine guns. The number of machine guns in the regiment increased considerably over the course of 1916. Within the regiment, each of the three infantry battalions had their own machine-gun company (with up to 12 08-type machine guns). Building on this firepower, the infantry squads held the ground also by applying stormtroop tactics offensively in the form of permanent counterstrokes *(Gegenstöße)*. These counterstrokes or the prepared counter-attack continued to be the flexible core and thus the main element of the German defence at the Somme. At the same time, the adoption of an offensive approach to fighting and the attempt to hold every inch of ground were the main causes of the immense losses suffered by the Germans. Under the permanent pressure of attacks from the Allies with their superior resources, the German divisions eventually expended their forces in battle more rapidly than could be replaced by the often hurried deployment of the few reserves.[15]

The German Army used its clashes with the enemy at Verdun and at the Somme to seek and find tactical solutions for modern combined arms combat. As shown above, this learning process was primarily based on the lessons-learned reports from front-line units. They had long circulated within and among the armies, allowing the new tactical knowledge to spread quickly. The German Army extended this system during the battle of the Somme from the regiment to the army group level in order to be able to withstand the extreme attrition in the battle of *matériel*.[16] Falkenhayn had made only a limited and selected number of lessons-learned reports from the OHL available in writing to the whole army. The problem was that these reports often presented conflicting conclusions. There was a lack of new command and control and training regulations combining the manifold lessons learned by the troops in uniform operational doctrines.[17] In 1916, cooperative combined arms combat was still far from being common knowledge among German officers. Only too often did familiar mental barriers reveal themselves: the infantry did not trust the artillery because artillery shells continued to accidentally land on their positions on a regular basis. This was due to the inadequate technical means of communication, poor ammunition and the increasing wear of artillery tubes resulting from the large number of rounds fired. There was still much controversy over battle management and fighting techniques, particularly as the interaction of the arms became increasingly complex as a result of the many new weapons employed. On the one hand, coordination required guidelines and orders that ranged from strict to pedantic. On the other hand, the individualization of tactics required forces to have the freedom of action they needed to implement *Auftragstaktik*. *Auftragstaktik* had been the prevailing leadership principle in the German Army since the turn of the century. It meant that a recipient of orders would act autonomously within the scope of the military leader's intent. This type of command inevitably implied downward delegation of responsibility as well as the rejection of tactical schematization. Above all, Falkenhayn had failed to enforce a conduct of war that avoided the wasteful use of resources, simply because this was not the main aim for him. It is therefore no wonder that an army order cautioned that practising 'reasonable thrift with human lives' should not result in a 'dread of losses'.[18] As a consequence, many commanders did not consider reducing losses a primary issue in battle management. On the contrary, aspirations for prestige and decorations misled many officers to send soldiers into the slaughter on the battlefield. As late as the summer of 1917, a Bavarian division commander accused his fellow officers of 'despicable ambition' that resulted in the 'useless slaughter of human beings'.[19] In the end, the soldier was and remained an abstract operand in the military machine, just like guns and grenades. In their contemporary parlance, the military leadership cynically called soldiers *'Menschenmaterial'* ('human material').

Addressing the changing character of war

As a consequence of the battles of Verdun and the Somme, Falkenhayn was removed from his office as Chief of the General Staff of the Field Army in August 1916. His two successors were the 'heroes of Tannenberg', Hindenburg and Ludendorff, who were popular with both the military and the civilian population.

In November 1916, Hindenburg, now Chief of the General Staff of the Field Army, was forced to openly announce to his officers that the 'character of war' and the 'means of waging war' had changed. These keywords are used in his memorandum entitled *Kriegführung und Generalstab* (*Warfare and the General Staff*), published on 22 November 1916.[20]

It was the result of the battles of *matériel* at Verdun and the Somme, both marked by their duration and the heavy losses incurred. The German armies involved in them had lost about 725,000 men.[21] It led to the

Erschöpfungskrieg (war of attrition) being at least temporarily acknowledged in operational thinking, a war in which Germany was forced to use men and war *matériel* more sparingly and to fight a defensive war. This was a painful realization and learning process for the majority of the officer corps, many of whom had been trained before the war in the spirit of being 'ruthlessly offensive' and 'gloriously deciding battles'.

The change in operational thinking was accompanied by the remarkably self-critical realization of what the 'means of waging war' were. Casting an analytical eye over the industrialized war being fought on the Western Front, Hindenburg wrote: 'We would be deluding ourselves if we were to deny that we have been slower to learn in some respects than our enemies.' By this he was not only referring to the gradual substitution of men by automatic weapons on the battlefield, but more importantly the complex interaction of old and new technological branches, including air forces, on the battlefield. The key lesson had been learned from the first fighting in 1914: anyone wanting to successfully engage in battle and win, with a minimum of losses, had to be better in reconciling the elements of technology, fire, and manoeuvre. This was just as true for small military units as it was for the conduct of major army operations. In order to be able to win the long war against an enemy with superior resources, the German Army simply had to learn to fight more efficiently, and this was the intent pursued by the German high command, OHL.

Hindenburg's memorandum *Kriegführung und Generalstab*, in combination with the directive on the lessons learned from the battle of the Somme issued on 25 September 1916, marked the beginning of an extensive modernization of the German Army's tactical doctrine. This was accompanied by a massive increase in the production of ammunition, guns, mine launchers, machine guns, and aircraft (the so-called Hindenburg Programme). On the battlefield, the focus turned to combined arms combat by better equipped and armed infantry divisions with standardized organizational structures. The lessons learned from Verdun and the Somme provided the key impetus: the former primarily for the further development of the attack in trench warfare, the latter for being regarded as the 'haute école of the German Army for defence in trench warfare'.[22] Massed fire assaults by the artillery aimed at breaking the morale of the enemy, the use of stormtroop tactics and the application of defence in depth were milestones. In late 1916, the insights of the front-line units served as an important foundation for the OHL in the preparation of new command and control as well as training regulations. These documents were then continuously updated to accommodate the new lessons learned and to permanently reflect the responses of the enemy. Tactical knowledge circulated between the commanders and troops on both a top-down and a bottom-up basis as well as between individual front-line units and theatres of war. In this way, the German Army experienced what British historians have for several years called the 'learning curve'[23] when referring to the British army in World War I.

Consequences for the conduct of battle in 1917/18

Hindenburg and Ludendorff implemented what Falkenhayn had merely initiated, proceeding much more resolutely and above all very quickly. The future guidelines for the German conduct of war were now unambiguous: Germany was to conserve its own forces while causing high attrition among the enemy. To successfully repel the expected Allied offensives on the Western Front, it was first necessary to focus on the further development of the defence in depth. In 1917, the defence no longer consisted of lines, but of several so-called deep combat zones. In order to be able to escape the attacker's annihilating artillery fire at least temporarily, the soldiers in the trenches were allowed to withdraw to a limited degree. The marked difference from Falkenhayn's concepts was that the rigid principle of holding ground at all cost was abandoned. Nevertheless, only senior commanders and, in exceptional cases, division commanders were allowed to order entire sections of terrain to be evacuated. The main elements of the elastic defence in depth – as it was now known – continued to be independent counterstrokes by local infantry reserves or planned counter-attacks by infantry reserves echeloned in depth and supported by cooperative and mission-oriented artillery volleys. The idea of this was to ensure that the decision in a battle could also be brought about in the defence by combining an overall defensive stance with offensive action against an attacking force that wore itself out in the depth of the defended area. So, careful consideration had to be given to making careful use of the scarce human and material resources available. In view of the few reserves available and force sustainability, the organization of the troops and the control of their use in trench warfare became tighter. This was a responsibility of the major commands from the corps to army group level. Following the procedure at the Somme, the staff at corps level (the *Generalkommando*) remained in their sections of the front *Bodenständig* (permanent and static) and commanded and controlled several divisions like a battle group headquarters. The conduct of combined arms combat was now the sole responsibility of the division. It was the 'combat unit of the battle front': one infantry brigade consisting of three regiments (nine machine-gun companies), an additional machine-gun sniper detachment, one field artillery regiment (a foot artillery battalion was added in the spring of 1918), one engineer battalion with a mine-launcher company as well as logistic and medical units including driver and signal teams. The divisions rotated continuously between the fronts and were employed either as a *Stellungsdivision* (trench division) or, to the rear, as an *Eingreifdivision* (counter-attack division) in reserve. Depending on the mission, additional army troops were placed under the operational control of the individual divisions (e.g. heavy artillery and air forces). In their positions, the infantry regiments of the *Stellungsdivision* were usually organized as *Kampf-, Bereitschafts-, Ruhebataillon* and rotated permanently in these roles (the division area was 1.5–2 miles wide). At the front, the commander of the *Kampfbataillon* exercised command more or less independently, whereas the troops moved in small combat teams applying stormtroop tactics. At the same time the infantry was increasingly equipped with powerful arms, primarily 08/15-type light machine guns, which also allowed further reduction in manpower without losing firepower within the deployed units – the machine was replacing man in battle. The small combat teams were utterly dependent on each other in the fight for survival on the front. The individualization of tactics took place in the 'emptiness of the battlefield'.

The OHL incorporated the innovative elastic defence in depth and the combined arms combat in a new regulation entitled *Grundsätze für die Führung der Abwehrschlacht im Stellungskriege* (*Principles for the Conduct of the Defensive Battle in Trench Warfare*). In 1917/18, the operational doctrine was continuously updated to accommodate the many and varied lessons-learned reports from the front-line troops. The new regulation was published in several revised versions, in an attempt to take account of the conditions of the latest decisive battles. In parallel, the OHL enforced the training of commanders, general staff officers and troops via an extensive network of schools, training areas and courses based on the permanently updated operational doctrine. New knowledge was also imparted to Germany's allies, for instance through their officers attending training courses. Ludendorff controlled and pushed ahead the tactical learning process in order to provide Germany with a mass army that was as widely qualified, and thus as hard-hitting, as possible.[24]

In early 1918, the OHL transformed the issues that had been originally intended for defensive operations in 1917 in a similar way into training and battle for attack operations. In January 1918, it issued a new central regulation entitled *Der Angriff im Stellungskrieg* (*The Attack in Trench Warfare*). The key foundations for offensive operations were the tried and tested element of surprise and the exploitation of the moral shock effect of mass artillery fire. Days of heavy preparatory artillery bombardment like that delivered during the methodical Allied attacks of 1917 were out of the question for Germany due to its inferiority in resources. A newly developed artillery technique allowed the abandonment of the tell-tale common practice of delivering artillery fire for days. This had been necessary in order to zero the artillery pieces in their positions and only a long bombardment was believed to deliver the required result of neutralizing or, preferably, destroying the enemy. The objective of the new, short preparatory was to neutralize the enemy's artillery and command structures unexpectedly and systematically, by using poison gas. This went hand in hand with a high expenditure of shells, so that this new short, heavy bombardment delivered the same amount of firepower to the enemy as the long and protected bombardment of earlier battles.

Protected by the rolling barrage, the forward infantry divisions had to quickly break through the weakest points of the enemy's positions and advance as far as possible. The infantry was to advance using stormtroop tactics, with close support from the artillery, engineers, and air forces. Reserves deployed close behind the first infantry wave were to sustain the attack. Divisions were the combat units for combined arms battle during attacks, although the corps and army staffs (*Generalkommando* or *Armeeoberkommando*) were earmarked to exercise centralized command with respect to the planning and opening of fire. From the OHL's viewpoint, the successful German counter-attack at Cambrai in late November 1917 confirmed the new offensive tactics.[25]

The implementation of operational doctrine developed for the defence and attack in 1917/18 remained greatly ambivalent in practice. As before, the operational doctrine left enough leeway to combine new and old as the situation and location permitted. Being a clever and extremely practical-minded tactician, Ludendorff even deliberately conceded deviations. He believed that no doctrine should contain wisdoms carved in stone, but should always be flexibly adapted to the battle at hand and the action of the enemy. The specific lessons learned by 1. Armee and Loßberg at the Somme formed the basis for the *Ausbildungsvorschrift für die Fußtruppen im Krieg* (AVF; *Training Regulation for the Infantry in War*), which was developed in late 1916 and later also revised. For example, the favoured approach in this regulation was to hold out in a position 'to the last man'.[26] There was no mention of withdrawal. The lessons-learned reports that were simultaneously disseminated among the troops often contained different tactical recommendations. This allowed the troops room for perseverance in training and battle in equal measure and the chance to make flexible use of innovations which the officers could not reject outright. Loßberg can be considered an example of an officer who implemented this compromise approach. What mattered in the end was success on the battlefield. If victory was achieved, there was promise of decorations, but if it was not, humiliating dismissal from command loomed. Ludendorff himself often used this leverage. It is therefore hardly surprising that the way war was waged on the front was often the result of numerous combinations of tactics. In addition to the innovative elastic defence in depth, there were many instances where the traditional static line defence was applied. And despite stormtroop tactics, the infantry still often attacked in dense skirmish lines in the spring of 1918.[27] This inconsistency was also reflected in the propagated *Auftragstaktik*. Like Loßberg, many senior officers considered the mass army a poorly trained militia compared to the pre-war army. They simply did not think these soldiers were capable of mastering and applying demanding fighting techniques within a short period. They feared the troops would run away when withdrawing in the elastic defence in depth. This scepticism was also reflected in the AVF. There were even reservations regarding the military capabilities of young general staff officers. This resulted in pedantic monitoring of lower echelons, which in turn muzzled the very individual initiative that was demanded. In the end, the strict supervision served a pragmatic purpose: it ensured that Ludendorff's main demand for efficient use to be made of the scarce personnel and *matériel* resources was met.[28]

Deciding the outcome of war

Despite all the contradictions, the compromise-based tactical learning that was so heavily influenced by the battles of Verdun and, in particular, the Somme, paid off. In 1917, the troops were able to successfully repel the mass Allied attacks in the main theatre of war on the Western Front and in the course of their spring offensives in 1918, the German attack divisions initially gained miles of ground, something neither side had achieved since 1914. However the German forces, which had only a few trucks and hardly any tanks and even suffered from a shortage of horses, simply lacked the mobility to follow up their successful breakthrough and decide the war. 'Indomitable will' and alleged better leadership were just not enough.

It was not only the hope of turning the war into a war of movement that proved to be a miscalculation. Despite all the supervision exercised, the pressure of the Allied major offensives rendered it impossible to adhere to Ludendorff's guidelines of conducting operations with a minimum of losses in 1917. At the battle of Third Ypres, the 4. Armee lost more than 250,000 troops, and the Spring Offensives in 1918 saw some 950,000 German casualties.[29] By mid-1918, there were hardly any replacements available. Numerous divisions had to be dissolved and the strengths of the infantry battalions had to be repeatedly reduced.

In the end, it was simply the side that was able to make better use of its superior resources for fighting the war that kept the upper hand. It was not progressive doctrines that decided the outcome of war in the industrial age. More important were strategic advantages that came in the form of human reserves and economic output, which really showed their faces for the first time during the battle of the Somme.

CHAPTER 9

BRITISH TACTICAL PRACTICE DURING THE SOMME CAMPAIGN

Dr Bill Mitchinson

The traditional view of the BEF's tactical approach to the Somme is that of waves of soldiers walking or wading resolutely towards fields of uncut wire and intact German defences. Critics of generals Haig, Rawlinson, and Gough point to the scores of cemeteries scattered across the rolling downland and the brutal testimony of the Thiepval Memorial to the Missing as evidence of the unimaginative and callous methods of assault. While this may, on occasion, represent a reasonable interpretation of the tactics employed, as the months passed the BEF demonstrated it was capable of learning from experience gained both before and during the various stages of the campaign. It was able to assimilate lessons, ideas, and new technology to develop new practices which, although not always evident in the engagements fought in the mud and winter of late 1916, laid the foundations for what in the following two years of war were to become the tactics and fighting methods employed which ultimately defeated the German Army.

General Sir Henry Rawlinson was appointed General Officer Commanding (GOC) Fourth Army on its creation in February 1916. Its task was to undertake the greater part of the forthcoming Somme Offensive and Rawlinson intended that the winter and spring would allow time for the New Armies to finish what, to him, had been their inadequate training. Incessant demands for labour meant that the infantry were called upon to perform endless working parties; these ate into what would otherwise have been valuable training time. Brigades and divisions did, however, form schools where groups of officers and men were instructed in particular skills; they in turn disseminated their knowledge to their own platoons and companies. War diaries are usually unspecific as to how the training was actually done but centrally produced syllabi, such as SS109, *Training Divisions for Offensive Action* of May 1916, and *Fourth Army's Tactical Notes* of the same month were widely distributed. These were in addition to training programmes issued by brigades, divisions, and corps instructing formations to undertake company, battalion, and brigade schemes, as well as plenty of rifle and bayonet work. Specialist training programmes for bombers, Lewis gunners and signallers were also produced, but '"tactics" is a notoriously difficult subject to teach unless one is in a genuinely "tactical situation" – that is, someone is shooting at you with live ammunition.'[1] The New Army and Territorial Force battalions used on the first day of the offensive may not, perhaps, have been as well instructed in tactical theory as their pre-war Regular Army counterparts, but their regional affiliations, the length of time served together and their – albeit for some, reasonably limited – experience on the Western Front, had given them a cohesion which to some theorists was more important than an advanced base of tactical knowledge.[2]

The first day of the Somme, 1 July 1916

Infantry tactics employed on the opening day of the Somme have long aroused considerable controversy. The usual view of successive waves of neatly spaced infantry with rifles at the port advancing at walking pace towards the German defences has been proved to be inaccurate for several sectors of the front on 1 July. Rawlinson's *Tactical Notes*, in fact, offered a series of contradictory suggestions as to how corps or divisional commanders might send their troops across no man's land.[3] The army commander seems to have allowed his subordinates to determine what they considered to be the most appropriate method for the terrain and anticipated defences in their sectors. He advocated that sections of troops unencumbered by heavy packs should rush across no man's land to effect quick entry to the enemy trenches; these would be followed and reinforced by companies or platoons advancing either in extended waves on a broad front or in smaller groups, possibly in column or even in single file, on a narrower frontage. The crucial point that Rawlinson did make clear in his *Notes*, however, was that tempo and momentum should be maintained by the regular arrival of successive companies who would either leapfrog the original platoons or act as supports and moppers-up to allow the leading platoons to continue the advance.

Whether Rawlinson deliberately left his *Notes* open to different interpretation or whether they were inadvertently ambiguous and poorly devised is unclear, but his subordinates decided they would adopt the tactics, and even vary the number of battalions within a brigade committed to the initial assault, which best suited their situation. In the hybrid 8th Division,[4] the two leading New Army battalions of 70th Brigade advanced in columns of platoons echeloned behind the one in front, while the support battalion advanced in two waves, each a half-battalion of two companies. In contrast the regular battalions of the division advanced in company waves. The two assaulting brigades of the 56th Division also adopted slightly different formations: two of the three attacking battalions in 169th Brigade advanced in six waves, with the third attacking with two companies in four leading waves followed by another company in support. To their right, 168th Brigade attacked with only two battalions, both with all four companies in four waves in column of platoons. The composition of the waves also varied across corps and divisions. For example, the leading waves of the London Rifle Brigade went across with lighter loads but did include bombers and Lewis gun teams within their ranks; the following waves were more heavily laden with tools and ammunition for consolidation. Other battalion commanding officers, conscious that the weapon was still in short supply, kept their Lewis guns behind the leading waves ready to be sent forward once the initial objectives had been reached. Another infantry support weapon, the light trench mortar, was also becoming more available but, like the Lewis, required considerable numbers of men to carry forward its ammunition. They came under brigade control but few, if any barrels were sent across to the enemy trenches on 1 July.[5] One weapon that was in wide supply was a reliable hand grenade. The various and unpredictable varieties of 1915 had been replaced by the increasing availability of the Mills bomb. Although it could not be thrown as far as the German stick grenade, and lacked the explosive power to clear larger dugouts, the Mills was an effective addition to the physical component of infantry fighting power.

Some lead battalions did clamber from their own trenches at 0730hrs when the barrage lifted onto the German second line; others were already in no man's land. Their commanders decided troops needed to be as close as possible to their first objectives before the enemy had time to recover from what was hoped to be the crushing effect of the barrage. Despite employing this sensible precaution, few troops of 23rd Brigade who had to cross the wide expanse of Mash Valley whilst enfiladed from both sides and under frontal fire, managed to reach the German front line. By contrast, the Ulstermen of the 36th Division surged forward from their positions halfway across a much narrower no man's land and entered the formidable Schwaben Redoubt before the defenders had emerged from their shelters. The Territorial troops of 8th Battalion Royal Warwickshire Regiment attached to the 4th Division advanced in 'rushes', as did some of the Pals battalions of the 31st Division. The nominally regular units of the 29th Division had no uniform manner, some walking and some rushing, while the 34th Division seems to have sent its battalions across at the walk. Undoubtedly, when fire opened some troops would naturally attempt to quicken their pace and evidence shows that even carrying 66lb, men could advance for short distances at a trot. If, however, they did then manage to enter the enemy trenches, they might well have been incapacitated for a few vital minutes.

The vagueness apparent in Rawlinson's *Notes* was perhaps because he considered the means of crossing no man's land to have been largely irrelevant. The opinion of many was that the bombardment would so smash and demoralize German front-line resistance that it would not matter how the British actually got into the enemy trenches. It was partly also for this reason that smoke candles were used to cover the advance on only a few sectors of front. Smoke had worked well on parts of the Loos front in 1915 but, despite this success, it was not exploited on 1 July because it was thought troops would lose direction and artillery spotting would be obscured. Both reasons have resonance but if the infantry were to be exposed during their crossing of no man's land, the artillery had to protect them. This it singly failed to do.

The lessons learnt at Neuve Chapelle in 1915 about the density of guns required per yard of trench had been ignored two months later at Aubers and then again at Loos. It was impossible to recreate the Neuve Chapelle density for 1 July owing to the much greater length of front to be attacked and the depth of its defences. What heavy and field guns there were, however, were not always used to best effect. Furthermore, although the supply of ammunition had improved significantly since 1915, the quality was hugely variable. Similarly, the output of guns had risen but there were still far too many obsolete or ineffective pieces and defects were becoming apparent in even the most recently produced marks. The purpose of the artillery was to cut gaps in the enemy wire, destroy the enemy's front-line defences, his morale and silence his guns. Some wire was cut and some trenches flattened by 1 July but even before 0730hrs, it had become obvious that those few batteries which had been tasked with counter-battery fire had failed completely to achieve their purpose. The Germans had rushed additional artillery brigades to the Somme in anticipation of the attack. Many of these remained silent until the offensive began and were, in any case, beyond the range of the British guns; others had been moved about during the preparatory phase. Cloudy weather had hampered aerial observation by the RFC, but even if visibility had been good and control of the air assured, the type and number of guns available for counter-battery fire would have made little impact on the bulk of the enemy batteries able to fire on the infantry assault.

It was the failure of the British artillery to locate and destroy the enemy batteries which doomed the infantry – in whichever tactical formation the divisions or brigades chose to employ – to slaughter. The only significant success occurred in the southern sector where a form of creeping barrage protected the troops as they advanced against defences that were not as deep as those in the north and where the density of German guns was less. In addition, the success of the 30th Division at Montauban was aided by a number of French batteries. It was not only that land–air and infantry–artillery tactical cooperation and communications needed to improve, but it was also the question of sufficient numbers and the reliability of the guns and munitions which had to be addressed.

Tactical developments

The attack by XII and XV Corps on 14–15 July did not mark any great tactical innovation but did address the issue of gun density. The 9th (Scottish) Division also demonstrated that a creeping barrage, principally of high explosive with delayed action fuses rather than shrapnel, had a greater effect on defenders' morale and made it easier for the attackers to keep direction.[6] This was especially important for this assault, because Rawlinson had managed to persuade a dubious Haig that a night attack in the southern sector would be successful in taking the German second line. Sound staff work allowed the assaulting troops to form up on tapes laid by Royal Engineers parties well into no man's land unhindered by German gunfire and protected by Lewis gun teams lying to their front. It is not known which tactical formations were employed by the battalions, but at zero hour they advanced into the German trenches and beyond. A degree of confusion, indifferent communications and poor command decisions, as well as stiffening enemy resistance, meant that further exploitation was not possible. Nonetheless, the night had proved to be a major success. The key had been in the significantly improved concentration of heavy guns which effectively destroyed the wire and enemy trenches, shattered German defensive cohesion and prevented the swift arrival of enemy reserves.[7] The two corps had achieved surprise, had concentrated force and shown tactical flexibility and adaptability. In reality, however, the terrain and the 1,000-yard wide no man's land suited this type of operation. It was really a case of the artillery gaining the ground and the infantry occupying it; in the central sector of the line, close to what had been the original axis of advance along the Albert–Bapaume road, significant infantry advances proved considerably harder to achieve.

July and August were characterized by small, often entirely uncoordinated actions by individual brigades or even battalions aimed at securing some local tactical advantage; these would serve as jumping-off points for larger operations. For example, the 48th (South Midland) Division conducted a number of fairly minor but costly operations to the north of Ovillers in the attempt to push up towards the Pozières Ridge and the road between it and Thiepval.[8] The division was faced by a succession of enemy posts and strongpoints positioned within a maze of trenches which could only be taken by a series of bombing operations. Five battalions from 144th and 145th Brigades were to assault at 0245hrs on 21 July behind a brief two-minute bombardment. They were to be supported by machine-gun and trench mortar barrages and, if the wind was favourable, a smoke screen. The infantry was to carry only essential equipment and ammunition, with shutter screens to signal the artillery the depth they had reached, and several cages of pigeons. The troops were instructed to be in the German trenches immediately the barrage lifted onto the enemy's reserve positions. The diarist of the 1st Buckingham Battalion, the Oxfordshire and Buckinghamshire Light Infantry, thought everything went 'like clockwork' until the assault actually began. The trench mortar barrage, which according to one report began ten minutes before the infantry attacked, attracted an immediate German response and another report declared the British bombardment had 'absolutely no effect' on the heavy machine-gun and rifle fire which lashed the Bucks' parapet. In contrast another, from 5th Battalion, The Gloucestershire Regiment, claimed the enemy's defensive fire was checked by the British artillery and that they reached within 100 yards of the German posts before being spotted. Another report from the same battalion, however, suggests that the assaulting platoons were fired on even before they left their own trenches. When they were close to the posts they were held up by wire, a 'very thick barrage of bombs' and by machine guns on the ridge behind firing over the heads of the posts' garrisons. The attacking companies were silhouetted against the rising moon and offered a 'good target' but some did get into the enemy posts. It did not take long for the Germans to organize counter-attacks which, in turn, forced most of the British troops back to their own start line. One platoon of 6th Gloucesters reported that it would have been able to hold the 'particularly unhealthy' Post 28, but its other two platoons withdrew from their gains because they had run out of rifle grenades, the supporting 2-inch Stokes trench mortars had exhausted their bombs and 7th Battalion, the Worcestershire Regiment on their right had failed to get forward. For its part, 7th Worcesters claimed it had withdrawn because its left flank was in the air owing to 6th Gloucesters having been 'badly held up'. One company commander of the Worcesters requested a platoon of the division's pioneer battalion be sent forward to help consolidate his newly won position, but 50 minutes later what was left of his company and the pioneers were struggling back over the broken ground to their own lines. A handwritten note by an officer of 5th Gloucesters declared that after three hours of continuous fighting against 'overwhelming odds' his men were exhausted and almost out of ammunition.

These bombing attacks were to set the scene for the next five nights. It is rare for war diaries to record the calling of conferences in advance of the attacks but, rather than division or brigade staffs simply issuing orders without any previous consultation, some officers' meetings must have taken place. 145th Brigade recorded one such conference involving infantry, artillery, and Royal Engineers commanders in preparation for the attacks in the early hours of 23 July. Divisional HQ wanted two new jumping-off trenches dug before the attack but staff orders as to who should do it were unclear. Originally, 145th Brigade was told to organize the digging with the pioneers of 5th Battalion the Royal Sussex Regiment, but this instruction was later contradicted. Consequently, 'through various misunderstanding and other causes which were never cleared up but remained the subject of much correspondence, little work was done.' The confusion continued when 144th Brigade's brigade major and company commanders of 6th Gloucesters went forward to establish jumping-off points and were fired on by both British and German artillery.

Under a barrage of high-explosive shells and flamethrowers, and with a section of Royal Engineers in support, three of the battalion's companies advanced at 0030hrs on 23 July in the sobering knowledge that if the attack failed they would be required to do it again at 0400hrs. Contact aircraft were scheduled to fly above the battalion at specified times to look for identification flares but these were not required because the Gloucesters were met immediately by heavy machine-gun fire. Some men did manage to enter the enemy trench but the last waves and the consolidation parties did not even enter the zone swept by the machine guns. Two of the companies lost all of their officers and only one officer of the third company returned. Instead of having to try again a few hours later the battalion was ordered to assist, with machine guns, rifle grenades and Stokes, a new attempt by the other two brigades.

To the right, 4th Ox and Bucks achieved rather more success. They approached Pozières from the west through the warren of trenches which covered the rising ground between it and Ovillers. The Oxfords found it heavy going, with at least one platoon getting too far forward and falling victim to its own barrage; others became disorganized and 'suffered heavily' from German fire. The platoons engaged in ferocious bombing exchanges but when 4th Battalion, the Royal Berkshire Regiment, brought forward a fresh supply of bombs the Oxfords succeeded in securing a stretch of enemy trenches. To try to straighten the line, the Bucks attacked over the ground from which 5th Gloucesters had earlier withdrawn. With one company 'seriously impeded' by their own barrage, the remaining companies stormed into the German trenches almost at the same time as the barrage lifted. An astonished German officer declared that he and his men were waiting for the barrage to move before emerging from their shelters. Bombing assaults and 'minor enterprises' continued through the night of 24–25 July with what was described as 'varying success.' Staff work suffered from the lack of reliable information and resulted in 'miscarriage of orders' but these small tactical operations proved that with suitable weapons, organization, inter-arms cooperation and determination, progress could be made.

Artillery-infantry cooperation

During major operations artillery brigades usually worked in groups, sometimes with the guns of other divisions attached for additional firepower. For these smaller, largely bombing attacks, half-batteries or even individual 18-pounders could be sent to forward positions if the situation or the infantry demanded close protection. The usual practice was, however, for the field guns and howitzers to be in pits behind the lines and connected to the infantry brigades and their attached forward observation officer by telephone. Enemy shelling, horsed transport and the encumbrances carried by infantry working parties frequently disrupted the lines with the result that, at times, infantry calls for fire support were not immediately met. Flares could sometimes be missed in the dust and smoke of battle and, if they arrived at all, messages by runners were often received too late to have an impact.

Reports show that the effectiveness of the artillery could vary between different battalions of the same division. While, for example, 1st Bucks praised the artillery for its accuracy, 6th Gloucesters described its covering barrage as 'quite useless' in keeping down Germans' heads. There were 'long periods' when no shells fell and so, 'having nothing to worry them [German machine gunners] were able to fire on the assaulting troops as they pleased.' Yet, despite the physical problems of remaining in contact with the infantry and of the contrary opinions as to their effectiveness, cooperation between gunners and infantry did gradually improve as the campaign progressed. The fire plan for the attacks during the night of 22–23 July was fairly typical of those devised for subsequent operations. The usual night-time barrage of about 40 rounds per battery was to be fired but every 15 minutes from four hours before zero, batteries were to fire salvoes of two or four guns at the enemy posts in order to mark them for the observing infantry. From dawn onwards one battery of 18-pounder guns was assigned to each of the attacking infantry brigades, with the battery commanders being themselves positioned at the infantry brigade headquarters ready to pass on any calls for immediate assistance. In addition to the main barrage, occasional rounds of up to about 30 per battery were to be fired at almost random points behind the German front line. The infantry were ordered to fire flares to mark their new positions both to the artillery and to contact aircraft at specified times. Batteries positioned sentries at those times with orders to observe specifically for the flares.

Attacks such as these offered little real opportunity to develop the conceptual component of fighting power. Distances between attacker and defender were sometimes too close to allow an effective barrage, whether creeping or lifts, to protect the initial approach. When out at rest, platoons practised assaulting strongpoints with Lewis guns to give covering flanking fire while the riflemen rushed them with bomb and bayonet under the protection of a light mortar barrage. 2-inch Stokes trench mortars were available in increasing numbers but they, like the Lewis, required a regular and heavy supply of ammunition. 145th Brigade recorded that an attack by 5th Gloucesters failed because insufficient Stokes ammunition had been brought forwards before dawn. Because the barrels were thus unable to cooperate with the infantry for as long as intended much of the enemy wire remained untouched and unbroken. 143rd Brigade also complained several times during July of the 'unsatisfactory nature of the work' of the Stokes. One report condemned the mortar crews for taking too long to get into action and another for killing six and wounding ten of the infantry when the guns fired short. This was thought to be the result of base plates shifting in the soft ground but if, as was suggested, they were adjusted every ten rounds the rate of fire would drop substantially. The Royal Warwickshire troops, on the receiving end of the shorts, were described as having been 'considerably shaken' and it was suggested that if, like the Lewis detachments, two guns and crews were attached to each battalion it would lead to greater tactical control and boost the infantry's confidence. The existing system, it was argued, created 'misunderstandings' which worked against efficient communications and effective coordination between the supporting and supported arms.

The physical as well as the conceptual component of fighting power improved when the supply of light support weapons increased and as their effective use was gradually assimilated into platoon and company tactics. Certain administrative and operational points were also becoming obvious. 4th Ox and Bucks was one of several battalions which noted the importance of battalion headquarters being informed in sufficient time to organize an attack. It compared the assaults made by the battalion on 19 July and 23 July and concluded there had been little hope of success for the first 'enterprise' because there was no time for officers to reconnoitre the objectives and troops reached their jumping-off point only 15 minutes before zero. In contrast, preparations for the action on 23 July had been considerably better paced. Officers had had time to study the front positions and to relay that knowledge to their platoon commanders and there was sufficient time between the issue of orders from battalion headquarters and the move forward for the troops to draw stores, eat, and rest. There were still, however, problems in coordinating movement of the infantry with the barrage's rate of advance; there also remained appalling omissions in the exchange of intelligence between neighbouring divisions and corps. The consequences of this lack of cross-boundary coordination became even more apparent during the period of rapidly and generally poorly organized local attacks in the middle period of the campaign.

Schwaben Redoubt

Perhaps one of the defining moments in the tactical development of the BEF on the Somme came in September with 18th Division's attack on the Schwaben Redoubt.[9] Although there was no significant difference in the way 53rd and 54th brigades conducted the actual attack compared with those of earlier attempts, the thorough practical preparations made by the brigades and battalions were to prove crucial in the assault against the heavily defended positions between the Leipzig Redoubt and Thiepval. Battalion commanding officers and company commanders were able to reconnoitre the ground before rehearsing their men over mock-up trenches in the rear, platoon commanders and non-commissioned officers (NCOs) knew their objectives, a shattering bombardment followed by an effective creeping barrage swamped the enemy positions and a machine-gun barrage soared overhead to disrupt the arrival of counter-attacking units. There was time for orders to be issued and for troops to be in their assembly positions rested and well in advance of zero. The follow-up battalions were not to be immediately ushered into the front trenches once the leading units attacked, a thoughtful and sensible instruction which meant that the expected German retaliatory barrage fell on almost empty trenches. The GOC division, Major-General Maxse, had a reputation within the BEF as one of the great trainers of men and, once convinced his subordinates knew their commander's intent, allowed them a good degree of mission command as to how they achieved it. Two of his brigade commanders were extremely able and experienced men and his battalion commanding officers were trusted and capable. Confident in the superiority of the physical and moral components of fighting power, the junior officers, NCOs, and other ranks showed command, leadership, courage, resilience, and perhaps above all, initiative. Despite the frequent arrival of drafts, unit cohesion and team spirit had been fostered assiduously over the preparatory period. There were no particularly innovative tactical features employed during the attack itself, battalion commanders being allowed to decide on or even invent the assault formation which best suited their purpose. Despite the excellent preparations, however, once the British platoons entered the labyrinth of German trenches and dugouts it developed into a series of brutal slogging matches of bombing attacks and counter-attacks. Nonetheless, the flexibility, sustainment, concentration of force and determination of the attackers managed to clear a large portion of the Schwaben and its network of neighbouring trenches.

Despite, however, this remarkable assault on exceptionally strong German positions, there was to be no breakthrough in how future tactical actions were to be fought before the Somme was officially closed down in November. The introduction of the tank on 15 September did lead to some local gains but most of the few troops who had had the opportunity to train with the leviathans before the attack, had been limited to about two hours' familiarization. Strides were made over the following winter in deciding how tanks could be most appropriately integrated with infantry but the end of the war was to arrive before any purposeful doctrine on the use of tanks had been established. On occasions, such as an attack by 141st Brigade of 47th Division towards Eaucourt l'Abbaye on 1 October, they did offer substantial support but their proclivity to break down or ditch made them unreliable partners. Other weapons, for example oil projectors which could drench a short-range objective in flame and smoke, could also be employed but unless knocked out by the accompanying barrage, garrisons either side of the targeted area would still bring machine guns and rifles to bear on the attacking troops.

The fighting of October and November offered little opportunity for the infantry to develop further tactical skills. The dreadful weather and appalling ground conditions precluded meaningful experimentation so operations tended to rely on heavy preliminary barrages of varying length, creeping barrages to lead the infantry and then the capture of perhaps a few score yards of trench. When practicable deception, such as false barrages and Chinese attacks, were made but often during these assaults autumn fog and mist and the shelled and waterlogged ground led to confusion and made communications with the artillery or contact aircraft impossible. Situation reports from forward troops to brigade and divisional headquarters were inevitably delayed so effective command and control was usually lost as soon as the leading platoons left their own jumping-off position. To add to the misery of the attacking troops, unstable firing platforms and worn barrels meant barrages often fell short. To avoid instances of 'blue on blue' the infantry were sometimes withdrawn from their hard-worn gains.[10] The dreadful experience of 50th Division during a series of attacks in October and November illustrates well how two of Clausewitz's often imponderable 'frictions' – terrain and weather – permitted the infantry little real opportunity to demonstrate any significant improvement of their tactical skills.

The Northumbrian Division began its slog towards the Flers Line, and eventually the Butte de Warlencourt, in early October. The first attack went remarkably well with, as an observing airman reported, a 'wall of fire' marching steadily towards the enemy line.[11] The infantry followed closely behind this creeping barrage and were untroubled by the 'promiscuous character and comparative lack of volume' of the enemy's counter-fire.[12] The division was back in the line in preparation for another attack scheduled for 26 October, but this was postponed when incessant rain transformed the battlefield into the quagmire and the ineluctable gas-soaked shell holes permanently associated with the wilderness of the Somme uplands. Further postponements followed but the exhausted, sodden and chilled troops continued to live and work in trenches thigh- and waist-deep in mud. It was decided the ground would be dry enough on 5 November, but during the night the heavens again opened and 6th Battalion, the Durham Light Infantry (DLI), reported several men drowned as they waited for zero. When the hour came, those who first managed literally to crawl from the trenches hauled out their comrades. Unsurprisingly, as the laden troops tried to make their way across the shell-pocked and flooded land, cohesion was quickly lost.[13] The curve of the German front lines allowed enfilade from both flanks and, to add to the chaos, the Northumbrians' own artillery began firing short, a Stokes battery wiped out a Lewis gun crew and the supporting Australian machine-gun barrage raked the 6th DLI's parapet from the rear. Despite these handicaps, the infantry managed to establish a post beyond the Butte but successive German counter-attacks and the inability of supports to get across meant the survivors were back in their jumping-off lines by the morning of 6 November. Another attempt was undertaken by 149th Brigade in the early hours of 14 November but, once more, and despite managing to get into parts of the enemy trenches, counter-attacks and heavy counter-barrages drove them back to their start line.

These were typical of many of the scores of attacks made during the latter part of the Somme campaign which produced no territorial gains. Tactically and operationally they were a disaster and did little to aid the maintenance of the moral component of fighting power. The cost in dead and wounded was invariably high and, to the troops in the morass of mud and flooded trenches, appeared futile. Many of them were, of course, simply that, but from the chaos, mud, blood, and disappointment, several important points on how future operations might be framed emerged. The 'want of control and direction from behind',[14] which had been cited as one of the reasons why, for example, 49th Division had failed in September, was being addressed. Only one divisional commander had been sacked for his part in the disaster of 1 July but in the following weeks many brigade and battalion commanders were replaced by men with trench experience and with growing reputations as commanders and leaders. If the accusation that the BEF was 'unsubtle and inflexible in its approach to battle'[15] ever had any solid foundation, that, too, was being addressed by promoting men on merit into positions where they could influence the character of future battles.

Applying the lessons of the Somme

New doctrine did emerge from the lessons learnt during the campaign. The *Memorandum on Trench to Trench Attack* appeared in October and an increasing number of post-battle reports were analysed by staffs and their conclusions passed down the chain of command. By December it was tacitly recognized that the platoon had replaced the company as the principal tactical unit and pamphlet *SS 135, Instructions for the Training of Divisions for Offensive Action* appeared soon afterwards. This gave guidance on how the tactical coordination of infantry weapons should be conducted. By January 1917, pressure to establish uniformity in the means of delivering tactical instruction across the BEF and training battalions in the UK was becoming irresistible. Codification of battle drills proceeded apace and in February 1917, *SS 143, Instructions for the Training of Platoons for Offensive Action* and *SS 144, Normal Formation for the Attack* laid down the composition of a new more or less self-contained platoon of four specialist weapon sections. These pamphlets marked a significant development in tactical evolution and were the result of experience gained on the Somme, the absorption of certain elements of French tactical doctrine and the increased availability of infantry support weapons such as the Lewis and a reliable rifle grenade. By emphasizing the platoon's increased firepower in trench and open warfare the pamphlets signalled a return to pre-war doctrine of fire and movement. They also helped to build small unit cohesion and partly addressed the problem of ill-trained troops going quickly to ground when coming under fire. It had been recognized that mutual confidence in each other's abilities and the fear of opprobrium and shame built understanding and unity in small, compact groups.

The new doctrine also helped to shift opinion on what many commanders believed had become the standard tactic of infantry attack. They had become increasingly concerned that rapidly trained conscripts from the UK had abandoned the rifle and bayonet in favour of the grenade.[16] It was this preference, some argued, that had caused many attacks to founder and fail. Instead of advancing across the open with bayonet poised to intimidate the enemy, troops preferred to throw bombs at each other from the protection of trenches. By instilling into drafts the spirit of the bayonet it would, thought General Hubert Gough, reduce if not eliminate the alleged lack of élan and 'martial spirit, discipline and resolution without which success is impossible.'[17]

Debate was to continue as to whether attacks were best launched during darkness, at dawn or midday, of the gaps between waves or echelons and of the coordination of what by the end of 1917 would be recognized as the developing 'all arms' battle. The experience of the Somme did confirm, however, that 're-skilling' of the BEF was firmly under way.[18] It also confirmed the growing primacy of the artillery as the major arbiter of the battlefield. There were still troughs as well as peaks, inconsistencies and contradictions to be negotiated in the so-called 'learning curve' but, while it may not have been obvious to the average soldier shivering with cold and fear in the trenches of the Western Front, the attrition of the Somme was to prove a significant period in the evolution of British tactical thought. In conjunction with advances in what can be seen as the development of the operational and strategic levels of warfare, this evolution was ultimately to ensure victory in 1918.

CHAPTER 10

THE GERMAN ARMY AT WAR

The 26. Reserve-Division during the first day of the battle of the Somme

Dr Matthias Strohn

For German soldiers in World War I their military 'home' was the regiment, and it was their regiment that they would identify with. However, the main fighting unit was not the regiment, but the division.[1] This chapter explores how German divisions fought in World War I, and provides a case study for the successful conduct of a defensive battle: the 26. (württembergische) Reserve-Division on the first day of the battle of the Somme. Several aspects make this division an interesting case study. It held a part of the front line that saw particularly heavy fighting and some of the places associated with the divisional sector, such as Thiepval and the Schwaben Redoubt, have entered the common history of the battle. Also, the division was not a Prussian division, but a unit from the kingdom of Württemberg in the south-west of Germany.

Most of the documents of the Prussian Army went up in flames during an air raid on Potsdam in 1945, but the files of the Württemberg Army survived World War II relatively unscathed. This enables the historian to conduct primary research on a level that is, on the whole, no longer possible for the Prussian Army. The reader might wonder why we talk of the Prussian and Württemberg armies here and not of the German Army. This is an important point and one that is often overlooked: it is technically wrong to speak of the German Army in World War I. The army that went to war in 1914 consisted of the armies of the kingdoms of Prussia, Bavaria, Saxony, and Württemberg. Other German areas, such as Baden or the small principality Lippe, formed units that served within the Prussian Army. Only in times of war did the Prussian king as Kaiser of Germany become the supreme warlord; during peacetime the crowned heads of Bavaria, Saxony and Württemberg held the command over their troops. Only with the end of World War I and the establishment of the preliminary Reichswehr in 1919 was a 'German' army established, even though local differences continued to exist and still exist in the army today.

When general mobilization was declared in 1914, Württemberg sent into the field its two active divisions (26. and 27.) which formed XIII. (königlich-württembergisches) Korps. In addition, 26. Reserve-Division was formed. It had the typical structure of a German infantry division, the so-called square structure: two infantry brigades, with two regiments per brigade. These were 51. Reserve-Infanterie-Brigade with Infanterie-Regiment 180 (the only active unit in the division) and Reserve-Infanterie-Regiment 121; and 52. Reserve-Infanterie-Brigade, which consisted of Reserve-Infanterie-Regimenter 119 and 120. Each regiment had three battalions of approximately 1,000 men each. Every battalion consisted of four companies. In addition to the infantry formations, 26. Reserve-Division also contained the württembergisches Reserve-Dragoner-Regiment, the Reserve-Feld-Artillerie-Regiment 26 and 4. Kompanie of IV. Pionier-Batallion.

At the outbreak of the war, the rank and file in active divisions were conscripts or reservists who had only recently left the colours. In reserve divisions the men were slightly older, with an average age of between

26. Reserve-Division on 30 June 1916

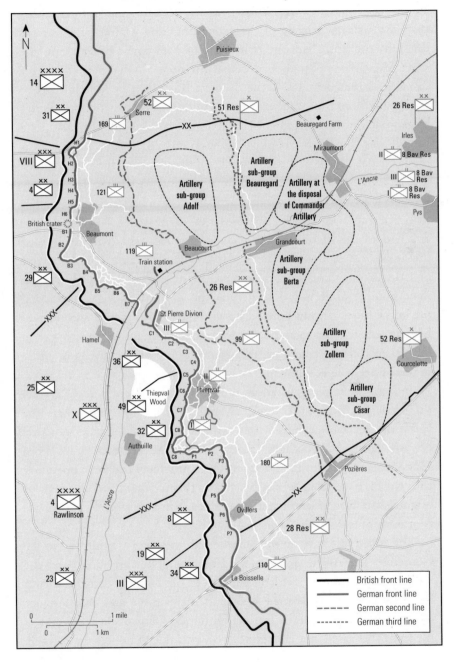

N

14

31

169 Serre

52

51 Res

Beauregard Farm

26 Res

Irles

VIII

4

121

Artillery sub-group Adolf

Artillery sub-group Beauregard

Artillery at the disposal of Commander Artillery

Miraumont

L'Ancre

Pys

II 8 Bav Res

III 8 Bav Res

I 8 Bav Res

British crater

Beaumont

119

Train station

Beaucourt

Grandcourt

Artillery sub-group Berta

29

St Pierre Divion

26 Res

Hamel

36

III

99

Artillery sub-group Zollern

52 Res

Courcelette

25

X

49 Thiepval Wood

32

II Thiepval

I

Artillery sub-group Cäsar

Authuille

180

Pozières

4 Rawlinson

8

Ovillers

28 Res

19

110

23

III

34

La Boiselle

	British front line
	German front line
	German second line
	German third line

0 ——— 1 mile

0 ——— 1 km

24 and 30. There was also less firepower in a reserve division – it contained an artillery regiment with six batteries, i.e. 36 field guns in total, rather than the artillery brigade of the active divisions. Unlike some reserve divisions the 26th had one machine-gun company per regiment, the same level of support as had active divisions. In light of the heavy casualties suffered in 1914, the decision was taken in March 1915 to change divisions from a square to a triangular structure with one infantry brigade with three regiments, practically making the brigade level superfluous. The brigade commander was retained, though, and served as the principal adviser to the divisional commander in all infantry matters. The regiments were reduced from four to three battalions. The artillery was also reorganized with the field artillery now in batteries of four rather than six guns. In return, two batteries of heavy '*Fußartillerie*' were attached to the division.[2] The changes applied first to newly formed divisions, existing divisions then adapted their structure over the course of 1915. At the same time, the reserve divisions were equipped with the same number of guns and artillery as the active divisions. Considering the heavy losses already suffered by all the divisions (active and reserve) by that time it is fair to argue that from this point onwards there was no longer any difference between the active and the reserve divisions, either in personnel or in equipment.

In light of the reorganization, the 26. Reserve-Division lost Reserve-Infanterie-Regiment 120 on 9 March 1915. However, when the battle of the Somme began, it was back to the old square structure of two brigades, because Reserve-Infanterie-Regiment 99 from Mönchengladbach (in the Prussian Rhine province) had been operating with the division since September 1915. This regiment had also kept its original structure of four battalions rather than adopting the now more common three-battalion structure.

The Allied offensive on the Somme did not come as a surprise to the Germans. The Allied preparations had not gone unnoticed and the artillery bombardment, which commenced on 24 June, convinced even the most optimistic German soldier in the Somme area that a major offensive was imminent. Unfortunately for the Germans in this sector of the front there were not enough reserves available to bolster the defence.

The battle at Verdun was continuing to use up the *Menschenmaterial*, and other fronts, especially in the East, needed German reinforcements. Accordingly the 2. Armee, which stood in the way of the Allied forces on the Somme, had to make do with what could only be described as insufficient forces: two corps, with XIV. Reserve-Korps positioned north of the Somme River and XVII. Armee-Korps to the south. The latter, under the command of General Günther von Pannewitz, contained the 121., 11., 35., and 36. Division next to the Gardekorps with 15. Landwehr-Division together with a corps reserve of the 185. Division and one third of the 10. bayerische Infanterie-Division. North of the river, Generalleutnant Hermann von Stein commanded XIV. Reserve-Korps which contained, from north to south, the 2. Garde-Reserve-Division and the 52. Division which held the ground around Gommecourt and Serre; to the south of this was the 26. Reserve-Division under the command of Generalleutnant Franz Freiherr von Soden. The division held the line from Serre, via Beaumont Hamel and Thiepval to Ovillers. The line around La Boisselle, Fricourt and Mametz was held by the 28. Reserve-Division. At the southern end of the corps sector, the 12. Division was placed around Montauban and also stretched south of the Somme River. During the course of the battle this command structure was changed twice. On 19 July, the 1. Armee was created north of the Somme River, under the command of General Fritz von Below, while the troops south of the river now came under the command of General Max von Gallwitz' 2. Armee. Gallwitz also held overall command over both armies. On 28 August another change in the command structure occurred when both armies were placed under the command of the newly created Heeresgruppe Kronprinz Rupprecht (Army Group Crown Prince Rupprecht), which made it easier to coordinate the overall defence in the Somme sector and also enabled the army group to use its reserves in the battle.

Preparing for the defensive battle

When the battle of the Somme began on 1 July 1916, the 26. Reserve-Division had one advantage over many of the other German units that would go through the *Materialschlacht* on the Somme. During the initial

German advance into Belgium and France in 1914, the division had been deployed in the Vosges Mountains, and then sent to the Somme area in September 1914.[3] The division then stayed in this sector of the front and thus, when the battle of the Somme began, it fought in terrain that was well known to the division and that its men had prepared for the defence. The divisional history notes that the rest of 1914 was quite uneventful for the division.[4] The main effort on the Western Front was not in the Somme sector and the division could concentrate on expanding the defensive position. The division had to control a 9-mile sector of the front line and nearly all the infantry was constantly deployed. Nevertheless, work continued on the defensive line. The positions were strengthened and the villages were prepared for defence. In line with the defensive doctrine of 1914, no second line of defence was built or prepared. The entire defence was organized for combat in the first position, with the intention that no ground would be surrendered to the enemy. As a consequence, casualties from enemy artillery fire were common even during these quiet days in the Somme sector.[5]

The end of 1914 and the beginning of 1915 was more eventful for the division and the engagements and battles fought during this time provided important lessons for the conduct of the defence in general and the battle of the Somme in particular. On 17 December 1914, the French 19e Régiment d'Infanterie launched an attack against Thiepval that ended in disaster and the defeat of the French troops. From 25 December 1914 the division, in particular Reserve-Infanterie-Regiment 120, fought for the possession of a farm complex (the 'Granathof') which was located in front of the defensive line and which did not have any tactical significance, but the possession of which became a 'question of honour' for both the French and the Germans. The French were able to occupy the farm and initial German counter-attacks remained unsuccessful, until a surprise attack without artillery support resulted in a German victory on 18 January 1915.

The following months were quiet, but on 6 June the French launched an attack in the area of Serre, just north of the border between the 26. Reserve-Division and 52. Division, and, despite the divisional boundaries, the 26. took part in the battle. The divisional history of the 26. Reserve-

Division acknowledged that this engagement was not a French attempt to break through the German lines, but rather an attempt to straighten the French front line. Nevertheless, it provided the Germans with lessons that would prove very important for the battle of the Somme. Despite thorough preparations for the defensive battle, the French were able to break into the German defensive positions. The reason for this failure on the German side was the heavy artillery bombardment that preceded the infantry attack. Hasty counter-attacks did not succeed and the Germans realised that without heavy artillery support they would not be able to regain their initial position. The engagement was bloody for the 26. Reserve-Division, which suffered 900 casualties. The division's experience in the summer of 1915 was mirrored by that of other units on the Western Front. As a consequence, the OHL issued a new doctrine for the conduct of the defensive battle in October 1915 which showed a considerable shift in thinking.[6] The defensive systems had to be expanded, so that they could be defended with a minimum of soldiers. To achieve this, a second line of resistance had to be erected behind the first one, with each line defendable on its own. On sectors of the front that were considered highly likely to be attacked, three or more lines might be suitable. The second line of resistance should be erected far enough to the rear that the enemy would not be able to hit it with concentrated artillery fire and that an attack on the second line of defence demanded a new deployment of the enemy's infantry and artillery.

However, the reality of trench warfare showed that these new regulations were not sufficient. They were an improvement on the pre-war doctrine, but they still placed too much attention on holding ground and on stiff resistance. Units on the Western Front soon went a step further and developed a deeper trench system which made it harder for the enemy artillery to shell all positions.[7] This was not yet the defence in depth that did away with trenches and which would see its heyday in 1917, but it was a move in that direction. In May 1916, XIV. Reserve-Korps issued its own guidelines on the erection of defensive positions.[8] In accordance with other doctrine, the emphasis was still on the first line of defence, which should stop the enemy if at all possible. Taking into consideration the lessons learned from the previous battles, the guidelines described how a successful defence in the corps sector should be conducted. Generalleutnant von Soden made it clear that he still considered the first line to be the main line of defence and that ground should not be ceded to the enemy. The front-line position or first position should consist of three trenches. Each trench should have rows of barbed wire in front in order to hamper the enemy's advance. Communication trenches were to be dug, so that within the company sectors troops could move between the trenches of the first position. Further to the rear, communication trenches would enable troops to leave the combat zone and to bring forward reinforcements. The *Zwischenstellung*, or intermediate position, and the second line of defence were to have two trenches each, also with barbed wire and communication trenches. Further to the rear, a third position was to be established, which would consist of a shallow trench, but whose strength would be several strongpoints, such as concrete bunkers and fortified houses. The defence in these would be organized around machine guns. The firepower of the machine guns would become the backbone of the German defence in the battle of the Somme. When the offensive hit the 26. Reserve-Division, it could rely on the firepower of eight machine-gun companies which had been reinforced by captured Russian and Belgian machine guns. In total, the division had 90 heavy machine guns and 30 *Musketen* ('muskets') which were the German version of a light machine gun, even though they were heavier and more static than the British Lewis machine gun.[9]

The lessons learned in previous battles and engagements and the new defensive guidelines set in motion a feverish activity in the 26. Reserve-Division's sector. The front line held by XIV. Reserve-Korps stretched for approximately 28 miles. Both the army commander, Below, and the corps commander, Stein, regarded the ridge between Pozières on the Albert–Bapaume road and St Pierre Divion in the Ancre River valley as the cornerstone of the German defences north of the river. This ridge was in the part of the front line held by the 26. Reserve-Division which therefore became the main focus of the German defensive preparations for the battle in the corps sector. All defensive lines were strengthened, including the intermediate line between the first and second lines of defence.[10] More communication trenches were built and prepared for the defence in case the enemy managed to break through the first line of defence. Several new positions were prepared for the artillery, so that possible artillery reinforcements could be deployed in times of need. The dugouts were strengthened and driven deeper into the ground. The aspiration was to dig them at least 20 feet deep, with two or three exits, so that the troops could leave the dugouts quickly and would also have a way to escape in case one or more of the exits were destroyed by artillery fire. The communication network was improved by the laying of more telephone cables, and sirens were brought forward to warn the troops in case of gas attacks. Bombproof ammunition depots were built in all lines of defence and hand grenades were stockpiled. The civilian population was moved out of the projected battle zone. The division particularly focused on strengthening strongpoints in its line of defence. The two most important were the so-called 'Grallsburg' east of Beaumont, and the 'Feste Schwaben' north of Thiepval. On the British side it would become infamous as the 'Schwaben Redoubt'. The importance of this position could not be exaggerated. If this position was lost, it would put the entire German front line in danger. The importance of the position was summed up by Matthäus Gerster, a reserve Leutnant who served in Reserve-Infanterie-Regiment 119. If the British occupied the position 'they would sit on the highest part of the Thiepval Plateau, and they would be able to see far into the [German] hinterland and overlook all the approach routes and battery positions [of the German artillery], in particular those north of the Ancre. Thiepval itself would have been threatened from the rear and St Pierre Divion would have been taken and Beaumont Hamel would have had to be surrendered, because it would have been overlooked from three sides.'[11] It was therefore not surprising that both XIV. Korps and the 26. Reserve-Division placed the highest importance on fortifying the approaches to the Pozières ridge.

Further to the north, in the sector of Reserve-Infanterie-Regiment 121, the spurs from Beaumont Hamel to Beaucourt and from Serre to Miraumont were equally important to the conduct of a successful defensive battle. The positions on the spurs offered good views of the Ancre valley and beyond to the heights of Thiepval and Pozières. Should the Serre heights fall into enemy hands, the consequence would have been that 'Beaumont [Hamel] and Thiepval would have automatically fallen'.[12] The importance attached to the 26. Reserve-Division's sector is also obvious from the fact that the division was given strong artillery support. In total, XIV. Reserve-Korps had 147 batteries with approximately 570 field and heavy guns.[13] Of these, the 26. Reserve-Division was allocated 39 batteries, of which 28 and a half were field artillery, and ten and a half were heavy batteries, in total 154 guns.[14] To put this into perspective, the 52. Division to the north had 28 batteries with 106 guns and to the south the 28. Reserve-Division had 33 batteries with 125 guns. The 2. Garde-Reserve-Division and 12. Division had even less artillery support with 22 batteries and 25 batteries, respectively.

When the Allied offensive started on 1 July, the division had made a great deal of progress in strengthening its defensive positions, but it had not reached the standard required by the corps commander. In total, the division had spent about one and a half years improving its positions, and by July 1916 the soldiers had prepared two defensive lines, the first with three trenches, the second one with two trenches. Strongpoints were the centre of the defence. In the first line the strongpoints and fortified positions were Heidenkopf, Beaumont village, Biberkolonie in the Ancre valley, St Pierre Divion with the Leilingtunnel, Thiepval village, Height 141, and Ovillers. Behind this defensive line the intermediate position, or *Zwischenstellung*, consisted mainly of strongpoints: Feste Soden, Grallsburg, Feste Alt-Württemberg with the train station and Beaucourt village, Feste Schwaben, Ferme du Mouquet and Pozières village. About a mile behind this was the second position which, similar to the first line of defence, consisted of a trench system and strongpoints to stiffen the defence. Here the strongpoints were Alte Gardestellung, Moulin ruiné, Feste Staufen, Feste Zollern. The third position had not been constructed yet.[15]

On 24 June the Allied artillery opened fire on the German positions. The impact of the artillery bombardment was remarkable and the fire became more deadly and devastating as it continued. On 27 June, Infanterie-Regiment 180 reported that the enemy artillery had caused severe casualties, while in the previous days the losses had only been light.[16] On that day, the regiment lost 19 dead, 38 men wounded and one missing. On 29 June, the position suffered severely and the regiment's sections of the forward defensive line were described as follows (for letters see the map): P1 totally destroyed. All entrances to dugout destroyed or heavily damaged. P2 partially flattened. P3 in good order. P4 first trench and forward position flattened. In the sector Ovillers south the first and second trenches were fully destroyed and the wire obstacles destroyed. On 30 June two dugouts in P6 were fully destroyed. The losses on that day were 60 dead, 85 wounded, one missing. Overall, the 26. Reserve-Division suffered approximately 900 casualties during the British preparatory bombardment.[17]

The first day of the Somme

The storm finally broke on the morning of 1 July when the British attacked the 26. Reserve-Division.[18] Reserve-Infanterie-Regiment 121 held the front line between Serre and Beaumont. South of the Heidenkopf position, British troops managed to enter the position of I. Bataillon and advanced against Feste Soden and the Serrewäldchen (Pendant Copse). If the British seized the heights the entire German front line would become untenable; accordingly, the Germans reacted rapidly and, in accordance with general German doctrine, launched a hasty counter-attack. The troops made available for this came from III. Bataillon, and were supported by troops from the neighbouring regiment, Infanterie-Regiment 169, and the artillery of the 52. Division. This attack required a great deal of coordination between the different units and its success is evidence of the high level of professionalism among the soldiers.

The front line between Beaumont and the Ancre was held by Reserve-Infanterie-Regiment 119. It was attacked by the 29th Division and parts of the 36th (Ulster) Division. The divisional account of the 26. Reserve-Division records, with a mild tone of understatement, that the regiment initially had a difficult stand because of the explosion of a mine near Beaumont village, on Hawthorn Ridge. The explosion created a 45-yard wide crater and killed many soldiers of 9. Kompanie. For a while, the situation in and around the crater was very tense, but reserves were rushed forward. Platoons from 7. and 12. Kompanie, accompanied by two automatic rifles raced forward from the third trench of the first defensive line and established a firing line which drove the British troops back.[19]

Approximately 550 yards to the south, the defenders of Leilingsschlucht were warned by the mine explosion. The British preparatory bombardment was lifted too early and thus the troops of III. Bataillon Reserve-Infanterie-Regiment 119 were able to reach their defensive positions before the British troops appeared. There was no race for the parapet and the Germans had been given what has been called 'a generous start'.[20] The result was predictable. The British soldiers never made it to the German positions. The war diary of III. Bataillon describes the destruction of the attacking enemy:

8.15am   Mine blown in B1
8.20am   B1–B3 under attack.
8.30am   The British are lying down 100 metres [110 yards] short of the first trench of B3. Own machine guns have opened fire.
8.35am   B2 reports: Attack stalled. Masses of British soldiers are lying in the hollow in front of Target Area 46. Machine guns are being moved forward from the second to the first trench.
8.40am   B2 reports: The British are lying in front of the first trench and are being shot to pieces. No defensive fire is coming down in the hollow in front of Target Area 46; a battalion is gathering there to launch an attack. Sector order: destroy them with machine-gun fire.[21]

A much tougher task faced the men of Reserve-Infanterie-Regiment 99, who held the front line between the Ancre at St Pierre Divion via Thiepval to Height 141 and Granatloch. The regiment was hit by the main attack of the 36th (Ulster) Division and parts of the 32nd Division. South of St Pierre Divion the British were able to overrun two German companies and to seize the Schwaben Redoubt. German artillery observers were moving forward at the same time and were also in the danger of being cut off. An official German report stated that:

The enemy attack on C2 and C3 was conducted with such aggression that the two machine guns could only fire for a short time before they were both overrun. More than half of both teams were killed or wounded by artillery fire. The remaining weapons in C1, C4 and the Strassburger

Steige were operated with outstanding effect… The Russian machine gun in the Schwaben Redoubt did not come into action, because a direct hit shortly before the assault buried the gun and quarters of its crew. Both the platoon commander and his runner, who hurried to the spot to dig them out, were killed by shrapnel.[22]

When the divisional commander, Soden, learned about the successful British attack in this sector, he immediately ordered a counter-attack. For this the divisional reserve, II. Bataillon of bayerisches Reserve-Infanterie-Regiment 8, was moved forward to the second defensive position. At 1035hrs the commander of 52. Reserve-Infanterie-Brigade, Generalleutnant Friedrich von Auwärter, was ordered to launch the counter-attack. But problems mounted: the reserve troops from the Bavarian regiment came under heavy fire, suffered casualties and could not advance. Also, misleading messages were reported which claimed that the Schwaben Redoubt had already been retaken by German troops. All this resulted in the attack not being carried out energetically and only at 1700hrs was a new order issued to carry out the attack. As a consequence, the redoubt could only be retaken during the night and with heavy artillery support.

The line Granatloch–Ovillers–La Boisselle was held by the men of Infanterie-Regiment 180. Heavy fighting occurred in particular in the area of I. Bataillon, at the regimental boundary with Reserve-Infanterie-Regiment 99 and in Ovillers village, which was temporarily seized by three British companies. Local, hasty counter-attacks drove the British back and by the end of the day the regiment could report that it was in full control of the German position.

On the whole, the first day of the battle of the Somme was a huge success for the 26. Reserve-Division. The principles on which the conduct of the defensive battle was founded had proven their worth. The move away from a static defence in only one trench to several defensive positions had been successful. Also, aggressive offensive spirit, as manifested in the hasty counter-attacks, had generally delivered success.

As a consequence of the successful defensive battle, the divisional commander issued an order of the day on 2 July in which he stated that 'After seven days of heavy artillery fire the division repulsed in heroic fighting all enemy attacks that had been carried out with superior troops and it is in full control of all its positions.'[23] But this was only one side of the story. Despite the overall successful conduct of the defensive battle the division had suffered severe casualties. On the same day that the order was published, the corps commander, Generalleutnant von Stein, reported that the 26. Reserve-Division should be relieved, because of the casualties it had sustained.[24]

The battle of the Somme had only just begun and it would continue for many weeks. The division continued to hold its position and was engaged in further fighting before finally being relieved and taken out of the front line between 6 and 10 October 1916. Some units of the division stayed behind and came under new command. Therefore it can be argued that the men of the division fought continuously in the battle of the Somme from its beginning on 1 July until its official end, which was set by the German High Command as 26 November.

Analysing the battle

After the battle, the commander of the 1. Armee, General von Below, issued a report in which he summed up the experiences of the 1. Armee in the battle of the Somme, including the lessons learned by the men of the 26. Reserve-Division.[25]

The report made clear that the divisions were the main combat units on the battlefield and that the conduct of the defensive battle was their responsibility:

> The real weight of the fighting rests on the shoulders of the Divisional Commanders, on whom devolves full responsibility for the maintenance of their sectors. Divisional Commanders must, therefore be given control of all the organs of action available in their sectors, with the exception of guns employed on special tasks and, in exceptional cases, Corps Artillery Groups detailed for special long-range objectives. They must at the right time allot to their subordinate both their own reserves and the reserves placed at their disposal by the superior authority; these subordinate commanders must, in their turn, make local arrangements for the

employment of these reserves on the battlefield. The divisional commander must exert a continuous and keen influence on the whole control of the action; this will be ensured by accurate reconnaissance on the ground, and by maintaining daily personal touch with his troops and their commanders.

The fight of the 26. Reserve-Division had evolved around vital ground that had to be defended in order to keep the entire German defensive line intact. The counter-attack in the sector of Reserve-Infanterie-Regiment 121 had shown that only the cooperation of several units would ensure victory. In this spirit, Below's report stated that the lateral boundaries of the battle sectors of armies, corps and divisions were primarily dictated by the ground, and, above all, by the facilities which they gave for the development of artillery fire and for artillery observation.

The counter-attack on the Schwaben Redoubt had shown that the chaos and confusion of battle made it difficult for orders to be sent from the rear to the combat troops in the trenches. Below's report was very clear about this:

> Every Higher Commander must clearly recognise that every report from the front to the rear and every order from rear to front required a very long time to reach its destination. During a defensive battle, the fighting zone lies almost continuously under the enemy's intense artillery bombardment. It has been frequently found that orders take 8 to 10 hours to reach the front line from Divisional Headquarters.

The importance of this was clear to Below, who stated in his report that the destruction of telephone lines during the battle frequently resulted in the total isolation of the higher command and in the absence of cooperation between the various arms. The infantry, heavily engaged, were often left to their own devices for hours and days at a time, or else the front-line trenches would be crammed with troops owing to the ignorance of the situation that prevailed in the rear. This resulted in unnecessary casualties and had a negative effect on the troops' morale. This state of affairs was aggravated by the enemy's superiority in the air, which, at first, was incontestable. Not only did the enemy's airmen direct the artillery fire undisturbed, but by day and by night they harassed the German infantry with bombs and machine guns, in their trenches and shell holes, as well as on the march to and from the trenches. Even although the losses thus caused were comparatively small, these attacks from the air had a disastrous effect on the morale of the men, who felt helpless.

It was clear that the 26. Reserve-Division's approach for the conduct of the defensive battle had been right, but the first day of the Somme (and subsequent fighting) showed that more had to be done if a breakthrough was to be avoided and manpower was to be spared. In the final analysis of the battle, Below therefore stated that for an obstinate defence of the front position, it was not sufficient to dig a few parallel lines of trenches one behind another; a broad defensive zone was necessary, a network of trenches disposed in depth, with plenty of cross trenches. Every fire trench, communication trench and approach trench had to be prepared for defence in case the enemy broke through the first defensive system, An enemy who penetrated the front line of trenches had to find himself opposed not only on his front, but on his flanks at the next line, and it had to be possible to counter-attack him from all sides.

However, the battle of the Somme had shown the power of the *Materialschlacht* and the impact of artillery on the modern battlefield. Even a position formed of broad, deep, defensive zones was not enough to stop breakthrough attempts launched by a strong and prepared enemy. The power of the concentrated artillery fire was so great that losses of ground would be inevitable even in the strongest positions. Behind the front-line position, therefore, there had to be at least two rearward positions, spaced far enough apart that the enemy had to be compelled to change the position of his artillery in order to attack them.

Below's report also stated that:

> Our infantry is superior to that of the enemy. In the Somme battle, wherever the enemy gained the upper hand, it was chiefly due to the perfected application of technical means, in particular to the employment of guns and ammunition in quantities, which had been hitherto inconceivable. It was also due to the exemplary manner in which infantry, artillery, and aeroplanes cooperated.

It might be true that the German soldiers were superior to their enemies on the Western Front. However, the bottom line is that World War I was not decided in the trenches of the Western Front, but in the factories of the belligerent nations. The high human cost borne by the German army could not avert final defeat. The fact that they tried is obvious in the horrendous casualties suffered by the soldiers in the battle of the Somme. For instance, Reserve-Infanterie-Regiment 99 alone lost 48 officers and 2,070 other ranks in the fighting on the Somme River,[26] roughly two thirds of its original strength. And that was only one regiment of many that fought in the summer and autumn of 1916. The fact that the 26. Reserve-Division was still classed as a 'first-rate division' by the US War Office in 1918 says a lot about the fighting spirit of these men, who, despite all their efforts and losses, could not avoid final defeat for Germany and Württemberg.

CHAPTER 11

THE EVOLUTION OF FRENCH TACTICS 1914–16

Dr Jonathan Krause

On 1 July 1916 French and British forces surged over the top north and south of the Somme River. The fate met by those thousands of young British soldiers is well known to the English-speaking world. It is widely seen as emblematic of the entire war on the Western Front: the brave sacrifice and foolish slaughter of countless infantrymen in hopeless, mismanaged, unimaginative frontal assaults against intact enemy trench systems. The machine guns tat-tat-tattering before Thiepval and Bapaume still hammer out the rhythm of most public perceptions of what the battle of the Somme was, and what it was like. The forever misquoted 56,886 casualties suffered by Britain on 1 July 1916 acts as a final argument unto itself against the folly of the Somme and the generals who lead the battle. The Anglophone focus on the battle of the Somme neglects the French contribution to the battle, despite the fact that more French soldiers took part in the battle of the Somme by its end than

British and Commonwealth soldiers! So dominant is this blind spot that most Anglophone maps of the Somme only include the northern British sector, content to just label the south of the river 'French forces' and leave it at that. This is not only a great disservice to those troops who fought to keep France alive and independent, it fundamentally skews and misrepresents the battle as it actually happened. It also ignores the feats of military skill that French forces were able to achieve. This chapter will look at French tactics during the battle of the Somme, how they were developed and why they were effective.

With red trousers...

The French Army that marched to war in 1914 had little in common with the one that would perform so well on the banks of the Somme two years later. French armed forces in the years before World War I were in a state of near-continual flux. Between controversies like the Dreyfus Affair and the *Affaires des Fiches* the army was held in particularly low regard in the early 1900s. Training was perfunctory, and lasted only two years, as opposed to the Germans' three. In those two years French troops would be lucky to visit one of France's limited number of large training camps even once for summer manoeuvres. Live-fire training was rare, as were exercises with combined arms. Artillerymen were trained only in the most basic techniques and were strongly discouraged from firing from defilade[1] (a methodology that would be critical during the war), or even from properly aiming their guns. French artillery training before 1914 frequently envisioned guns firing over open sights directly at advancing hordes of enemy troops marching in close order. Instead of carefully focusing on hitting their target gun crews were instructed to simply inundate an area with shrapnel in a grand, 20th-century form of volley fire so as to maximize the number of casualties they might inflict. French artillery doctrine from 1903 was clear: 'speed of fire is the essential property for field artillery'.[2] Ferdinand Foch, who would later go on to lead the French forces on the Somme before finding himself Supreme Allied Commander in 1918, stated in 1903 that 'A quarter of an hour's quick fire by mass artillery on a clearly determined objective will generally suffice to break its resistance, or at any rate make it uninhabitable, and therefore uninhabited'.[3] The reality of trench warfare on the Western Front would quickly render such aphorisms laughably obsolete.

When French forces clashed with their German counterparts along the Western Front in August 1914 the results were usually appalling. French troops too often attacked without the support of neighbouring units, or even the support of their own artillery. Intelligence was all but non-existent and the blind, groping advance of French formations frequently led to their being held up by German formations half their size. The bumbling mixture of laziness in the day-to-day necessities of warfare like reconnaissance and liaison, and suicidal audacity in the face of enemy firepower led French forces to lose some 300,000 dead in the opening five months of the war from August to December 1914. The French fared so poorly that these five months very nearly made 1914 the deadliest year of the war for French forces (a dubious honour that instead falls to 1915, which cost France nearly 350,000 dead and over 1 million missing or wounded). The French Army needed drastic change, and quickly, if the German armies rapidly advancing through France and Belgium were going to be stopped. It fell to Commander-in-Chief Joseph Joffre to make those changes.

Joseph Joffre was named chef d'état-major (Chief of the General Staff) in 1911. Already he had a monumental task before him. The French Army had no clear, recognizable doctrine and Joffre made it his top priority to provide one. France had fallen significantly behind Germany in artillery production, especially in heavy artillery, of which the French had hardly any, and the nation could not yet safely rely on Russia and Britain to intervene in a timely manner – or at all! – should Germany invade. Joffre made significant progress in all three areas between 1911 and 1913, especially in convincing Russia to quickly respond to any German aggression by invading eastern Germany, but still went to war with a force that was seriously outmatched by its opponent. One of the critical failings was in the leadership and management capabilities of the French officer corps. Partially as a result of the disastrous series of controversies that dogged the French Army in the early 1900s, including the systematic weeding out of conservative and Catholic officers in favour of officers with proven republican leanings, and partially out of a lack of serious war-fighting since 1871, French officers were older and less competent than their German counterparts when the war broke out. In a desperate attempt to right the ship and prevent the French Army from buckling under its own mistakes and inadequacies Joffre began to fire senior commanders at a furious pace. In the end some 40 per cent of corps and army level commanders would be sacked by Joffre in the autumn of 1914. These men were largely sent to Limoges, a small town southwest of Paris where they could do no more harm (hence the French term for these men: the *limogé*[4]). As a result of this vigorous house-cleaning the French army leadership was quickly rejuvenated. The army that defeated and repulsed the Germans on the Marne was already a different animal to that which had marched to war mere weeks earlier.

Trench warfare

After repulsing the Germans in a counter-attack now immortalized as the 'miracle of the Marne' in September, and failing to outflank German forces during the 'race to the sea' the French Army found itself all of a sudden facing a new challenge: trench warfare. If French forces were unprepared for mobile warfare against Germany they were doubly unprepared for trench warfare. Whereas the Germans marched to war with hundreds of modern, high-arcing mortars and heavy artillery from Krupp and Skoda, the French had only a small number of truly modern heavy guns (about 140), instead having chosen to rely on their 75mm field gun. This is generally seen as an example of the Germans thinking ahead and entering the war more prepared than the French, but we should be careful with this interpretation. The Germans, after all, had been planning an offensive war for years and as such had the benefit of preparing for a war that they could anticipate, and in fact could probably bring about at a time of their choosing.

German planning since Schlieffen first set down his 'Schlieffen Plan' in 1905 envisioned a rapid sweep through Belgium and eastern France, which necessitated the conquest of several major fortifications: Liège, Namur, Verdun, and possibly Belfort and Toul. Knowing that this was a specific challenge they would have to overcome, the Germans committed to producing (or otherwise obtaining) the tools required to take these key fortifications – and ultimately did so with great success, at least in Belgium. The French found themselves in a completely different situation. The French Army needed a means to break up what they imagined would be large columns of advancing German infantry. Field guns rapidly firing over open sights were a great way to do that. As archaic and 19th century as this scenario sounds it was a regular fixture of war-fighting in 1914, thus (perhaps dangerously) proving that French pre-war tactical thinking was not as moribund as some historians would suggest. Nevertheless, the 75mm was ill-suited to trench warfare. It was not powerful enough, and its flat trajectory made it impossible for the gun to hit targets sited in defilade. It would have to give up its role as the principal French artillery piece – although it would remain the most common piece right through to 1918 – and make way for heavy artillery like the Rimailho 155CTR.[5]

The French Army's first forays into trench warfare were largely disastrous. French forces attacked in Artois in December 1914 as the trench line between the Alps and the North Sea began to settle into place. Lacking in heavy artillery, the 10e Armée Française under Général Louis d'Maud'huy had to stagger their initial assault over three days. Instead of 10e, 21e and 33e Corps d'Armée (army corps) attacking simultaneously, they attacked in turn from 16 to 18 December. Each day the 10e Armée's heavy artillery would turn, re-register targets on another corps' front and prepare for the upcoming attack. This paucity of resources and rapid reorientation made an already difficult preparation simply impossible. French forces made no progress and suffered heavy losses.

This battle and the second and third battles of Artois in 1915 would have a direct impact on French fighting on the Somme. They were in theory overseen by Ferdinand Foch, who was then commander of the Groupe Provisoire du Nord (Provisional Northern Army Group) and would later be commander of the Groupe d'Armées du Nord (Northern Army Group) under which the French forces of the Somme would serve. Général Marie Émile Fayolle, who would command the 6e Armée on the Somme, also commanded formations in the Artois battles. During the first and second battles of Artois he was commander of the 70e Division d'Infanterie before becoming commander of 33e Corps d'Armée in time for the third battle of Artois in September 1915. These men cut their teeth commanding troops among the slag heaps, hillocks, and industrial towns of the Artois region; their relative caution and methodical approach to warfare would come to characterize French efforts on the Somme.

In the days leading up to the first battle of Artois Foch urged his subordinates that 'it is less important to advance rapidly, but essential to move securely, step by step, as each objective is gained'.[6] Rather than pray that French forces would swarm over German defences and rapidly conquer large swaths of dense trench networks Foch realized that progress would always be slow, and require substantial preparation. Fayolle was even more devoted to a slow, cautious, and methodical approach to trench warfare; he excoriated his superiors, including Foch, in his diary (later published as *Cahiers secrets de la grande guerre*) for ordering him to attack before he felt he was ready. Both men by 1915 were entirely convinced that only a methodical artillery preparation would give the infantry a chance to attack and conquer enemy trenches without undue loss of life – even though successful attacks might still incur substantial casualties. This impression would be solidified by their conduct of the second battle of Artois, and would shape how they later managed the Somme battle.

From 9 May to 18 June, the 10e Armée Française, then under Général Viktor d'Urbal (Maud'huy had been moved aside after his initial tactical failures), waged the French Army's first sustained, coalition trench battle with the British attacking adjacent to French positions at Aubers Ridge on 9 May and again at Festubert 14–20 May. The spearhead of the attack would be 33e Corps d'Armée, commanded by future president and marshal of France Philippe Pétain (Fayolle's 70e Division d'Infanterie was part of 33e Corps d'Armée). On 9 May elements of 33e Corps d'Armée, principally the Division Marocaine[7] and the 77e Division d'Infanterie, surged forward over battered German trenches, advancing just under 3 miles in a mere hour and a half and storming Vimy Ridge in the process; this would be the largest single advance the French would make in 1915. They were able to advance so quickly and effectively in part owing to revised trench warfare doctrine that had been written the month before and which would form the basis for French doctrine on the Somme a year later. This doctrine was entitled *But et conditions d'une action offensive d'ensemble* (*Goal and Conditions of a General Offensive*, or Note 5779).[8]

Released on 16 April 1915, Note 5779 was the culmination of months of work by the Grand Quartier Général (French General Headquarters, GQG) in an effort to rapidly create a new, functional doctrine for trench warfare. Based on reports and lessons learned from their failures in Artois in December 1914 and also the halting, costly slog in Champagne in February and March 1915 (a battle in which French losses were double that of their German opponents), Note 5779 came in four parts with a short main text laying out general principles and goals followed by three annexes which looked more in depth at issues of infantry tactics, the artillery, and defensive tactics. Its most important tactical precepts, the ones that came to shape French action for the rest of the war, were its codifications of two key trench-fighting methods: the rolling barrage and an early incarnation of what we would now call infiltration tactics. Unfortunately, the doctrine also included concepts that were already hopelessly outdated, and would condemn the French to further disasters in the autumn of 1915.

Note 5779 opens with the sentence: 'The goal of an offensive action is not only to take a line of enemy trenches, but to chase the enemy *as a whole* from his position and *defeat* him without giving him time to re-establish himself'.[9] In short, French doctrine would still cling to the illusory goal of creating a *percée* or 'breakthrough' of the German trench network. Rather than admitting that the limited means available to the French Army at the time necessitated a commensurate limiting of their tactical goals, the GQG urged senior operational commanders to think big – too big. At the same time, and indeed in the very next sentence, Note 5779 told commanders that 'an ... operation does not improvise itself. Repeated experiences have shown that a detailed organization and preparation are the indispensable conditions of success. This preparation ought to leave nothing to chance and realize, before the launching of an attack, all the conditions favourable to its execution.'[10] There is here a small glimpse into the intellectual battle that raged amongst French commanders regarding how best to fight trench warfare. Most senior commanders who, owing to their position tended to think more about strategy than tactics, favoured big, risky pushes. In the short term casualties would be higher, no doubt, but they were under pressure to win a grand strategic victory. The quickest way to do so was crushing, or at least severely mangling, enemy forces in a single battle the way commanders of the last two centuries had managed to do. Other commanders, Foch, Fayolle, and Pétain foremost among them, saw that the nature of trench warfare made large advances and rapid strategic victories an impossibility. While each of the three men frequently, even acrimoniously, disagreed, their ideas were far more similar than they were different. Fundamentally, they believed in a slower, methodical, *matériel*-intensive approach that above all else sought to redress the gross imbalance in casualties that were dogging the French Army (in both 1914 and 1915 the French consistently lost twice as many casualties as they managed to inflict on the Germans). Some of the methods they would use were laid out in the annexes of Note 5779.

In contrast to the often vague main body of the new doctrine, which was a mere three pages long, the annexes dealing with infantry, artillery, and defensive tactics were much more substantial and detailed. The artillery annex stated clearly that,

> The artillery will, by *a systematic fire on the successive lines of the enemy*, destroy the accessory defences, destroy the dugouts, their communication trenches and their flanking positions; it will demoralize the enemy by repeated shocks and will be prepared to effectively support infantry attacks for their duration, not just on their first objective, but on their further objectives [as well].[11]

After just eight months of war the French doctrine machine had clearly and unequivocally abandoned the pre-war doctrine which stated that artillery was merely there to 'support' attacks (to help the infantry cross the 'killing zone'), rather than preparing attacks through lengthy bombardments. The annex also codified for the first time the French use of the rolling barrage, stating: 'at the hour fixed for the infantry attack the artillery will increase its range *progressively* to make, in front and on the flanks of the attack, a longitudinal and transversal barrage to shelter the infantry so they can advance'.[12] Contrary to conventional historiographical wisdom which views the rolling barrage as a rarity even through 1916 it was actually core French doctrine as early as April 1915, and was used extensively in every major battle from that point on.

The infantry doctrine set forth in the infantry annex of Note 5779 was very much reminiscent of the precepts set forth in the main body: side by side sat good, solid tactical ideas and hopelessly outdated, dangerous anachronisms. The infantry annex on the one hand enshrined the idea of the breakthrough (stating that the infantry should aim for distant objectives), in direct contrast to the artillery annex which stated that infantry should only be asked to take one position at a time, with enough time in between attacks to rebuild destroyed trenches, logistical networks, rest, and care for the wounded.[13] It did however reaffirm pre-war doctrine which stated that infantry should attack in loose formation 'as skirmishers' rather than in lines or columns, formations that had no hope of standing up to modern firepower. The most inventive part of the new doctrine dealt with 'nettoyeurs de tranchée' or 'trench clearers' ('moppers-up' in British terminology). Whereas the initial assault waves would be trained to bypass enemy strongpoints and penetrate as far into the enemy trench network as quickly as possible these secondary waves of infantry would be specially armed with trench knives, revolvers, and grenades to go in behind the assault waves and take out the bypassed machine guns and strongpoints. This is a tactic that the French used very well on the Somme, and the failure of the British to implement similar concepts was one of the principal reasons for their early failures in the battle. These ideas of a rapid penetration bypassing enemy strongpoints followed up by specially trained and equipped secondary waves can also be seen as an early incarnation of what would later be called 'infiltration' or 'stormtroop' tactics, a tactical system normally attributed to the Germans.[14]

As much as these tactical advancements helped the French win astounding early successes in the Artois they ultimately proved insufficient. The Moroccans and alpine troops may have broken through in the centre, but on both flanks French forces from 20e Corps d'Armée (the famous 'Iron Corps' formerly led by Foch) and 21e Corps d'Armée found themselves unable to rapidly advance against dense German defences set up in the stone villages of the region. The tactics were continually upgraded and refined over the next year, but French attacks seemed incapable of making that final step and turning their initial successes into lasting strategic victories. In 1916, on the banks of the Somme the French, for the first time acting as junior partners to the smaller, less experienced British forces, would attempt to win a strategic victory with their first offensive trench battle lasting more than just a month or two.

French tactics for the battle of the Somme

The tactics that the French Army would employ on the Somme had their deepest origins in the doctrine of April 1915 (Note 5779). Since that time, however, the French, and especially Ferdinand Foch, had engaged in a continual process of reflection and constantly refined their methods. This process was not linear, nor was it necessarily happening at any constant rate throughout the French Army. Large segments of the army, especially those serving under certain senior commanders (like Général Noël Édouard de Castelnau) still clung to the belief that a 'continuous' breakthrough battle was possible and that it held out the best prospects for winning a major strategic victory on the battlefield (as opposed to the slow grind of attrition and blockade that eventually won the war for the Allies). The main French effort in autumn 1915 – the second battle of Champagne – would put this continued belief to the test. Castelnau sold the offensive by boasting to Joffre that his troops would be able to advance 6–7.5 miles in 24 to 48 hours 'with rifles at the shoulder' i.e. not even having to engage with the German infantry, who would have been destroyed by French artillery.

Unfortunately, the French infantry would not have it so lucky. The second battle of Champagne opened up with a stunning advance made by elements of the 2e Armée (now under command of Pétain, who had been promoted and replaced as commander of 33e Corps d'Armée by Fayolle). Within a few days, however, the attack bogged down and then slowly devolved into an attritional slog which ultimately favoured the Germans. The failure was sufficiently clear that even the French official history (*Les Armées Françaises dans la Grande Guerre*) stated that:

After the battles of Champagne and Artois a very clear evolution came to manifest itself in the minds of the command. For the first time, all of the participants [of the battles of 1915] were in accordance on the following capital point: *the rupture of an enemy front probably could not be realized in a single bound, but* [only] *by a series of successive and prolonged efforts.*[15]

The methodology proposed by senior commanders like Foch, Pétain, and Fayolle seemed to finally have been accepted by the GQG. The next grand battle would be given to two of these men (Foch as commander of the Groupe d'Armées du Nord, and Fayolle as the newly minted commander of the 6e Armée), who would be sure to develop a more careful and methodical battle plan as they liaised with their allies the British fighting astride the Somme River.

When the battle of the Somme was proposed in December 1915 it was envisioned as another French-led, British-supported battle in the same vein as the second battle of Artois, albeit, with the implication of better cooperation between the French and British forces. With this in mind, and full of fresh reflections on the failures of 1915, Foch sat down to pen the first of two doctrinal documents that would be the basis for the French conduct of operations during the Somme. The first, completed in December 1915, was called *Enseignements à tirer de nos dernières attaques* (*Lessons to take from our last/most recent attacks*). This document is largely an expansion upon the ideas laid down in Note 5779 and Foch's own thinking about trench warfare to date. Above all else he championed a slow, *matériel*-intensive approach that expended munitions instead of French lives to achieve tactical objectives. Where Foch hit on new ground was in the scope he envisioned.

While Foch had been supporting a methodical battle since late 1914, more or less as soon as the trenches were dug, Foch no longer saw the capture of one or two important pieces of terrain as sufficient objectives for a major battle such as the Somme. The war was in its second year and saw no signs of abating (quite the opposite in fact, the war had only been expanding). Foch realized that the French needed to not just fight smarter, but also to substantially scale up their efforts. He wrote that instead of just lasting a few weeks battles must instead consist of 'deep action …

of a duration not known until now.'[16] The capture of terrain was less important than the unrelenting, rhythmic hammering of German positions in a given area for months on end. Instead of fighting for six weeks at a time the French would aim to fight for six months or more, pinning the Germans down, exhausting them, and methodically destroying whatever forces they committed to the battle. The only way to sustain a battle for so long was to cut the staggering losses that battles had entailed for French forces since the start of the war.

To that effect Foch recommended that a much greater emphasis be laid on good aerial observation and better liaison between air forces and the artillery. Artillery shells were a precious commodity, even when being fired by the million, and needed to be husbanded almost as closely as the lives of French infantrymen. Instead of attacking with distant targets in mind attacks should only aim to capture a narrow band of enemy trenches. Attacks would be short and sharp, then quickly followed up by renewed attacks with fresh artillery preparations (a methodology the British would call 'bite and hold'). This would greatly reduce French casualties, most of which usually occurred not in the initial assault, but in subsequent waves as French forces continued to surge forward, even in the face of renewed enemy resistance, and allow the French to only attack when they had an overwhelming chance of success.[17] In effect Foch had solved the problem that had set tactics and strategy against each other for much of the war: the best tactical methodologies could not produce victories of strategic value, and more ambitious battles could not guarantee tactical success. Foch chose to take the most tactically viable model and scale it up to strategic significance by sheer duration and tempo. Foch expanded upon this theory in *La Bataille Offensive* (*The Offensive Battle*), a piece of doctrine he wrote in the spring of 1916, just a few months before the opening of the Somme battle.

La Bataille Offensive was not really a work of original scholarship – if we can use that word. Foch expressly based it on existing French doctrine as espoused by the GQG, including periodic updates to the doctrine released in April 1915 (Note 5779), i.e. doctrinal documents that he himself had helped compose in late 1915.[18] As such we should see this as Foch taking a generalized doctrine and preparing it for the specific circumstances the

French would face on the Somme. He wrote that 'in the current situation an offensive battle requires the conquest of a series of enemy positions organized and arrayed in depth.'[19] This being the case that 'the battle, once engaged, [must be] a long-term operation which ought to be conducted methodically and pursued until the enemy's capacity for resistance has been broken by the [enemy's] moral[e], material and physical destruction, without weakening our own offensive capabilities.'[20] Instead of a short, sharp series of battles moving laterally up and down the front (an idea Foch would return to as Supreme Allied Commander in 1918) Foch was proposing a modern 'operation': a series of discrete tactical engagements working together to achieve a strategic goal.

Foch consistently pressed home the need for the battle to maintain tempo. In order to keep the Germans off balance he believed that 'battle, once engaged, ought to be pursued without interruption: to this effect each progression of the infantry is [must be] immediately followed by the progression of the artillery needed to begin, without delay, the new preparation [of the enemy's next line of trenches].'[21] This method of picking a sore point and applying sustained pressure against German defences would allow the French to break through at Flaucourt in July and Bouchavesnes in September 1916. After two months of hammering the German line simply ceased to exist beyond the village of Bouchavesnes; for a brief time there was nothing between French troops and Berlin but open fields.

Under Foch and Fayolle the French were destroying and capturing trench networks faster than the Germans could build them. To maintain this tempo the French had to vigorously rotate units in and out of the front to keep them fresh and up to date, a method pioneered by Pétain at Verdun, but taken up quickly by Foch in his planning for the Somme.[22] This rotation of units and the sustained rhythmic hammering of German trench systems could only be achieved by a careful manipulation of available artillery. Foch wrote that 'the artillery preparation is the definitive measure of the possibilities of the infantry … the depth of terrain [bombarded] by the artillery fixes the space one can assign the infantry to conquer. [This space] is not considerable: 2, 3, 4 kilometres.'[23] The battle of the Somme would be an artillery battle, with the management of artillery resources determining the efficacy (or lack thereof) of any individual attack. With this in mind Foch assigned specific roles to various types of artillery (medium guns and mortars against barbed wire and machine-gun nests, heavier guns against pillboxes and fortified villages, etc.). This would ensure a basic level of efficiency that comes with using the right tool for the right job.

Foch laid especial importance on counter-battery fire, and for good reason. In 1915 French attacks had been blunted by massed enemy artillery barrages. As French troops surged forward *en masse* all German artillery had to do was fire at likely avenues of transit (communication trenches, etc), erecting walls of fire and steel through which French infantry units would have to cross. The casualties inflicted by these barrages severely reduced the French infantry's ability to push ahead and continue the fight. Knowing this, Foch suggested inundating enemy artillery batteries (discovered by aerial reconnaissance) with artillery, including poison gas, a tactic his Groupe Provisoire du Nord pioneered in June 1915. In *La Bataille Offensive* he stated that, 'the weight of calibre is not very important, so long as the fire is <u>rapid</u> … it is necessary to average two rounds a minute against each enemy gun; [thus] a section of 75s can neutralize a battery of enemy field guns. [underline in original].'[24]

The last important detail Foch provides in *La Bataille Offensive* is regarding the rolling barrage. By spring and summer 1916 it had become an expected component of any French attack. It remained, however, a very complicated tactic to implement consistently, and was often a source of problems in and of itself: if the barrage advanced too quickly it out-ran the infantry, leaving them exposed; if it advanced too slowly it left infantry stuck out in the open and vulnerable to enemy counter-barrages. Even a well-timed rolling barrage was dangerous if advancing infantry tried to follow it too closely, which was an understandable tactic for infantrymen wanting to ensure that they win the 'race to the parapet' and get into German trenches before the defenders could get out of their deep dugouts and start manning machine-gun posts. Foch reminded his subordinates that the 'danger zone' for a rolling barrage might be anywhere from 65 to 160 yards deep, and even then stray shells would often fall beyond those parameters. The fact that many trench positions along the Western Front were sited only 55–160 yards away from the enemy should give us some understanding of just what a serious problem this was: the rolling barrage, as effective a tool as it was, was not a panacea.

French performance during the battle of the Somme

Putting all of this together inevitably brings us back to the beginning: to 1 July 1916. Was all of this tactical navel-gazing by French commanders of any real value on the ground? Perhaps. On 1 July 1916 some 12 French divisions advanced along a 6-mile front. They captured all of their objectives and were in sufficiently good order that they could continue the attack the next day. When and where minor hold-ups presented themselves (intact barbed wire or surviving machine-gun positions) good local command and infantry–artillery liaison quickly cleared them up and allowed the French infantry to continue surging forwards. The cost? A mere 1,560 casualties, according to Foch. Joseph Joffre, Commander-in-Chief of the French Army, gave credit squarely to the French artillery, which had done the job well. He also felt that the Germans had not taken as many precautions against the French as in the northern sector of the battlefield, assuming that the still-raging battle of Verdun precluded French attacks anywhere else on the front.[25] Such simple observations probably do not give enough credit to the thousands of hours of preparation and the hard work and fighting of French troops.

The French, many of them jubilant after their relatively easy success on 1 July, did not stop there. Each day a fresh artillery preparation caught increasingly unprepared Germans and troops (often fresh from the rear) surged forward to capture new positions. In the first 48 hours the French broke through the German lines across a 5-mile front.[26] It was an image of the high-tempo, artillery-intensive hammering that Foch had planned for, and it worked. The Germans simply could not re-establish themselves or their positions under such unrelenting pressure. By 5 July the men under Foch and Fayolle's command had advanced 3 miles and had taken 9,000 prisoners for a cost of fewer than 8,000 casualties. By 10 July, the

6e Armée found itself in possession of the whole of the Flaucourt plateau, with nothing but the river itself now keeping them out of their grand strategic objective: Péronne.

It was here that things bogged down. With the river blocking the path to Péronne and the abysmal opening attacks of the British to the north of the river the French had nowhere left to go. Eventually the attack would be extended southwards, but French forces would never manage to cross the River Somme; such were the pitfalls of coalition war-making. This leaves us with the question, perhaps unanswerable, of whether or not French efforts won any real strategic objectives. Arguments can be made regarding the loss of irreplaceable German troops (the Allies had substantial manpower, which would only improve once the Americans joined the war a few months after the end of the Somme), and the lifting of the German pressure at Verdun. Does this really equate to strategic significance? It is hard to say. What we can say is that the French advanced over 5 miles across a 12-mile front, and suffered a little over 200,000 casualties in doing so. They committed more troops to the Somme than the British by its end, and suffered only half the casualties. Their tactical performance should put the British efforts on the Somme into stark context, although we should be careful to not use French success as a rod against British struggles. The French had already had their 1 July 1916 many times over: in 1915 the French nearly lost as many soldiers dead as British forces did over the whole of World War II. It was a horrendous learning process that should not be glossed over. Experience in war is best learned first-hand; unfortunately the cost of that learning can sometimes be steep, even pyrrhic.

CHAPTER 12

THE LONG SHADOWS OF THE SOMME

Major General (Ret'd) Mungo Melvin CB OBE

The official figure for British losses in killed, wounded, and missing in action at the battle of the Somme in 1916 is 419,654 men. A century on, the slaughter still haunts us: no other land battle has generated such a profound impact on the British perception of war. Impressions of heroic sacrifice, of futility and waste, and of the professional incompetence of the generals (echoing Victorian criticisms of the Crimean War) continue to frame popular opinions. The British Army that fought in France and Flanders during World War I was one of Empire: the various national contingents from Australia, Canada, India, Newfoundland, New Zealand and South Africa have their own memories and proud monuments to the fallen. Yet this long battle fought in Picardy from 1 July to 18 November 1916 – the largest the British Army has ever fought in terms of the numbers of men committed over time – cut particularly deeply into the hearts of the peoples of the United Kingdom. The huge losses incurred on the Somme battlefield affected official policy and public attitude during the remainder of the war. These scars persisted during the inter-war period, into World War II and for decades long after. Notwithstanding the ultimate victory in late 1918, John Keegan observed the battle 'marked the end of an age of vital optimism in British life that has never been recovered'. His thesis rests on the view that the Somme represents the 'greatest military tragedy of the twentieth century [and] indeed of [our] national military history'.[1] The fate of Kitchener's New Army volunteers, including the 'Pals battalions', significantly contributed to this sense of calamity. As Lyn Macdonald has noted, 'it seemed at the time the country would never get over it – and it never has'.[2] Unsurprisingly, therefore, the aftershocks of the Somme continue to reverberate today.

The list of British national centennial commemorations of World War I announced by David Cameron on 11 October 2012 included, significantly, the first day of the battle of the Somme, but not the stunning triumph (the 'Black Day of the German Army' according to Ludendorff) of 8 August 1918.[3] For some reason, the British government appeared unwilling to remember the battle of Amiens, which heralded the 'Hundred Days' to the armistice on 11 November 1918 when the guns fell silent on the Western Front. In the selection criteria of such events, the magnitude of the sacrifice involved seems to have weighed more heavily than the success gained. It is a strange metric, but hardly surprising if one agrees with Jeremy Paxman's opinion that 'those military events which have the greatest imaginative resonance in the English mind are not necessarily triumphs at all'.[4] In citing famous actions such as the Charge of the Light Brigade (1854), Gallipoli (1915) and Dunkirk (1940), Paxman may be making a semi-valid point: but the 'disaster of the Somme', which he includes in his drum-beat of disparagement, surely deserves closer enquiry.

Revulsion to the mass casualties of the battle of the Somme and condemnation of the generals, however, was not instantaneous – it had over a decade's gestation. Indeed, during World War I, the film made of the battle, seen by millions in cinemas up and down the land in Britain and in the Dominions alike, had evinced an attitude of sticking it out until the job was done and the war won. Senior officers such as Field Marshal Sir Douglas Haig, if not universally revered, were regarded at the war's end as the very necessary architects and standard-bearers of victory. Over 1 million people turned out to witness Haig's state funeral in London on 3 February 1928, a testament to the very high regard in which he was held at the time. Such stoicism and deference to rank, however, were beginning to run their natural course. By then the Somme – and, more generally, the experience of World War I – had begun to strike a more discordant tone in Britain's national folklore. The public mood slowly but surely shifted to one of disquiet – if not disgust – towards such industrial-scale bloodletting for so little tangible gain.

A rich literature and a haunting legacy

Both the Western Front generally, and the Somme specifically, have found poignant literary expression since the late 1920s. This chapter makes no attempt to review the vast literature of the Somme in a manner similar to works such as Paul Fussell's groundbreaking *The Great War and Modern Memory* (1975). Nor does it try to tread the same ground as much more recent, and widely acclaimed, research by scholars such as Robin Prior and Trevor Wilson, Hew Strachan, Gary Sheffield, Dan Todman and William Philpott. The latter's study of the legacy of the Somme in *Bloody Victory* (2009), however, has provided a starting point for this present contribution. In particular, Philpott's trenchant criticism of Winston Churchill's account of the battle, who described the 'graveyards of Kitchener's Army', set a number of hares running in this author's mind.[5] To what extent, for example, did the experience of the Somme distort policy and military strategy during World War II? Did a widespread aversion to fielding a large expeditionary force lead to Montgomery only commanding two armies in 1944–45 as opposed to Haig's five in 1916–18? This, of course, is by no means an original observation; many other factors, not least the constraints on army manpower posed by the various requirements of the RAF, the coal mines and other war-essential industries, were surely at work. Keegan again, however, provides a strong clue, quoting an exchange between the United States' General George Marshall and Churchill's scientific advisor Lord

Cherwell. When the former provided the 'most cogent and logical arguments in favour of a prompt invasion of the Continent', the latter is reported as remarking 'It's no use – you are arguing against the casualties of the Somme'.[6]

British schoolchildren today are fed a rich diet of evocative poetry[7] and prose including the wartime works of Wilfred Owen (such as 'Anthem for Doomed Youth' and 'Dulce Et Decorum Est'), Edmund Blunden's *Undertones of War* (1928), Robert Graves' *Good-bye to All That* (1929), Siegfried Sassoon's *Memoirs of a Fox-Hunting Man* (1928) and *Memoirs of an Infantry Officer* (1930) and, more recently, Sebastian Faulks' *Birdsong* (1993), which has also been broadcast as a television film (2012). Their parents and grandparents were entertained by popular parodies such as the stage production *Oh What A Lovely War!* (1963) and later film (1969), based on the alluring 'lions led by donkeys' thesis advanced by Alan Clark in 1961.[8] The BBC's *Blackadder Goes Forth!* television series of 1989 was but another well-received reprise of the same theme. In contrast, the rather more sober fictional pictures painted by C. S. Forrester in *The General* (1936) and in John Masters' magisterial 'Loss of Eden' trilogy[9] (1979–81) have found less resonance.

For understanding the realities of the war on the Western Front, including the Somme fighting, however, perhaps one volume stands out: Captain J. C. Dunn's privately published *The War the Infantry Knew 1914–1919* (1938). Thanks to the efforts of the military historian and editor Keith Simpson, this 'Chronicle of Service in France and Belgium with The Second Battalion of His Majesty's Twenty-Third Foot, The Royal Welch Fusiliers', has been back in print since 1987 and continues to sell very well, demonstrating the enduring public interest in this conflict.[10] A more specific work, Martin Middlebrook's *The First Day of the Somme* (1971), has introduced many historians and enthusiasts alike to the battle; that said, its focus on the initial and most costly episode of the offensive from a British perspective has perhaps distorted some views. Equally important are the first-hand accounts of 'the most devastating battle of the Great War', collated in Joshua Levine's *Forgotten Voices of the Somme* (2008), which drew on the wealth of material contained in the Imperial War Museum's sound archive.

The first organized tours of the battlefields following World War I were predominately 'pilgrimages' for the comrades and bereaved to pay their respects to fallen friends and loved ones at the newly opened cemeteries of the Imperial (later Commonwealth) War Graves Commission. During World War II many thousands of British soldiers of a certain age passed through familiar terrain once again: many did not return. Senior politicians also knew the ground well. On 11 November 1939, for example, a former Rifle Brigade officer, Anthony Eden, now Dominions Minister, drove from Paris through the Somme battlefield to visit the British Expeditionary Force headquarters near Arras. 'Memories from the last war were still vivid', he recalled, when crossing 'the same grim sector, from Delville Wood forward to Factory Corner and the Gird Ridge'.[11]

Today, groups of all ages visit the war cemeteries and memorials of the Somme, the latter including Thiepval and Ulster Tower. The inevitable consequences of war, the losses, rather than its causes or dynamics, remain the focus of such trips. Although countless monuments and serried ranks of graves have dominated the Somme landscape for nearly a century, their legacy in abstract terms is as important as the physical one so solemnly on display. John Keegan opined famously in his classic study *The Face of Battle* (1976), the 'principal memorial which the Somme left to the British nation is not one of headstones and inscriptions', but rather the realization that 'war could threaten with death the young manhood of a whole nation'.[12] The unprecedented losses of this battle have framed much of the military accounts, academic analyses and popular narratives of World War I.

The main protagonists in this brief study include those who fought in World War I and who then went on to have major roles in World War II, surviving both conflicts to reflect on their experiences and to shape their positions in history. Both Churchill and Montgomery, for example, had their own axes to grind: their accounts of the Somme, however, would fuel rather than follow the popular debate. Historians such as Sir Llewellyn Woodward in *Great Britain and the War of 1914–1918* (1967) provided academic underpinning to others' compelling – if not entirely accurate – critiques of the generals.

Politicians and generals

For a number of modern historians of the Somme, Churchill has become a bogeyman, if not a principal target of complaint. Their criticisms hit hard both the man and his method. Gary Sheffield has described Churchill's description of the Somme as a combination of 'a blithe disregard for what was possible in 1916 with an astonishing lack of understanding of the realities of combat on the Western Front'.[13] Philpott goes further, not only accusing Churchill of manufacturing 'one of Britain's great historical myths', but also lambasting his work in terms of the 'nostrums and cavils [which] have become the familiar staples of First World War literature, recycled again and again to a credulous public'.[14] Against such attacks, it is only fair to briefly review Churchill's direct experience of World War I conditions and to examine the charges he makes against the planning and conduct of the battle of the Somme.

Winston Churchill neither knew the battlefield nor witnessed the fighting at the Somme. To his credit, however, he had served on the Western Front. His experience of the trenches was limited to a period between 18 November 1915 and 7 May 1916, in which he was attached initially to the 2nd Battalion of the Grenadier Guards before assuming command of the 6th Royal Scots Fusiliers on 1 January 1916. His commentary of the Somme in *The World Crisis* drew heavily on a paper, which he had circulated to the British cabinet on 1 August 1916, one month after the opening of the battle. Having questioned the strategic rationale for the offensive ('what are Péronne and Bapaume, even if we were likely to take them?'), Churchill summed up its futility: 'In *personnel* the results of the operation have been disastrous; in *terrain* they have been absolutely barren.'[15] By his own admission, however, Churchill's memorandum was 'repudiated both in the Cabinet and at General Headquarters' in France.[16] There appeared to be little alternative but to continue with the battle despite its terrible cost: Churchill had offered no new course of action.

In *The World Crisis*, Churchill criticized Haig's intelligence staff, observing 'The temptation to tell a Chief in a great position the things he most likes to hear is one of the commonest explanations of mistaken policy'. More generally, he flagged up the 'whole habit of mind of a military staff is based upon subordination of opinion'.[17] Yet as to where Haig could have found a source of more challenging staff officers, Churchill gave no clue. David Lloyd George highlighted the over-optimistic nature of Haig's intelligence in his self-serving memoirs.[18] With the battles of both the Somme and third Ypres in mind, Lloyd George would claim that 'the Flanders offensive [of 1917] would have been turned down' by the War Committee had the 'whole truth' been exposed at the time.[19] This was but one example of the politicians trying to distance themselves from the generals after the disastrous events of battle. Meanwhile, Churchill's disdain for Haig and other senior officers was evident in a digression he inserted into his life of Marlborough, written in the early 1930s.[20] Portraying an astonishing ignorance of the real pressures of higher command in the 20th century as opposed to 17th, he penned:

> The generalissimo of an army of 2 million men, already for ten days in desperate battle, has little or nothing to do except to keep himself fit and cool. ... There is no need for the modern commander to wear boots and breeches: he will never ride a horse except for the purposes of health. In the height of his largest battles, when twenty thousand men are falling every day, time will hang heavily on his hands.

In a sketch worthy of Blackadder's General Sir Anthony Cecil Hogmanay Melchett, Churchill's fictional commander-in-chief is served by an anonymous staff moving 'flags upon his map, or perhaps the Chief of Staff himself will draw a blue line or a brown line or make a strong arrow upon it'. Moreover, the commander-in-chief's 'hardest trials are reduced to great simplicity'; orders are reduced to: '"Advance," "Hold," or "Retreat."' The caricature continues unabated: 'There is nearly always leisure for a conference even in the gravest crises'.[21] However, life in the GHQ was far from idle: '[Haig] and his staff had an overwhelming amount of work to get through'.[22] But brilliant writers such as Churchill never allowed the inconvenient facts to interfere with the telling of a good story.

In his works, Churchill skilfully planted the seed of the myth set out in Alan Clark's polemic *The Donkeys*. Clark, although he had studied history at Oxford, and had briefly served as a subaltern in the Household Cavalry, was an expert neither in military affairs nor of World War I. Yet his book struck a chord with his gripping narratives of the battles of 1915 and vivid pen portraits of the senior generals involved, including French, Haig, Rawlinson, and Wilson. As Max Hastings has emphasized in his fine introduction to a recent reprint of Forrester's *The General* (originally published in 1936), Clark's work, though influential, was 'wildly unscholarly'.[23] Furthermore, it would appear that Clark had invented the very memorable invective 'lions led by donkeys' exchange between Ludendorff and Hoffman that prefaces his book.[24] Yet this sort of mud has a particular adhesive quality. As bloodbaths rather than victories loom large in the popular memory of World War I, the myth continues to stick.

At times during World War II Churchill could hardly constrain his contempt for the British Army's senior leaders. 'Deep down', as David Reynolds has pointed out in his masterly study of Churchill's history of that conflict, 'he yearned to be a great general'.[25] Indeed, he probably thought he could do better himself, as a latter-day Marlborough or Napoleon – but certainly not as either an unimaginative Haig or a hapless Auchinleck (whom Churchill sacked in August 1942 as Commander-in-Chief Middle East). According to Alan Brooke, the CIGS for the majority of World War II, during the dark days of defeat in North Africa and in the Far East during early 1942, Churchill 'came out continually with remarks such as: "Have you not got a single general in the army who can win battles, have none of them any ideas, must we continually lose battles in this way?"'[26] In November of that year Churchill was to find in Bernard Law Montgomery a general who could, finally, deliver a noteworthy victory – at El Alamein.

Montgomery's bitter experiences of World War I did much to shape his approach to high command in World War II. Such was Monty's influence on the British Army, moreover, that the impact of his particular methods endured long after he retired. If one accepts such a

'Montgomery effect' existed, then the post-war army was as much the product of World War I as of World War II, and the received wisdom of the Somme had played a major part in forming that legacy. 'Monty' knew the realities of warfare only too well from an early stage of his career. When serving as an infantry platoon commander in the Royal Warwickshire Regiment, he had been very nearly killed on 13 October 1914 at the village of Meteren during the first battle of Ypres. For his conspicuous gallantry in this action he was awarded the Distinguished Service Order. As his sympathetic biographer, Nigel Hamilton, has noted, following Montgomery's recovery from near-mortal wounds, 'he would wear the bright red collar tabs of a staff officer' from February 1915.[27] Although no longer in an infantry battalion, and thus spared many of the attendant risks of direct combat, Montgomery would serve until the end of the war as a general staff officer at the right hand of brigade and divisional commanders in dug-outs positioned close to the front line, not in some distant headquarters housed in some safe château.

During the battle of the Somme, Montgomery served as the brigade major of 104th Brigade, 35th (Bantam) Division. His memoirs of this period reveal complaints not only about the way operations were conducted, but also about the poor relationships between the commanders and members of staff on the one hand and the troops on the other. Montgomery claimed:

> There was little contact between the generals and the soldiers. I went through the whole war on the Western Front, except during the period I was in England after being wounded; I never once saw the British Commander-in-Chief, neither French nor Haig, and only twice did I see an Army Commander.[28]

Furthermore, he felt that the 'higher staffs were out of touch with the troops'. Montgomery observed scathingly: 'At most large headquarters in back areas the doctrine seemed to be that the troops existed for the benefit of the staff'. More acutely, perhaps, the 'frightful casualties' appalled him. He noted that the 'so-called "good fighting generals" of the war appeared ... to be those who had a complete disregard for human life'.[29] As he explained in his memoirs, Montgomery made a particular point of keeping 'in close touch with [the] casualty figures' arising from the Normandy campaign of June–August 1944.[30] He documented them perhaps for two reasons: first, to show his real concern for the human cost of war; and secondly, to indicate the British share of the fighting in comparison with the American. Sensitivity to casualties characterized much of the British Army's approach to World War II: the employment of firepower and armour as opposed to infantry were to dominate much of its thinking if not practice.

A dominant theme – shared by politicians, public, and soldiers alike – was to avoid fighting another very costly battle like the Somme. Part of the way this was achieved was by limiting the potential liability in terms of forces committed over time and space. For example, the British and Canadian losses in the battle for Normandy from 6 June to 11 August 1944 amounted to 68,000.[31] If one reckons, however, that the military effort – in strictly manpower terms – of the 21st Army Group (First Canadian and Second British Armies) represented about a third of that expended by Haig's Fourth and Reserve (later Fifth) Armies at the Somme over double the period, then the *relative* casualty tolls look similar. What distorted the figures for the Somme was the enormous and largely single-sided loss on the first day of battle. Furthermore, had the British and Canadian armies fought the Germans in the north-west European campaign longer than the 11 months from 6 June 1944 to 7 May 1945, the butcher's bill would have lengthened commensurately. There is no escape from the simple fact that a high-intensity war against a first-class, formidable opponent will cost very great numbers of lives, however skilfully fought.[32] The other fact that cannot be forgotten is that the bulk of the German Army was destroyed by the Red Army on the Eastern Front during World War II: in stark contrast, during World War I the British Expeditionary Force took a much larger proportionate share of the burden of defeating its major opponent.[33] However distasteful it may appear to some modern eyes, the battle of the Somme in 1916 formed a very necessary part of this wearing-down – attritional – process.

In his *A History of Warfare* (1968), Montgomery criticized both the value of the battle of the Somme and the quality of the British Army's leadership. At a cost to each side of 'about 500,000 men killed, wounded or taken prisoner', he noted, 'the Allies gained thereby a wedge of muddy ground, at no point more than about nine miles deep on a front of some twenty miles or so – and of no strategic value'.[34] Quite apart from the fact that the battle had a very damaging effect on the German Army, Montgomery understated the Allied losses, presumably because he discounted much of the French effort. According to him, the forces at the Somme 'were nearly all British', which was manifestly not the case.[35] Such side-lining of allies reflected a personal blind spot that limited his utility as a multinational commander, as demonstrated in his inept handling of the American media at a press conference on 7 January 1945 during the battle of the Bulge in World War II. Unfortunately, a dispatch of the conference was intercepted and re-broadcast in modified form by German radio in which it was reported that Montgomery had saved the day rather than troops of the US Army. The distortion 'started an uproar', thus sowing quite unnecessary dissent between the Allies.[36]

Returning to his account of the previous conflict, Montgomery highlighted the 'remarkable, and disgraceful fact' that 'a high proportion of the most senior officers were ignorant of the conditions in which the soldiers were fighting' – presumably in stark contrast to thoroughly modern generals such as himself. In his view, 'the soldiers [of World War I] were worthy of better generalship; on the whole they were better than their generals, although among these there were a few notable exceptions'.[37] With such robust claims, Montgomery provides an unlikely member of the 'lions led by donkeys' school. After all, Alan Clark had made a similar point. Writing of the sacrifice of the Canadians at the second battle of Ypres in resisting a German gas attack on an exposed position (from which they should have been withdrawn), he wrote of 'yet one more example of the gallantry of individual soldiers saving the commanders from the effects that should have followed on their own folly'.[38]

There is an ironic twist to Montgomery's critique of World War I generalship. While his military standing is probably in decline, Haig's appears to be in the ascendant. According to the audience at a National Army Museum celebrity speaker event on 9 April 2011, the joint winners of the accolade of 'Britain's Greatest General' were the Duke of Wellington and Field Marshal Sir William Slim.[39] Rather surprisingly, however, the runner-up was Haig rather than Montgomery as might otherwise have been expected. One suspects that Monty turned in his grave at this outcome. Haig, however, remains a controversial figure, not least for his handling of the Somme and the third battle of Ypres in 1917. But he has many supporters still in his native Scotland if the 2009 outcry over the moving of his equestrian statue from the foot of Edinburgh Castle's esplanade is anything to go by.[40]

Some historians' views

The historians' treatment of the battle of the Somme in 1916 has been critical, leading – if not reflecting – much of the prevailing public mood. Such writing, as ever, must be seen in its political and temporal context. Basil Liddell Hart's history of World War I, first published as *The Real War 1914–1918* (1930), although representing a major assault on the quality of the British Army's generalship, provides a more balanced view of the Somme, albeit the battle had 'proved both the glory and the graveyard of "Kitchener's Army"'. Although the first day of the battle was a 'military failure', in Liddell Hart's view it represented none the less 'an epic of heroism and, better still, the proof of the moral quality of the new armies of Britain'.[41] Arthur Bryant adopted a similar approach in his *English Saga 1840–1940*. Published in 1940, when the nation was at war with Germany for the second time within a generation, Bryant stuck a heroic note of endurance:

> On the first day of the battle alone, 60,000 casualties were sustained – the very flower of England. And week by week, as the brazen fury continued and the whole countryside was churned into a slimy mire

of death, victory was realized to be an indefinitely distant goal, far beyond the reach of most of those striving for it.[42]

He was also to point out the ability of writers such as Sassoon to observe 'beauty above the carnage', and not least to highlight the stoicism of the British public to the lengthening lists of casualties. Reaching new purple heights in his lyrical treatment of the past war to inform the present, Bryant noted that the grim resolution of the people in 1914–18 was needed 'before the English came to their journey's end'. Thinking no doubt of the Somme and other, further far-flung, battles such as Gallipoli, he reminded his readers: 'There were disasters in distant places of the earth; allies – broken by the storm – fell away, and, as offensive after offensive with all their high delusive hopes failed, the angel of death beat his wings against the panes of innumerable homes.'[43] Such bulldog determination, intertwined with a defiant Dunkirkian 'we're now on our own' spirit was written during the dark summer of 1940 with France out of the war and a German invasion expected.

Bryant, however, failed to allude to the reason for Britain's strategic weakness at that time, and not least the political grounds for the recent humiliating military defeat in France. As John Terraine wisely reminded his readers in his compelling study of myths and anti-myths of war – *The Smoke and the Fire* (1980), the 'birds [of appeasement had] finally come home to roost'. To underline his point, he quoted from the diary of General Sir Edmund Ironside, the recently appointed Commander-in-Chief Home Forces, who had noted in June 1940: 'The saying that we were never to again to have "the bloody massacres of the Somme" has deluded the people. Nobody has been educated to the horrors of modern war. I don't believe the people understand it yet.'[44] Ironside's concerns were all too clear. Heroism and endurance were very necessary, but surely insufficient conditions for success in contemporary warfare: the armed services needed not only the necessary manpower, *matériel*, and techniques for battle, but also the popular and political will to expend the required resources beforehand. There is also surely a lesson for World War II and subsequent conflicts: while we may not wish to fight another battle of the Somme, and do all in our power sensibly to avoid one, at some stage we may have no option other than to fight costly and protracted engagements. There is always, however, the allure of the tactical or strategic short-cut or policy panacea in the hope that war, if it is to be waged at all, can be done so in the most economic if not novel manner.

Liddell Hart is principally famous for his advocacy of the strategic 'indirect approach', which was not followed at the Somme. Surprise plays a large part in this concept. In his description of the battle, he praised – *unsurprisingly* – Rawlinson's dawn attack of 14 July 1916 as it 'revived the use of surprise, which lay rusting throughout the greater part of the war'.[45] He condemned, however, the missed opportunity to exploit its initial success, particular to the front of the 7th Division towards High Wood. Likewise, Liddell Hart criticized the fighting during the following two months in which the 'infantry on both sides served as compressed cannon-fodder for artillery consumption'.[46] Like Churchill, he deprecated the premature employment of the new tanks at the attack of Flers-Courcelette of 15 September 1916. Although they had 'rendered useful aid, especially in capturing Flers', their employment in insufficient numbers had meant that 'the greater prize – of a great surprise stroke – was a heavy forfeit to pay for redeeming in a limited degree the failure of the Somme offensive'.[47] That said, Liddell Hart was neither completely negative about the outcome nor one-sided in his treatment of the battle. He also criticized the German commanders concerned, and particularly General Fritz von Below (Commander-in-Chief of 2. Armee) for his orders to retake by counter-attack any German trench or position lost.[48] 'If German mistakes do not condone British mistakes', Liddell Hart maintained, 'they at least helped to balance the British loss'.[49] Indeed, the 'true texture' of the Somme fighting, as Terraine highlighted, was 'attack, counter-attack; attack again, counter-attack again'. For that reason, 'the Germans, both in the army at the front and at the back to talk with horror about the 'bloodbath of the Somme''.[50]

A. J. P. Taylor, in his popular and eminently readable illustrated *History of the First World War* (1963), described the battle of the Somme as 'an unredeemed defeat' without any of Liddell Hart's qualifications. In pithy terms, he condemned the overall deleterious effect of the offensive on the British Army:

> Idealism perished on the Somme. The enthusiastic volunteers were enthusiastic no longer. They had lost faith in their cause, in their leaders, in everything except loyalty to their fighting comrades. The war ceased to have a purpose. It went on for its own sake, as a contest in endurance.

Moreover, in Taylor's opinion, the 'Somme set the picture by which future generations saw World War I; brave helpless soldiers; blundering obstinate generals; nothing achieved. After the Somme men decided that the war would go on for ever'.[51] If his first hypothesis had been true, then it might have been expected that the British Army would have ceased to be an effective fighting force for the remainder of the war, or even mutinied as sections of the French Army did in 1917. The fact that some hard-won lessons were learned, that tactics and techniques improved accordingly, and in consequence more successful actions would follow, albeit at a high cost in casualties, seems to have been ignored. None the less, the combined views of critics such as Churchill, Clark, and Taylor have proved very resilient to revision; Liddell Hart's more nuanced approach – while certainly not uncritical of Haig – has found less resonance in the popular narrative of the battle. Likewise Terraine, while very well regarded in historical circles, has failed to dent the image of the bungling generals.

Heavyweight, more scholarly accounts of World War I have also damned British generalship of World War I, and of the Somme more specifically. Take, for example, Sir Llewellyn Woodward's *Great Britain and the War of 1914–1918* (1967). In his view, before the battle, 'the commanders in the field had no "plan of attack" beyond the accumulation of masses of men, guns, and munitions, and they had shewn almost no interest in devising new methods of dealing with the problems of capturing and advancing beyond a series of strongly defended positions'.[52] Woodward's greater criticism appeared to be reserved for the civilian ministers who, abler than their military counterparts, 'ought to have remembered that the rifle and machine gun were mechanical contrivances, and that other contrivances might counter their effects'. Hence 'no mere tactical improvements in methods of advance' by an attacking force would 'enable men to get the better of machine guns'. In his opinion, and echoing the earlier criticisms, it was a 'fundamental error', moreover, 'not to have produced on much larger scale the "tank" surprise which might have changed the result of the Somme battles'.[53] In other words, the Somme should not have been attempted until sufficient numbers of tanks were available, reprising Churchill's and Liddell Hart's criticism of their precipitate use at the Somme on 15 September 1916.

Yet there was another strong thread that ran through much of Woodward's writing of World War I – the mediocrity of the generals. Having served in the army during the conflict, he recalled being alarmed by the 'lowness of the professional competence among the higher ranks'. While 'no one doubted their personal courage', they lacked both 'imagination' and 'free intelligence'. Woodward maintained that the 'intellectual requirements for entrance into the army were far below those laid down for entrance into the higher reaches of the civil service'.[54] Indeed, in his rambling personal introduction to his history, he appeared to take considerable delight in retelling an incident in 1919 on his return to academe in Oxford, having been elected a fellow of All Souls College. When 'complaining of the low mental state of our military leadership', one of his colleagues observed that the 'army was run by pass men'. Nevertheless Woodward declined to 'put the whole blame upon the army commanders, individually or collectively, for their mental illiteracy' – the nation as a whole was at fault. In his view, the 'English people' had been willing enough to 'leave the fate of a generation in the hands of a custom-bound clique which would not have been permitted to take over the management of any other important department of state or of a great business'.[55] In other words, the country received no better than it deserved. If the British Army's senior leadership was that incompetent, then it remains rather surprising that the war on the Western Front was won at all in 1918.

Although written nearly 60 years ago, Woodward's critique has a modern ring to it, particularly at a time when the heads of Britain's armed services (the chiefs of staff) have been marginalized by successive prime ministers and secretaries of state for Defence. Under the so-called Levene 'reforms' of 2011, they have now been banished from the Defence Board and rusticated from London.[56] Defence policy and management is now largely civilian driven. Tensions between soldiers and statesmen are nothing new: the struggle of the latter to control the former has an enduring quality.[57]

Conclusion

This chapter has done no more than scratch the surface of a huge subject. The legacy of the battle of the Somme from a British perspective has been analysed in depth in a literature that had already grown vast by the beginning of World War II. This brief, admittedly very selective survey, has none the less attempted to show that the Somme retains a particularly hallowed place in Britain's collective memory. One small further example may underline this assertion. The national ballot for 8,000 places for members of the public to attend the centenary commemoration of the battle at the Thiepval memorial on 1 July 2016 was almost immediately sold out. The battle continues to cast long shadows not only on perceptions of World War I, but also on both the morality and utility of applying brute force (and thereby wasting the nation's most cherished resource – its people) in the pursuit of military strategic, and ultimately political, war ends. Furthermore, while criticism of the British Army's generalship at the Somme is well deserved in specific cases, a blanket condemnation of the military leaders is surely not. The partial rehabilitation of senior commanders such as Haig represents an appropriate piece of historical rebalancing.

Yet one uncomfortable fact stands out: the British popular fascination with World War I, and the battles of the Western Front in particular, including the Somme of 1916, is not matched in other participating nations. For states such as France and Germany, and particularly Russia, the momentous events of World War II eclipsed memories of, and interest in, the previous conflict. This background presumably explains why the Western Front Association is a peculiarly British institution and the

Somme is seen as a British tragedy rather than a French or German one. Had the British Army fought in north-west Europe for an equivalent period during World War II, and suffered proportionate losses, perhaps the sacrifice of the Somme and Passchendaele would have been more quietly honoured – yet never forgotten. Nevertheless, the Somme is likely to be remembered on 1 July 2116 as the bicentenary of Waterloo was commemorated on 18 June 2015. For good and ill, the battle will retain – rightly – a firm lodgement in our national story – a moving saga of sacrifice, courage, and endurance, despite all the odds. Meanwhile, the debate over the quality of the British generalship will continue to run and run.

ENDNOTES

Chapter 1

1   Gerard Fassy, *Le Commandement Français en Orient (Octobre 1915–Novembre 1918)* (Paris: Economica, 2003), pp. 82–6, 103–11, 125–9; Leon, Greece and the Great Powers, pp. 436 ff.

2   Jan K. Tannenbaum, *General Maurice Sarrail (1856–1929): The French Army and Left-wing Politics* (Chapel Hill: University of North Carolina Press, 1974), pp. 51–63, 82–90; David Dutton, *The Politics of Diplomacy: Britain and France in the Balkans in the First World War* (London: Tauris, 1998).

3   Edmund Glaise-Horstenau (ed.), *Österreich-Ungarns letzter Krieg 1914–1918*, vol. 4 (Vienna: Verlag der Militärwissenschaftlichen Mitteilungen, 1933), p. 186; Mark Thompson, *The White War: Life and Death on the Italian Front 1915–1919* (London: Faber and Faber, 2008), pp. 159–66; Gianni Rocca, *Cadorna: Il Generalissimo di Caporetto* (Milano: Mondadori, 1985), pp. 128–44.

4   Piero Melograni, *Storia politica della Grande guerra 1915–1918* (Milano: Mondadori, 1998), pp. 171–86.

5   Wolfgang Pyta, *Hindenburg: Herrschaft zwischen Hohenzollern und Hitler* (Munich: Beck, 2009); Manfred Nebelin, *Ludendorff: Diktator im Ersten Weltkrieg* (Munich: Siedler Verlag, 2010).

6   See the table in Reichskriegsministerium (ed.), *Der Weltkrieg 1914–1918: Die militärischen Operationen zu Lande, vol. 10: Die Operationen des Jahres 1916* (Berlin: Mittler, 1936), p. 564.

7   Thompson, *The White War*, pp. 169–76; Rocca, *Cadorna*, pp. 159–68.

8   Glenn Torrey, 'Rumania's Decision to Intervene: Bratianu and the Entente, June–July 1916', in *Rumanian Studies* (2, 1973), pp. 3–29; reprinted in Glenn Torrey, *Romania and World War I* (Jasi/Oxford, 1998).

9   Gary Sheffield, *The Somme* (London: Cassell, 2003), p. 156.

10   Glenn Torrey, *The Romanian Battlefront in World War I* (Lawrence: University Press of Kansas, 2011), p. 21.

11   Michael Barrett, *Prelude to Blitzkrieg: The Austro-German Campaign in Romania* (Bloomington: Indiana UP, 2013); Giorgio Secca, 'Svishtov, novembre 1916', in *La Grande guerra* (17, October 2014), pp. 32–44; Torrey, *Romanian Battlefront*, pp. 137–53.

12   Lothar Höbelt, '*Stehen oder Fallen?' Österreichische Politik im ersten Weltkrieg* (Vienna: Boehlau, 2015), pp. 52 ff.

13   Höbelt, '*Stehen oder Fallen?*', pp. 101–7.

14   Gerhard Groß, 'Ein Nebenkriegsschauplatz: Die deutschen Operationen gegen Rumänien 1916' in Jürgen Angelow (ed.), *Der Erste Weltkrieg auf dem Balkan: Perspektiven der Forschung* (Berlin: be-bra, 2011), pp. 143–58.

15   Holger Afflerbach, 'Wilhelm II as Supreme Warlord in the First World War', in *War in History 4* (1998), pp. 427–49.

16   German commander Admiral Scheer himself once quipped that future historians would never cease wondering what he had had in mind when he courted that risk a second time. The solution, he said, was: 'nothing at all'. Werner Rahn, 'Die Seeschlacht vor dem Skaggerak. Verlauf und Analyse aus deutscher Perspektive', in Michael Epkenhans, Jörg Hillmann & Frank Nägler (eds.), *Skagerrakschlacht: Vorgeschichte – Ereignis – Verarbeitung* (Munich: Oldenbourg, 2009), pp. 139–286; here: p. 175.

17   Andrew Gordon, *The Rules of the Game: Jutland and British Naval Command* (London: John Murray, 1996), pp. 490, 562.

18   On the 'day after', the British disposed of 24 serviceable dreadnoughts, the German only ten. The Germans needed 650 dry-dock days to repair their ships vs. only 350 for the British (Gordon, *The Rules of the Game*, pp. 498, 514).

19   Jellicoe's caution and Beatty's 'gerrymandering of history' (ibid., p. 547) sparked a bitter controversy between critics and defenders of both admirals. Gordon's study and John Brooks, *Dreadnought Gunnery and the Battle of Jutland: The Question of Fire Control* (London: Routledge, 2005), represent the most recent and most sophisticated examples of this ongoing debate.

20   Rahn, *Seeschlacht*, p. 192 ff; Gordon, *Rules of the Game*, p. 515.

21   Bernd Stegemann, *Die deutsche Marinepolitik 1916–1918* (Berlin: Duncker & Humblot, 1970), pp. 47 f., 55–9, 63, 73–5, 101; Joachim Schröder, *Die U-Boote des Kaisers: Die Geschichte des deutschen U-Boot-Krieges gegen Großbritannien im Ersten Weltkrieg* (Bonn: Bernard & Graefe, 2003).

22   John Milton Cooper Jr., 'The Command of Gold Reversed: American Loans to Britain, 1915–1917', in *Pacific Historical Review* (45, 1976), pp. 209–30; here: p. 228.

23 Charles Townshend, *When God Made Hell: The British Invasion of Mesopotamia and the Creation of Iraq, 1914–1921* (London: Faber & Faber, 2010), pp. 259, 521; David French, 'The Dardanelles, Mecca and Kut: Prestige as a Factor in British Eastern Strategy', in *War and Society* (5, 1987), pp. 45–61.

24 Mansoureh Ettehadiyyeh, 'The Iranian Provisional Government', in Touraj Atabaki (ed.), *Iran and the First World War: Battleground of the Great Powers* (London: I.B. Tauris, 2006), pp. 9–27.

25 Alexander Will, *Kein Griff nach der Weltmacht: Geheime Dienste und Propaganda im deutsch-österreichisch-türkischen Bündnis 1914–1918* (Köln: Böhlau, 2012), pp. 230, 256–261.

26 Reichsarchiv (ed.), *Der Weltkrieg*, vol. 10 (Berlin 1945), pp. 606–10; Paul G. Halpern, *A Naval History of World War I* (London 1994), pp. 236–45; Edward Erickson, *Ordered to Die: A History of the Ottoman Army in the First World War* (Westport: Praeger, 2001), pp. 136 ff; Andrew Mango, *Atatürk* (London: John Murray, 1999), pp. 159–62.

27 Jacob Goldberg, 'The Origins of British-Saudi Relations: The 1915 Anglo-Saudi Treaty Revisited', in *Historical Journal* (28, 1985), pp. 693–703; R. H. Lieshout, 'Keeping better educated Moslems busy': Sir Reginald Wingate and the Origin of the Husayn-McMahon Correspondence', in *Historical Journal* (27, 1984), pp. 453–63; Townshend, *When God Made Hell*, pp. 265–9.

28 On a more optimistic note: David Murphy, 'A Sideshow of a Sideshow? The Arab Revolt (1916–18) and the development of Modern Desert warfare', in: Matthias Strohn (ed.), *World War I Companion* (Oxford: Osprey, 2013), pp. 176–94.

29 Hew Strachan, *The First World War in Africa* (Oxford: OUP, 2004), pp. 138–49, 171, 183; Anne Samson, *World War I in Africa: The Forgotten Conflict* (London: I.B. Tauris, 2013), pp. 112–6, 140, 150, 222; Ross Anderson, *The Forgotten Front: The East African Campaign* (Stroud: Tempus, 2004), pp. 101–80.

30 Russell McGuirk, *The Sanusi's Little War: The Amazing Story of a Forgotten Conflict in the Western Desert, 1915–1917* (London: Arabian Publishing, 2007), pp. 220–7, 260–2; Angelo Del Boca, *Gli Italiani in Libia: Tripoli bel suol d'amore 1860–1922* (Rome: Mondadori, 1986), pp. 293–7, 318.

31 Strachan, *War in Africa*, pp. 54–9.

32 Arthur S. Link, *Wilson*, vol. 4 (Princeton: Princeton University Press, 1964), pp. 102–38; Daniel Larsen, 'War Pessimism in Britain and an American Peace in Early 1916', in *International History Review* (34, 2012), pp. 795–817.

33 Link, *Wilson*, vol. 5, p. 202.

34 Frank Hadler (ed.), *Weg von Österreich! Das Weltkriegsexil von Masaryk und Benes im Spiegel ihrer Briefe und Aufzeichnungen aus den Jahren 1914 bis*

1918 (Berlin: Akademie Verlag, 1995), p. 409; T. G. Otte (ed.), *An Historian in War and Peace: The Diaries of Harold Temperley* (Farnham: Ashgate, 2014), pp. 106 (22.2.1917), 163 (4.7.1917), 196 (8.10.1917).

35 For recent additions to the literature see Georges-Henri Soutou, *La Grande Illusion: Quand la France perdait la paix 1914–1920* (Paris: Tallandier, 2015), pp. 180–202, 235–45.

Chapter 2

1 See Stephen Walsh, 'The Imperial Russian Army and the Eastern Front in World War I, 1914–1917', in Matthias Strohn (ed.), *World War I Companion* (Oxford: Osprey, 2013), pp. 151–5.

2 Gerhard P. Groß, *Mythos und Wirklichkeit: Geschichte des operativen Denkens im deutschen Heer von Moltke d. Ä. bis Heusinger* (Paderborn: Ferdinand Schöningh, 2012), pp. 131–6.

3 Personal war diary of General der Infanterie (retired) von Kuhl, diary entry of 28 November 1915, Bundesarchiv-Militärarchiv Freiburg im Breisgau, RH 61/970, p. 4.

4 Holger Afflerbach, *Falkenhayn: Politisches Denken und Handeln im Kaiserreich* (Munich: Oldenbourg 1994), pp. 211–7.

5 Groß, *Mythos und Wirklichkeit*, pp. 121–2.

6 Quoted from Afflerbach, *Falkenhayn*, p. 198.

7 See Afflerbach, *Falkenhayn*, pp. 218–32.

8 See Afflerbach, *Falkenhayn*, pp. 344–50.

9 See Erich von Falkenhayn, *General Headquarters 1914–1916 and its Critical Decisions* (London: Hutchinson 1919).

10 Kronprinz Rupprecht, *Mein Kriegstagebuch*, vol. 1 (Munich, 1929), entry of 12 February 1916.

11 Olaf Jessen, *Verdun 1916. Urschlacht des Jahrhunderts* (Munich: Beck 2014).

12 Personal war diary of General der Infanterie (retired) von Kuhl, diary entry of 25 May 1916, Bundesarchiv-Militärarchiv Freiburg im Breisgau, RH 61/970.

13 On the development of German tactics see: Matthias Strohn, 'German Tactical Doctrine and the Defensive Battle on the Western Front', in idem (ed.), *World War I Companion* (Oxford: Osprey, 2013), pp. 107–20 and Christian Stachelbeck's article in this book.

Chapter 3

1 Yannis G. Mourélos, *L'intervention de la Grèce dans la Grande Guerre* (Athens: Collection de l'Institut français d'Athènes, 1983).

2   Georges-Henri Soutou, *L'Or et le Sang: Les buts de guerre économiques de la première guerre mondiale* (Paris: Fayard, 1989) (henceforth quoted as Soutou, *L'Or*), p. 146.

3   General der Artillerie a. D. von Kressenstein (ed. D. Paitschadze), *Meine Mission im Kaukasus* (Tbilissi: Verlag Samschoblo, 2001).

4   Marjorie Farrar, *French Blockade Policy 1914–1916: A Study in Economic Warfare* (Stanford: StanfordUP PhD, 1968) (Ann Arbor Microfilm, pp. 162–3).

5   For Briand and Romania, see Georges Suarez, *Briand, vol. III: 1914–1916* (Paris: Plon, 1939), pp. 352ff; for Greece, see Mourélos, *L'intervention de la Grèce.*

6   Centre de Recherche de l'Historial de la Grande Guerre, *La Bataille de la Somme dans la Grande Guerre, Actes du Colloque des 1er, 2, 3, 4 juillet 1996* (Péronne, 2000).

7   Gérard Fassy, *Le Commandement Français en Orient (Octobre 1915– Novembre 1918)* (Paris: Economica, 2003), pp. 438–39.

8   Alan Kramer, 'Blockade and Economic Warfare', in Jay Winter (ed.), *The First World War* (Cambridge: CUP, 2014), vol. II.

9   Farrar, *French Blockade Policy 1914–1916*, pp. 162–3.

10 Georges Suarez, *Briand, vol. III: 1914–1916* (Paris: Plon, 1939), pp. 226, 230.

11 Général Edmond Buat, *Journal 1914–1923* (Paris: Librairie Academique Perrin, 2015) (Entry of 17 March 1916)

12 Georges-Henri Soutou, *L'Or*, pp. 246–60.

13 Suarez, *Briand*, p. 237 and Poincaré, *Au service de la France, vol. VIII: Verdun* (Paris: Plon, 1931), p. 159.

14 Joffre, *Mémoires du Maréchal Joffre* (Paris: Plon, 1932), vol. 2, pp. 95–140.

15 Ibid., pp. 161–8.

16 Général F. Gambiez and Colonel F. Suire, *Histoire de la Première Guerre Mondiale* (Paris: Fayard, 1968), vol. 1, pp. 327–8.

17 Ibid., pp. 313–4.

18 Joffre, *Mémoires,* p. 219.

19 Maréchal Fayolle, *Carnets Secrets de la Grande Guerre* (Paris: Plon, 1964), pp. 166–7, 179, 182.

20 They have been published by Colonel Frédéric Guelton: Général Edmond Buat: *Journal 1914–1923* (Paris: Librairie Academique Perrin, 2015)

21 Entries for 12 and 16 April.

22 Various entries in April and May.

23 Gambiez and Suire, *Histoire de la Première Guerre Mondiale*, p. 330–1.

24 Fayolle, *Carnets Secrets de la Grande Guerre,* p. 159. This was a not

infrequent view since Napoleon; it was still very present in many French circles at the time of Vichy.

25 Ministère des Affaires étrangères, Dépôt de Nantes, Ambassade de Londres, 1914–1920, carton 36.

26 Soutou, *L'Or*, p. 382.

27 Bundesarchiv, R 13/1, Verein deutscher Eisen-und Stahlindustrieller.

28 Wolfgang Steglich, *Bündnissicherung oder Verständigungsfrieden: Untersuchungen zu dem Friedensangebot der Mittelmächte vom 12. Dezember 1916* (Göttingen: Musterschmidt, 1958).

29 Soutou, *L'Or*, pp. 383–9.

30 Georges-Henri Soutou, *La Grande Illusion: Quand la France perdait la paix 1914–1920* (Paris: Tallandier, 2015).

31 Soutou, *La Grande Illusion*, pp. 89–131.

32 Ibid., pp. 171–88.

33 Joffre, *Mémoires,* p. 341.

34 Ibid., pp. 341 ff. Raymond Poincaré, *Au service de la France, T. IX*, pp. 15, 22.

35 Joffre, *Mémoires,* pp. 346 ff.

36 Operation plan for 1917, on 25 January 1917, in Commandant de Civrieux, *L'offensive de 1917 et le commandement du Général Nivelle*, Paris, 1919, pp. 42 ff.

37 Soutou, *La Grande illusion*, pp. 184–96.

38 Joffre, *Mémoires,* p. 264.

39 Gambiez and Suire, *Histoire de la Première Guerre Mondiale*, pp. 337–8.

Chapter 4

1 Dennis Showalter, *Tannenberg: Clash of Empires* (Hamden: Archon Books, 1991), pp. 152–3, 169–70, 192, 311–2. See also Peter Supf, *Die Geschichte des deutschen Flugwesens* (Berlin: Verlagsanstalt Hermann Klemm, 1935), vol. II, pp. 257–63.

2 Supf, *Die Geschichte des deutschen Flugwesens*, p. 262.

3 Francis Crosby, *A Handbook of Fighter Aircraft* (London: Anness Publishing Ltd, 2002), p. 70.

4 Alistair Horne, *The Price of Glory: Verdun 1916* (London: Penguin, 1962), pp. 54–55, 241.

5 On the Verdun air battle see Richard Hallion, *Rise of the Fighter Aircraft 1914–1918* (Baltimore: Nautical and Aviation Press, 1984), pp. 15–7, 28. At 97mph and with a 15,000-foot ceiling the Nieuport 11 significantly outperformed the Fokker Eindecker. John Slessor, *Air Power and Armies* (London, Oxford University Press, 1936), p. 19.

6   Charles Christienne and Pierre Lissarague, *A History of French Military Aviation* (Washington, DC: Smithsonian Institution Press, 1986), pp. 95–98.

7   Alex Revell, *British Fighter Units on the Western Front 1914–1918* (London: Osprey, 1978), p. 22.

8   Ibid.

9   On 1 July 1916, the RFC in the Somme sector had 410 serviceable aircraft, of these 219 were artillery spotting/observation planes, See Revell, *British Fighter Units on the Western Front*, p. 22, and Lieutenant-Colonel Thomas G. Bradbeer, *The Battle for Air Supremacy over the Somme, 1 June 1916–30 November 1916* (MA Thesis US Army Command and General Staff College, 2004), p. 130.

10 Richard Hallion, *Rise of the Fighter Aircraft, 1914–1918* (Annapolis: Nautical and Aviation Press, 1984).

11 See Hallion, *Rise of the Fighter Aircraft, 1914–1918*, pp. 33–34.

12 Revell, *British Fighter Units on the Western Front*, pp. 46–47.

13 Peter Kilduff, *Germany's First Air Force 1914–1918* (Osceola WI: Motorbooks International, 1991), p. 67.

14 Bradbeer, *The Battle for Air Supremacy over the Somme*, pp. 130–131.

15 John Morrow, *The Great War in the Air: Military Aviation from 1909 to 1921* (Washington: Smithsonian Institution Press, 1993), pp. 369, 371.

16 Ibid., p. 278.

17 Revell, *British Fighter Units on the Western Front*, pp. 18–9.

18 Henry Probert, *Bomber Harris: His Life and Times* (London: Greenhill Books, 2002), p. 36.

19 Ibid., pp. 38–9.

20 Ibid., p. 39.

21 Richard Hallion, *Rise of the Fighter Aircraft, 1914–1918*, pp. 72–3, 160–1.

22 Dennis Winter, *The First of the Few: Fighter Pilots of the First World War* (Athens: University of Georgia Press, 1983), p. 36.

23 Georg Neumann, *Die deutschen Luftstreitkräfte im Weltkrieg* (Berlin: E. S. Mittler und Sohn, 1921), pp. 268–9.

24 Revell, *British Fighter Units on the Western Front*, pp. 46–7.

25 Terry Treadwell, Alan Wood, *German Fighter Aces of World War I* (Stroud UK: Tempus, 2003), pp. 208–9, 214–7.

26 E. Christopher Cole, *Royal Flying Corps 1915–1916 (Communiques)* (London: William Kimber, 1969), p. 227.

27 Peter Hart, *Somme Success: The Royal Flying Corps and the Battle of the Somme* (Barnsley: Leo Cooper, 2001), p. 129.

28 Bradbeer, *The Battle for Air Supremacy over the Somme,* pp. 103–4.

29 Major a. D. von Bose, 'Wie war die Wirkung feindlicher Angriffe auf Bahnhoefe', Kriegsgeschichtliches Forschungsamt Study, 17 June 1934, in Bundesarchiv/Militärarchiv Freiburg, Doc W-10/ 50, 163.

30 Bradbeer, *The Battle for Air Supremacy over the Somme,* p. 130.

31 Hart, *Somme Success,* pp. 157–8, 174–5.

32 Ibid., p. 21.

33 Bradbeer, *The Battle for Air Supremacy over the Somme,* pp. 130–1.

34 A complete table of organization of the Luftstreitkräfte Headquarters and an army aviation headquarters is provided in Hermann Cron (ed.), *Reichsarchiv, Die Organisation des deutschen Heeres im Weltkriege,* Part V (Berlin: E. S. Mittler und Sohn, 1923), pp. 88–95.

35 On World War I fighter development see Richard Hallion, *Rise of the Fighter Aircraft, 1914–1918* (Annapolis: Nautical and Aviation Press, 1984).

36 Robert T. Foley, 'Learning War's Lessons: The German Army and the Battle of the Somme 1916', *Journal of Military History* (April 2011), pp. 471–504. See pp. 492–6.

Chapter 5

1   It should be noted that Third Army was confined to a largely subsidiary role (the diversionary attack at Gommecourt for example) and played very little part in the wider battle.

2   David French, *British Strategy and War Aims: 1914–1916* (London: Routledge, 1986) pp. xi–xiv, 120.

3   David Lloyd George, 'Memorandum to War Council', December 1914, quoted in *War Memoirs of David Lloyd George,* vol. I (London: Odhams Press, 1938), p. 222.

4   William Philpott, *Bloody Victory: The Sacrifice on the Somme and the Making of the Twentieth Century* (London: Little Brown, 2009) pp. 75–7.

5   Ibid., p. 58.

6   Ibid., p. 108.

7   Ibid., p. 122.

8   Gary Sheffield, *The Chief: Douglas Haig and the British Army* (London: Aurum Press, 2011), p.168.

9   'Report of the Army Commander's remarks at the conference held at Fourth Army Headquarters, 22 June 1916', Fourth Army Papers, vol. 6, quoted in Robin Prior and Trevor Wilson, *Command on the Western Front: Military Career of Sir Henry Rawlinson, 1914–1918* (London: Leo Cooper, 1992), p.155.

10 Prior and Wilson, *Command on the Western Front*, pp. 153, 155; Robin Prior and Trevor Wilson, *The Somme* (London: Yale University Press, 2005), p. 51; Tim Travers, *The Killing Ground* (Barnsley, Pen and Sword, 2003; originally published in 1987) p. 137.

11 Travers, *The Killing Ground*, p. 137.

12 Perth and Kinross Council Archive (PKCA), Rycroft Papers, MS35/50, Horace Smith-Dorrien to William Rycroft, 20 August 1916.

13 Prior and Wilson, *The Somme*, pp. 102, 107.

14 Christopher Duffy, *Through German Eyes: The British and the Somme 1916* (London: Weidenfeld and Nicolson, 2006), p. 171.

15 Prior and Wilson, *Command on the Western Front*, p. 191.

16 Sheffield and Bourne (eds.), *Douglas Haig: War Diaries and Letters*, p. 201.

17 Ibid., p. 205.

18 Prior and Wilson, *The Somme*, p. 217.

19 Duffy, *Through German Eyes* pp. 208–9.

20 Sheffield, *The Chief*, pp. 188–9.

21 Prior and Wilson, *The Somme*, pp. 221–2; Sheffield and Bourne, *Douglas Haig War Diaries and Letters*, p. 227.

22 Sheffield, *The Somme*, p. 121; Prior and Wilson, *The Somme* p. 236.

23 Prior and Wilson, *The Somme*, p. 226.

24 Nugent to his wife, 20 December 1916, quoted in Nicholas Perry, *Major-General Sir Oliver Nugent and the Ulster Division 1915–1918* (Stroud: Sutton, 2007), p. 126.

25 Prior and Wilson, *The Somme*, pp. 96–7; The National Archives, WO 95/2368, 'Captn. Spiers to C. G. S. [Launcelot Kiggell], 2 July 1918'.

26 Jonathan Krause, *Early Trench Tactics in the French Army: The Second Battle of Artois May–June 1915* (Farnham: Ashgate, 2013), pp. 29–30, 44.

27 Paddy Griffith, *Battle Tactics of the Western Front: The British Army's Art of Attack, 1916–1918* (London: Yale University Press, 1994), p. 143.

28 The National Archives, WO 95/2368, 32nd Division Notes on Operations, 27 October 1916.

29 XXVI Reserve Corps, *Erfahrungen in der Sommeschlacht*, 24 October 1916, quoted in Duffy, *Through German Eyes*, p. 292.

30 Prior and Wilson, *The Somme*, p. 71; TNA, WO 95/2392, The 1st Battalion the Dorset Regiment, 1 July 1916.

31 The National Archives, WO 95/2368 32nd Div. General Staff, 1 July 1916, 11.45am, 11.57am, 1.50pm; Cab 45/191 R. B. Warton, 155th Brigade RFA to Edmonds 26 May 1930; Edmonds, OH 1916, vol. 1 (1932), pp.410–1.

32 Peter Simkins, *From the Somme to Victory: The British Army's Experience on the Western Front 1916–1918* (Barnsley: Pen and Sword, 2014) p. 93.

Chapter 6

1   It would suffer a similar fate at Monchy, and after the battle of Cambrai was reduced in numbers to 250 all ranks despite 6,241 Newfoundlanders (only Newfoundlanders were eligible) having joined its ranks. An additional 3,296 Newfoundlanders joined the CEF. 'Newfoundland and the Great War', http://www.heritage.nf.ca/greatwar/articles/nfldatwar.html.

2   William Philpott, *Bloody Victory: The Sacrifice on the Somme and the Making of the Twentieth Century* (London: Little Brown, 2009), pp. 196–197.

3   Bill Nasson, *Springboks on the Somme: South Africa in the Great War 1914–1918* (Johannesburg Penguin, 2007), pp. 129–136; Philpott, *Bloody Victory*, p. 251.

4   Bill Rawling, *Surviving Trench Warfare: Technology and the Canadian Corps, 1914–1918* (Toronto University of Toronto Press, 1992), p.68.

5   C. E. W. Bean, *The Australian Imperial Force in France 1916* (Sydney: Angus & Robertson, 1935), pp. 328–447; Paul Cobb, *Fromelles 1916* (Stroud: Tempus, 2007).

6   Bean, *The Australian Imperial Force in France 1916*, pp. 32–49.

7   Ibid., p. 468.

8   General Staff Circular Memo No. 54 dated 14 July 1916 and General Staff Circular Memo No. 56 dated 18 July 1916 1st Australian Division War Diaries, WO95/3516, NA.

9   Ibid.

10 'Report on the Operations of First Australian Division at Pozieres', 1st Australian Division War Diary, WO95/3516, NA.

11 Birdwood to Walker dated 27 July 1916, 1st Australian Division War Diary, WO95/3516, NA.

12 Summary of Operations for week ending 6 pm, Friday 4 August 1916, I ANZAC GS War Diary August 1916–December 1916, WO 95/981, NA.

13 'Western Front', in Peter Dennis, Jeffrey Grey, Ewan Morris, Robin Prior with John Connor (eds.), *The Oxford Companion to Australian Military History* (Melbourne: OUP, 1955), pp. 653–67.

14 G. D. Sheffield, 'The Australians at Pozières: Command and Control on the Somme, 1916', in David French and Brian Holden Reid (eds.), *The British General Staff: Reform and Innovation, 1890–1939* (London: Cass, 2002).

15 Memorandum by Army Commander Reserve Army dated 3 August 1916, reissued 3 October 1916, Fifth Army, 'Notes and Lessons on 1916 Operations,' WO158/344, NA.

16 Philpott, *Bloody Victory*, pp. 244–9.

17   Christopher Pugsley, *The Anzac Experience: New Zealand, Australia and Empire in the First World War* (Auckland: Reed, 2004), p. 254.

18   Ibid., pp. 255–7.

19   Peter Stanley, *Bad Characters: Sex, Crime, Mutiny, Murder and the Australian Imperial Force* (Millers Point, NSW: Pier 9, 2010), pp. 90–93. See table on p. 158 and discussion on pp. 156–160, Pugsley, *The Anzac Experience*. See also Christopher Pugsley, *On the Fringe of Hell: New Zealanders and Military Discipline in the First World War* (Auckland: Hodder & Stoughton, 1991).

20   1st ANZAC Corps Admin Staff War Diary, 1–31 December 1916, HQ 1st ANZAC Corps April 1916–March 1917, WO95/988, NA.

21   C. E. W. Bean, 'The Somme Winter and Bullecourt', in Sir Charles Lucas, *The Empire at War, Volume III* (London: OUP, 1924), pp. 128–9.

22   Stanley, *Bad Characters*, pp. 203–19.

23   Gary Sheffield, *The Somme* (London: Cassell, 2003), pp. 121–2; David Bercuson and J. L. Granatstein, *Dictionary of Canadian Military History* (Toronto: OUP, 1992), pp. 200–201.

24   Rawling, *Surviving Trench Warfare*, pp. 68–9.

25   Tim Cook, *At the Sharp End: Canadians Fighting the Great War 1914–1916* (Toronto: Viking Canada, 2007), pp. 507–19; Sheffield, *The Somme*, pp. 130–1; Bercuson and Granatstein, *Dictionary of Canadian Military History*, pp. 200–1.

26   Rawling, *Surviving Trench Warfare*, pp.74–5.

27   Rawling, *Surviving Trench Warfare*, p. 81; Philpott, *Bloody Victory*, p. 331.

28   'Canadian Corps Training School. Formation', RG9, III, C1, Vol 3870, Folder 113, File 3. National Archives of Canada (NAC).

29   Rawling, *Surviving Trench Warfare*, pp. 81–6. Cook, *At the Sharp End*, pp. 502–4.

30   Canadian Corps G340 dated 27 December 1916, Battalion Organization (Army and Corps Scheme) RG 9, III, C1, Vol 3864, Folder 99, File 3, NAC.

31   Ibid.

32   GHQ to First Army OB 1919, dated 7 February 1917, signed Kiggell, Lt-General CGS. Canadian Corps to First Army G519, S.109/1 dated 13 February 1917. Battalion Organization (Army and Corps Scheme) RG 9, III, C1, Vol 3864, Folder 99, File 3, NAC.

33   2nd Canadian Div G42/538 dated 10 May 1917, NAC.

34   Colonel H. Stewart, *The New Zealand Division 1916–1919* (Wellington: Whitcombe & Tombs, 1921), p. 64.

35   'Preliminary Notes of the Tactical Lessons of Recent Operations' (S.S. 119, July 1916) See General Staff, S.S. 135. O.B./1 635, *Instructions for the Training of Divisions for Offensive Action*, December 1916, Harrison & Sons, London.

36 New Zealand Division, 'The Offensive, with regard to Bombardment and Barrages in particular', NZ War Diary, Archive New Zealand (ANZ).

37 R. F. Gambrill (ed.), *The Russell Family Saga*, vol. III, *World War 1, 1914–1919* (Manuscript qMS-0822, National Library of New Zealand).

38 Stewart, *The New Zealand Division*, pp. 119–122. Andrew Macdonald, *On My Way to the Somme: New Zealanders and the bloody offensive of 1916* (Auckland: HarperCollins, 2005).

39 Russell to Allen quoted in Pugsley, *The Anzac Experience*, p. 213.

40 Simon Robbins, *British Generalship on the Western Front 1914–1918: Defeat into Victory* (London: Frank Cass, 2005), pp. 57–60.

41 Christopher Duffy, *Through German Eyes: The British and the Somme 1916* (London: Weidenfeld & Nicolson, 2006), pp. 320–32; Cook, pp. 521–526.

42 Jonathan Walker, *The Blood Tub: General Gough and the Battle of Bullecourt, 1917* (Staplehurst: Spellmount, 1998), pp. 189–190.

Chapter 7

1 Robert Doughty, *Pyrrhic Victory: French Strategy and Operations in the Great War* (Cambridge, Massachusetts: Belknap Press of Harvard University Press, 2005) and William Philpott, *Bloody Victory: The Sacrifice on the Somme and the Making of the Twentieth Century* (London: Little, Brown, 2009) have done much to help set the record straight.

2 Alistair Horne, *The Price of Glory: Verdun 1916* (London: Penguin, 1962) helped to set the vision of Verdun for a generation or more of English-speaking readers. Paul Jankowski, *Verdun: The Longest Battle of the Great War* (New York: Oxford University Press, 2014) offers a much more sophisticated and nuanced history.

3 Spencer Cosby Papers, Box 4, Folder 12, *Progress of the War,* May 31, 1916, United States Army Heritage and Education Center, Carlisle, Pennsylvania.

4 Elizabeth Greenhalgh, *Foch in Command: The Forging of a First World War General* (Cambridge: Cambridge University Press, 2011), p. 154.

5 Chatinières et al., *Les Armées Françaises dans la Grande Guerre*, tome 4 (Paris: Imprimerie Nationale, 1927), vol. 1, p. 44.

6 The best study of this process is Michel Goya, *La Chair et L'Acier: L'invention de la Guerre Moderne, 1914–1918* (Paris: Tallandier, 2004), especially chapter seven.

7 Chatinières et al., *Les Armées Françaises*, tome 4, vol. 1, pp. 45–7.

8 Ibid., pp. 50–51.

9 Spencer Cosby Papers, Box 4, Folder 20, *Progress of the War,* July 7, 1916.

10 Chatinières et al., *Les Armées Françaises*, tome 4, vol. 2, p. 282.

11 Ibid., p. 173.

12 Maréchal Fayolle, *Cahiers Secrets de la Grande Guerre* (Paris: Plon, 1964), pp. 155–6, 159.

13 Chatinières et al., *Les Armées Françaises*, tome 4, vol. 2, p. 196.

14 Maxime Weygand, *Foch* (Paris: Flammarion, 1947), p. 138.

15 Ferdinand Foch, *The Memoirs of Marshal Foch* (Garden City, New York: Doubleday, Doran, and Company, 1931), p. 215.

16 Fayolle, *Cahiers Secrets*, p. 159.

17 Doughty, *Pyrrhic Victory*, p. 286.

18 Fayolle, *Cahiers Secrets*, p. 165.

19 Greenhalgh, *Foch in Command*, p. 170.

20 Philpott, *Bloody Victory*, p. 177.

21 Fayolle, *Cahiers Secrets*, p. 166.

22 Doughty, *Pyrrhic Victory*, p. 294.

23 Philpott, *Bloody Victory*, p. 205.

24 Chatinières et al., *Les Armées Françaises*, tome 4, vol. 2, p. 237.

25 Doughty, *Pyrrhic Victory*, p. 297.

26 Chatinières et al., *Les Armées Françaises*, tome 4, vol. 2, p. 242.

27 Ibid., p. 266.

28 Ibid., pp. 273–4.

29 Ibid., p. 278.

30 Abel Ferry, *Carnets Secrets, 1914–1918* (Paris: Grosset, 2005), pp. 202–3. I am grateful to my good friend Jean-Christophe Noël for helping me with this source.

31 Philpott, *Bloody Victory*, pp. 346–347.

32 Doughty, *Pyrrhic Victory*, p. 297.

33 Philpott, *Bloody Victory*, chapter 10.

34 Chatinières et al., *Les Armées Françaises*, tome 4, vol. 2, p. 305.

35 Ibid., p. 292.

36 Greenhalgh, *Foch in Command*, p. 180.

37 Chatinières et al., *Les Armées Françaises*, tome 4, vol. 3, pp. 210, 249.

38 Quoted in Philpott, *Bloody Victory*, p. 383.

39 Greenhalgh, *Foch in Command*, chapter 9.

40 Michael S. Neiberg, *Foch: Supreme Allied Commander in the Great War* (Washington, DC: Brassey's, 2003), pp. 50–51.

41 The citation from the English translation is Sébastien Japrisot, *A Very Long Engagement* (New York: Picador, 2004), pp. 254–5.

42 Doughty, *Pyrrhic Victory*, pp. 343–4.

Chapter 8

1   Olaf Jessen, *Verdun 1916: Urschlacht des Jahrhunderts* (Munich: C.H. Beck, 2014), p. 335.

2   Günter Riederer and Ulrich Ott (eds.), *Harry Graf Kessler: Das Tagebuch 1880–1937*, 9 vols. (Stuttgart: Klett-Cotta, 2008), vol. 5, p. 530.

3   cf. Robert T. Foley, *German Strategy and the Path to Verdun* (Cambridge: Cambridge University Press, 2005), pp. 191–7.

4   *Der Weltkrieg 1914–1918*, vol. 10 (Berlin: Mittler, 1936), pp. 56–68.

5   Wilhelm Solger, *Die Entwicklung des Stellungskrieges 1914–1917* in Bundesarchiv/Militärarchiv Freiburg im Breisgau (BArch), RH 61/1188, pp. 75–86; Wilhelm Solger, *Die Entwicklung des deutschen Angriffsverfahrens* in BArch, RH 61/1168, p. 7; Chef des Generalstabes des Feldheeres, No. 27956 op *Einige Erfahrungen aus den Kämpfen im Maasgebiet (Februar und März 1916)*, 15.5.1916 in BArch, RH 61/1687.

6   AOK 5, Ia Nr. 491, *Verwendung der Flammenwerfer, 6.2.1916* in Bayerisches Hauptstaatsarchiv/Kriegsarchiv (BHStA/KA) 11. Bayerische Infanteriedivision, Bund 5.

7   Erich Ludendorff, *Meine Kriegserinnerungen 1914–1918* (Berlin: Mittler, 1919), p. 306 ff.

8   BArch, RH 61/1188, pp. 66–9.

9   Stellvertretendes Generalkommando XII Dresden (ed.), *Studie über den Angriff im gegenwärtigen Zeitabschnitt des Krieges: Eindrücke und Betrachtungen eines Kompagnieführers, von Capitaine Laffargue du 153e Regiment d'Infanterie, 25.8.1915*, found near Reserve-Jäger 13 after the attack on 25 September 1915.

10 *Der Weltkrieg 1914–1918*, vol. 11 (Berlin: Mittler, 1938), pp. 103–5 and vol. 12, p. 39; *Sanitätsbericht über das Deutsche Heer im Weltkriege 1914/18*, 3 vols., vol. 3 (Berlin: Mittler, 1934), p. 49.

11 Robert T. Foley, 'Learning War's Lessons: The German Army and the Battle of the Somme 1916' in *The Journal of Military History* vol. 75 number 2 (2011), p. 471–504.

12 Chef des Generalstabes des Feldheeres, Nr. 17411 Op., *Erfahrungen aus den letzten Kämpfen*, 3.11.1915 in BHStA/KA, 11. Bayerische Infanteriedivision, Bund 99; OHL 27793 op, 12.5.1916 in BArch, RH 61/1687.

13 Fritz von Loßberg, *Meine Tätigkeit im Weltkriege, 1914–1918* (Berlin: Mittler, 1939), p. 222.

14 Otto von Moser, *Die Württemberger im Weltkriege: Ein Geschichts-, Erinnerungs- und Volksbuch* (Stuttgart: Belser, second edition, 1928), p. 55.

15 cf. Foley, *Learning War's Lessons*, pp. 471–504.

16 Ibid., p. 473.

17   BArch, RH 61/1188, pp. 61–86, 99. Nevertheless, individual regulations for trench warfare like *Gesichtspunkte für den Stellungskrieg* of 13 September 1915 or *Stellungsbau* of 20 June 1916 had been developed under Falkenhayn.

18   AOK 11, Ia Nr.1225, 23.10.1915 in BHStA/KA 11. Bayerische Infanteriedivision, Bund 99.

19   Paul Ritter von Kneußl, *Tagebuch XIV*, Eintrag vom 7.7.1917 in BHStA/KA Nachlass Kneußl.

20   Forschungsanstalt für Kriegs- und Heeresgeschichte (ed.), *Der Weltkrieg 1914–1918*, 14 vols., vol. 12 (Berlin: Mittler, 1939), pp. 56–7.

21   Heeres-Sanitätsinspektion des Reichswehrministeriums (ed.), *Sanitätsbericht*, vol 3, pp. 49 ff. Troops killed, missing, wounded and sick after deducting those who had become fit for service again during the battles.

22   *Der Weltkrieg 1914–1918*, vol. 12, pp. 32–4.

23   See a recent comparative approach to this: Robert T. Foley, 'Dumb donkeys or cunning foxes? Learning in the British and German Armies during the Great War', in *International Affairs* (90/2, 2014), pp. 279–98.

24   Christian Stachelbeck, *Militärische Effektivität im Ersten Weltkrieg: Die 11. Bayerische Infanteriedivision 1915–1918* (Paderborn: Schöningh, 2010), pp. 161–80, 343; *Grundsätze für die Führung der Abwehrschlacht im Stellungskrieg* (Berlin: December 1916/March and September 1917); BArch, RH 61/1188, pp. 115–60.

25   Der Angriff im Stellungskrieg, (Berlin: 1918); BArch RH 61/1168, p. 1-41.

26   *Ausbildungsvorschrift für die Fußtruppen im Krieg (AVF)*, January 1917, Nr. 178 and January 1918, Nr. 198.

27   Gerhard P. Groß, 'Das Dogma der Beweglichkeit. Überlegungen zur Genese der deutschen Heerestaktik im Zeitalter der Weltkriege', in Bruno Thoß and Hans-Erich Volkmann (eds.), *Erster Weltkrieg-Zweiter Weltkrieg. Ein Vergleich* (Paderborn: Schöningh, 2002), pp. 152 ff.

28   Hermann von Kuhl, *Der deutsche Generalstab in Vorbereitung und Durchführung des Weltkrieges* (Berlin: Mittler, 1920), p. 108.

29   *Sanitätsbericht*, vol. 3, p. 53; *Der Weltkrieg 1914–1918*, vol. 14 (Berlin: Mittler, 1944), p. 516.

Chapter 9

1   P. Griffith, *Battle Tactics on the Western Front* (New Haven: YUP, 1994), p. 52.

2   Ibid., p. 229.

3   For *Fourth Army Tactical Notes*, see J. Edmonds, *History of the Great War based on official documents by direction of the Historical Section of the Committee of Imperial Defence. Military Operations. France and Belgium, 1916*, vol. 1: *Sir Douglas Haig's Command to 1 July; Battle of the Somme* (London: Macmillan, 1932), Appendix 18.

4   The points following are taken from unit war diaries.

5   The disadvantage of this tactic became obvious on 3 September when 146th Brigade placed all its support weapons in the follow-up waves. These caught the full fury of the German counter-bombardment.

6   P. Griffith (ed.), *British Fighting Methods in the Great War* (London: Cass, 1996), p. 12.

7   On occasions bombardments could be *too* effective in that if they obliterated German trenches the infantry might be unable to ascertain where they actually were. Furthermore, a levelled trench offered little protection during a counter-attack.

8   The following paragraphs are compiled from the war diaries in the National Archives WO95 of the various units and headquarters of 48th (South Midland) Division.

9   P. Simkins, *From the Somme to Victory: The British Army's Experience on the Western Front 1916–1918* (London: Pen and Sword, 2014), pp. 86–102.

10 Dirty ammunition and problems with resupply also added to the difficulties in maintaining accuracy.

11 E. Wyrall, *The Fiftieth Division 1914–1919* (Uckfield: Naval & Military Press, no date given), p. 167.

12 Ibid.

13 Six Vickers guns of 151st Brigade MGC were hauled across to offer close support. Despite the appalling conditions and the difficulties of manhandling the 50lb weapons and numerous ammunition boxes across the swamp, they did come into action. At this stage of the Somme this was, however, an unusual tactic to employ. Some divisions had sent Vickers across no man's land on 1 July but they had been quickly destroyed by the counter-barrage. It was generally accepted that they were of much more use if kept in the British lines to provide overhead covering fire and to let the more mobile Lewis concentrate on offering close support.

14 National Archives, WO95.2766, General Staff War Diary of 49th Division. Report by Lieutenant-General Jacob.

15 M. Samuels, *Doctrine and Dogma: German and British Infantry Tactics in the First World War* (Santa Barbara: Greenwood Press, 1992), p. 180.

16 See Griffith, *Battle Tactics*, pp. 67–73

17 National Archives, General Staff War Diary of WO95.2766, Note by Gough.

18 J. Bourne, 'The BEF on the Somme: Some Career Aspects', in *Gun Fire* (No. 35, 1996), pp. 2–14.

Chapter 10

1   See, for this, Christian Stachelbeck, *Militärische Effektivität im Ersten Weltkrieg: Die 11. Bayerische Infanteriedivision 1915 bis 1918* (Paderborn: Schöningh, 2010), p. 3.

2   For the structure of the divisions and their changes during the war, see Edgar Graf von Matuschka, *Organisationsgeschichte des Heeres 1890–1918* (=Handbuch zur Deutschen Militärgeschichte, vol 3, part 5), (Munich: Bernard and Graefe, 1983), pp. 227–9.

3   Soden, *Die 26. (württ.) Reserve-Division im Weltkriege* (=Württembergs Heer im Weltkrieg, vol. 6) (Stuttgart: Berger, 1939), p. 51.

4   Ibid., p. 65.

5   Ibid., p. 67.

6   Chef des Generalstabes (ed.), *Gesichtspunkte für den Stellungskrieg* (Berlin, 1915).

7   For a discussion on how armies learned in World War I, see Robert Foley, 'Dumb donkeys or cunning Foxes. Learning in the British and German armies during the Great War', in *International Affairs* (90/2, 2014), pp. 279–98.

8   SS 490, *The Principles of Trench Warfare as Laid Down in the XIV Reserve Corps* (19 May 1916, translated 13 Oct 1916).

9   Soden, *Die 26. (württ.) Reserve-Division im Weltkriege*, p. 97.

10 For the improvement to the defensive works, see Soden, *Die 26. (württ.) Reserve-Division im Weltkriege*, p. 98.

11 Matthäus Gerster, *Die Schwaben an der Ancre. Aus den Kämpfen der 26. Reserve Division* (Heilbronn: Salzer, 1918), p. 117.

12 Freiherr Georg vom Holtz, *Die württembergischen Regimenter im Weltkrieg 1914–1918*, vol. 20, *Das Württembergische Reserve-Inf.-Regiment Nr. 121 im Weltkrieg 1914–1918* (Stuttgart: Chr. Belsersche Verlagsbuchhandlung, 1922), p. 34.

13 The number of guns is taken from appendix 1 in Albrecht von Stosch, *Schlachten des Weltkrieges*, vol. 20, *Somme Nord. I. Teil: Die Brennpunkte der Schlacht im Juli 1916* (Oldenburg: Stalling, 1927), pp. 249–59.

14 Soden, *Die 26. (württ.) Reserve-Division im Weltkriege*, p. 96.

15 Ibid., p. 106.

16 For the bombardment of 180 Regiment, see Fischer, *Das Württ. Infanterie-Regiment Nr 180 im Weltkrieg* (Stuttgart: Chr. Belsersche Verlagsbuchhandlung, 1921), pp. 31–6.

17 Soden, *Die 26. (württ.) Reserve-Division im Weltkriege*, p. 107.

18 Unless otherwise stated, the accounts for the first day of the Somme are taken from Soden, *Die 26. (württ.) Reserve-Division im Weltkriege*, pp. 108–12.

19 Matthäus Gerster, *Das Württembergische Reserve-Infanterie Regiment 119 im Weltkrieg 1914–1918* (Stuttgart: Belser, 1920), p. 53.

20 Jack Sheldon, *The German Army on the Somme, 1914–1916* (Barnsley: Pen & Sword, 2007), p. 146.

21 Hauptstaatsarchiv Stuttgart M107 Bü42/103. The translation here is taken from Sheldon, *The German Army on the Somme*, pp. 146–7.

22 Hauptstaatsarchiv Stuttgart M43/19RIR99. The translation here is taken from Sheldon, *The German Army on the Somme*, p.147.

23 Soden, *Die 26. (württ.) Reserve-Division im Weltkriege*, p. 112.

24 Reichskriegsministerium (ed.), *Der Weltkrieg 1914–1918, vol. 10, Die Operationen des Jahres 1916 bis zum Wechsel in der Obersten Heeresleitung* (Berlin: Mittler, 1936), p. 356.

25 *Experience of the German 1st Army in the Somme Battle by General von Below* (translation of a German document) British Library, document 9086.C.9.

26 *Histories of two hundred and fifty one divisions of the German army which participated in the war (1914–1918)* (London: Stamp Exchange, 1989; reprint of US War Office, 1920), p. 366.

Chapter 11

1 Firing from the rear side of an incline or hill, such that the artillery battery cannot see the target.

2 France (1903), *Règlement provisoire de manouvre de l'artillerie de campagne*, p. 66; '*La rapidité du tir … est la propriété essentielle du canon de campagne*'.

3 Joseph C. Arnold, 'French Tactical Doctrine 1870–1914', *Military Affairs* (42/2, 1978), p. 64.

4 This word doubles as a verb … if sacked a person was said to be '*limogé*'.

5 *court tir rapide* or 'short [barrel] rapid fire'.

6 Quoted in General Sir James Marshall-Cornwall (), *Foch as Military Commander* (London: Willmer Brothers Ltd, 1972), p. 150.

7 The Moroccan Division was a division made up primarily of white French colonial troops who had been sent to police Morocco, rather than soldiers from Morocco. These troops were bolstered by substantial numbers of Foreign Legion troops, notably with large Greek, Polish, Russian and Czech contingents.

8 This doctrinal document never had a standard reference name. I am using the document number simply because it is the shortest and most distinct way to refer to the document. French commanders typically referred to it as 'the doctrine of April 1915'.

9   Service Historique de la Défense, 19N735 'But et conditions et d'une action offensive d'ensemble'; 'Le but d'une action offensive n'est pas uniquement de s'emparer de une ligne de tranchées adverses, mais bien de chasser l'ennemi de l'ensemble de sa position et de le battre, sans lui laisser le temps de se rétablir'.

10 Ibid., 'une … opération ne s'improvise pas. Des expériences répétées ont montré qu'une organization et une préparation minutieuses sont les conditions indispensable du succès. Cette preparation doit ne rien laisser au hasard et réaliser, avant le déclanchement de l'attaque, toutes les conditions favorables à son exécution'.

11 Ibid., 'L'artillerie aura dû, par un tir systématique, sur les lignes successives de l'ennemi, détruire les défenses accessoires, bouleverser les abris, ses boyaux des communication et ses organes de flanquement; elle aura déprimé par des chocs répétés le moral des défenseurs et sera préparée à appuyer efficacement les attaques de l'infanterie pendant tout leur durée, non seulement sur son premier objectif, mais sur les objectifs ultérieurs'.

12 Ibid., 'à l'heure fixée pour l'attaque de l'infanterie, l'artillerie allonge progressivement son tir, pour faire, en avant et sur les flancs de l'attaque, un barrage longitudinal et transversal à l'abri duquel l'infanterie peut progresser'.

13 Ibid., 'de transmettre aux batteries les besoins de l'infanterie'; 'dont la possession affirmera que le premier résultat à attendre – percer le ligne ennemi – a été obtenu'.

14 Bruce I. Gudmundsson, *Stormtroop Tactics: Innovation in the German Army, 1914–1918* (Westport, Connecticut: Praeger, 1989), p. 173.

15 Chatinières, Janet, Lefranc and Landousie, *Les Armées Français dans la Grande Guerre* (Paris: Imprimerie Nationale, 1923), p. 563.

16 Maréchal Foch, *Œuvres complètes,* Tome II, *Les Inédits: Nos Dernières Attaques* (Paris: Economica, 2008), p. 439.

17 Ibid., p. 440.

18 Elizabeth Greenhalgh, *Foch in Command: The Forging of a First World War General* (Cambridge: Cambridge University Press, 2011), p. 140.

19 *Service Historique de la Défense*, 18N148; *'La Bataille Offensive'.*

20 Ibid.

21 Ibid.

22 Chatinières et al., *Les Armées Françaises*, tome IV, annex 1282, *'Projet d'attaque dans la région entre Somme et Oise' Groupe d'Armées du Nord (GAN), 16 Mars 1916.*

23 *Service Historique de la Défense*, 18N148; *'La Bataille Offensive'.*

24 Ibid.

25 William Philpott, *Bloody Victory: The Sacrifice on the Somme and the Making of the Twentieth Century* (London: Little, Brown, 2009), p. 205.

26 Ibid., p. 214.

Chapter 12

1   John Keegan, *The First World War* (London: Hutchinson, 1998), p. 321.

2   Lyn Macdonald, *Somme* (London: Penguin, 1993; originally published by Michael Joseph in 1983), p. xiii. Contrary to some opinion, however, the Somme was not the first blooding of Kitchener's New Army: 10th (Irish), 11th (Northern) and 13th (Western) divisions fought at Gallipoli; 9th (Scottish), 12th (Eastern), 15th (Scottish), 21st and 24th divisions were engaged in the battle of Loos on the Western Front in September–October 1915.

3   The transcript is at https://www.gov.uk/government/speeches/speech-at-imperial-war-museum-on-first-world-war-centenary-plans, accessed on 21 October 2015.

4   Jeremy Paxman, *The English* (London: Penguin, 2007; originally published by Michael Joseph in 1998), p. 87.

5   Winston Churchill, *The World Crisis*, vol. iii (London: Butterworth, 1927), p. 195.

6   Ibid.

7   War poetry remains a fertile source of illustration and inquiry. See, for example, the anthology edited by Max Egremont, *Some Desperate Glory: The First World War the Poets Knew* (London: Picador, 2014).

8   Alan Clark, *The Donkeys* (London: Pimlico, 1991; originally published by Hutchinson, 1961). The focus of Clark's withering critique of the British Army's generalship was not the battle of the Somme of 1916, but rather the major engagements of the previous year: Neuve Chapelle, Second Ypres, Aubers Ridge and Loos.

9   *Now, God be Thanked* (1979); *Heart of War* (1980) and *By the Green of Spring* (1981). The second volume covers the battle of the Somme.

10   In one of those remarkable coincidences of history, Robert Graves and Siegfried Sassoon both served briefly in this battalion, whose Regimental Medical Officer for much of the war was Dunn.

11   The Earl of Avon, *The Eden Memoirs: The Reckoning* (London: Cassell, 1965), p. 77.

12   John Keegan, *The Face of Battle: A Study of Agincourt, Waterloo and the Somme* (London: Barrie & Jenkins, 1988; Originally published by Jonathan Cape in 1976), p. 248.

13   Gary Sheffield, *Forgotten Victory. The First World War: Myths and Realities* (London: Review, 2002), p. 177.

14   William Philpott, *Bloody Victory: The Sacrifice on the Somme* (London: Abacus, 2010; originally published by Little, Brown, 2009) pp. 4–5.

15   Quoted by Churchill, *The World Crisis*, vol. iii, p. 191.

16   Ibid., p. 193.

17   Ibid., p. 194.

18 The real flaws are exposed in Jim Beach, *Haig's Intelligence: GHQ and the German Army, 1916–1918* (Cambridge: Cambridge University Press, 2013).

19 David Lloyd George, *War Memoirs*, vol. 4 (London: Ivor Nicholson & Watson, 1934) p. 2192.

20 Martin Gilbert, *Churchill: The Power of Words* (London: Bantam Press, 2010), pp. 126–127, drew attention to 'The trials of our latter-day generals' in Churchill's biography of Marlborough.

21 Winston S. Churchill, *Marlborough: His Life and Times, Book One* (London: Harrap, 1947) pp. 570–1.

22 Peter Hart, *The Great War* (London: Profile Books, 2013) p. 210.

23 C. S. Forrester, *The General* (London: William Collins, 2014) p. vi.

24 (As according to Alan Clark) *Ludendorff:* 'The English soldiers fight like lions.' *Hoffman:* 'True. But don't we know that they are lions led by donkeys.'

25 David Reynolds, *In Command of History: Churchill Fighting and Writing the Second World War* (London: Allen Lane, 2004), p. xxiii.

26 Field Marshal Lord Alanbrooke (ed. Alex Danchev and Daniel Todman), *War Diaries 1939–1945* (London: Phoenix, 2002), p. 226.

27 Nigel Hamilton, *Monty*, vol. 1: *The Making of a General 1887–1942* (London: Hamish Hamilton, 1981), p. 84.

28 Field Marshal the Viscount Montgomery of Alamein, *The Memoirs* (London: Collins, 1958), p. 35.

29 Ibid.

30 Ibid., p. 258.

31 Ibid., p. 262. By way of very crude comparison, if the severe fighting during the battle of Normandy of 1944 had lasted as long as the Somme in 1916, and had consumed the equivalent number of divisions, then the British and Canadian casualty toll might have been six-fold: 408,000 rather than 68,000 men.

32 Captain Dunn in his preface to *The War the Infantry Knew* made a related and equally valid point: 'War in the battle-zone between antagonists of equal tenacity and resource is prolonged drudgery ... but drudgery with fearful moments'.

33 As Max Hastings has pointed out in his introduction C. S. Forrester's *The General,* (p. xxiv): '... the dominant reality of World War II was that Alanbrooke and Marshall, Montgomery and Eisenhower were spared the odium of presiding over bloodbaths comparable with those of 1914–1918 not by their own genius, but because the Russians did most of the killing and dying undertaken by British Tommies and French *poilu*s a generation earlier.'

34 Montgomery of Alamein, *A History of Warfare* (London: Collins, 1968), p. 470.

35 Ibid., p. 477.

36 To be fair, Montgomery showed considerable contrition for this ill-advised action in his memoirs (p. 314): 'Distorted or not, I think now that I should never have held that Press conference. So great was the feeling against me on the part of the American generals, that whatever I said was bound to be wrong. I therefore should have said nothing.'

37 Montgomery, *History of Warfare*, p. 476.

38 Clark, *The Donkeys,* p. 90.

39 As posted at http://www.nam.ac.uk/exhibitions/online-exhibitions/britains-greatest-general, accessed on 18 October 2015.

40 Details from Internet press reports, 'After 85 years, Haig's statue finally retreats inside Edinburgh Castle', *The Scotsman* (16 June 2009), http://www.scotsman.com/news/scotland/top-stories/after-85-years-haig-s-statue-finally-retreats-inside-edinburgh-castle-1-1042602#axzz3p0pVYxax; and 'Renovated Earl Haig monument rededicated', *The Southern* Reporter (25 March 2011), http://www.thesouthernreporter.co.uk/news/local-headlines/renovated-earl-haig-monument-rededicated-1-1534508, both accessed on 19 October 2015.

41 Basil Liddell Hart, *A History of the First World War* (London: Pan Books, 1972; originally published by Cassell, 1970) p. 231.

42 Arthur Bryant, *English Saga 1840–1940* (London: Collins, 1940) p. 288.

43 Ibid., pp. 289–90.

44 John Terraine, *The Smoke and the Fire: Myths and Anti-Myths of War 1861–1945* (London: Sidgwick & Jackson, 1980) p. 103.

45 Liddell Hart, *A History of the First World War*, p. 246.

46 Ibid., p. 249.

47 Ibid., p. 251.

48 The strict policy of retaking every lost position was originally mandated by General Erich von Falkenhayn. See Terraine, *The Smoke and the Fire*, p. 120, for details.

49 Liddell Hart, *A History of the First World War*, p. 253.

50 Terraine, *The Smoke and the Fire*, pp. 121–2.

51 A. J. P. Taylor, *The First World War: an Illustrated History* (London: Hamish Hamilton, 1963), p. 140. [Page ref. to the Penguin Books edition of 1966.]

52 Sir Llewellyn Woodward, *Great Britain and the War of 1914–1918* (London: Methuen, 1967) p. 146.

53 Ibid.

54 Ibid., p. xviii.

55 Ibid., pp. xix–xx.

56 The Chief of Defence Staff and Vice Chief of Defence Staff remain in London and continue to serve on the Defence Board.

57 See, for example, Mungo Melvin, 'Soldiers, Statesmen and Strategy', *RUSI Journal* (157/1, February/March 2012), pp. 20–7.

BIBLIOGRAPHY

Chapter 1

Barrett, Michael, *Prelude to Blitzkrieg: The Austro-German Campaign in Romania* (Bloomington: Indiana UP, 2013)

Dutton, David, *The Politics of Diplomacy: Britain and France in the Balkans in the First World War* (London: IB Tauris, 1998)

Gordon, Andrew, *The Rules of the Game: Jutland and British Naval Command* (London: John Murray, 1996)

Halpern, Paul G., *A Naval History of World War I* (London: Naval Institute Press, 1994)

Höbelt, Lothar, *'Stehen oder Fallen?' Österreichische Politik im ersten Weltkrieg* (Vienna: Boehlau, 2015)

Shanafelt, Gary, *The Secret Enemy: Austria-Hungary and the German Alliance 1914–1918* (New York: Columbia University Press, 1985)

Soutou, Georges-Henri, *L'Or et le Sang: Les buts de guerre économiques de la première guerre mondiale* (Paris: Fayard, 1989)

Strachan, Hew, *The First World War in Africa* (Oxford: OUP, 2004)

Thompson, Mark, *The White War: Life and Death on the Italian Front 1915–1919* (London: Faber and Faber, 2008)

Torrey, Glenn, *The Romanian Battlefront in World War I* (Lawrence: University Press of Kansas, 2011)

Townshend, Charles, *When God Made Hell: The British Invasion of Mesopotamia and the Creation of Iraq, 1914–1921* (London: Faber & Faber, 2010)

Chapter 2

Afflerbach, Holger, *Falkenhayn: Politisches Denken und Handeln im Kaiserreich* (Munich: Oldenbourg 1994)

Afflerbach, Holger, 'Die militärischen Planungen des Deutschen Reiches im Ersten

Weltkrieg' in *Der Erste Weltkrieg Wirkung – Wahrnehmung – Analyse* (Weyarn: Seehammer 1997)

Falkenhayn, Erich von, *General Headquarters 1914–1916 and its Critical Decisions* (London: Hutchinson 1919)

Foley, Robert T., *German Strategy and the path to Verdun: Erich von Falkenhayn and the Development of Attrition 1870–1916* (Cambridge: Cambridge University Press 2005)

Groß, Gerhard P., 'Das Dogma der Beweglichkeit. Überlegungen zur Genese der deutschen Heerestaktik im Zeitalter der Weltkriege' in *Erster Weltkrieg – Zweiter Weltkrieg. Ein Vergleich* (Paderborn: Schöningh 2002)

Groß, Gerhard P., *Mythos und Wirklichkeit: Geschichte des operativen Denkens im deutschen Heer von Moltke d.Ä. bis Heusinger* (Paderborn: Ferdinand Schöningh 2012)

Jessen, Olaf, *Verdun 1916: Urschlacht des Jahrhunderts* (Munich: Beck 2014)

Strohn, Matthias, 'German Tactical Doctrine and the Defensive Battle on the Western Front' in *World War I Companion* (Oxford: Osprey 2013)

Wendt, Hermann, *Verdun 1916: Der Angriff Falkenhayns im Maasgebiet mit Richtung auf Verdun als strategisches Problem* (Berlin: Mittler, 1931).

Reichskriegsministerium, ed., *Der Weltkrieg 1914–1918, vol. 10, Die Operationen des Jahres 1916 bis zum Wechsel in der Obersten Heeresleitung* (Berlin: Mittler, 1936)

Chapter 3

Clayton, Anthony, *Paths of Glory: The French Army 1914–1918* (London: Cassel, 2003)

Cochet, François, *1914–1918: Fin d'un monde, début d'un siècle* (Paris: Perrin, 2014)

Doughty, Robert A., *Pyrrhic Victory: French Strategy and Operations in the Great War* (Harvard: HUP, 2005)

Fayolle, Maréchal Marie Émile, *Carnets Secrets de la Grande Guerre* (Paris: Plon, 1964)

Horne, Alistair, *The French Army and Politics, 1870–1970* (Basingstoke: Macmillan, 1984)

Joffre, Maréchal Joseph, *Mémoires du Maréchal Joffre* (Paris: Plon, 1932)

Neiberg, Michael S., *Foch: Supreme Allied Commander in the Great War* (Washington: Potomac Books, 2003)

Poincaré, Raymond, *Au service de la France*, (Paris: Plon, 1931)

Soutou, Georges-Henri, *L'Or et le Sang. Les buts de guerre économiques de la première guerre mondiale* (Paris: Fayard, 1989)

Soutou, Georges-Henri, *La Grande Illusion. Quand la France perdait la paix 1914–1920* (Paris: Tallandier, 2015)

Chapter 4

Budiansky, Stephen, *Air Power* (New York: Viking Press, 2003)

Corum, James and Muller, Richard, *The Luftwaffe's Way of War: German Air Doctrine 1911–1945* (Baltimore: Nautical and Aviation Press, 1998)

Franks, Norman, Guest, Russell and Bailey, Frank, *Bloody April ... Black September* (London: Grub Street, 1995)

Kennett, Lee, *The First Air War 1914–1918* (New York: The Free Press, 1991)

Kilduff, Peter, *Germany's First Air Force 1914–1918* (Osceola WI: Motorbooks International, 1991)

Morrow, John, *German Air Power in World War I* (Lincoln: University of Nebraska Press, 1982)

Morrow, John, *The Great War in the Air: Military Aviation from 1909 to 1921* (Washington: Smithsonian Institution Press, 1993)

Shores, Christopher, Franks, Norman and Guest, Russell, *Above the Trenches* (London: Grub Street, 1990)

Winter, Dennis, *The First of the Few; Fighter Pilots of the First World War* (Athens: University of Georgia Press, 1983)

Chapter 5

Ashurst, G. (ed. Holmes, Richard), *My Bit: A Lancashire Fusilier at War, 1914–1918* (Marlborough: Crowood, 1987)

Carrington, Charles, *Soldier from the Wars Returning* (London: Hutchinson & Co, 1965)

Dunn, Captain J. C., *The War the Infantry Knew 1914–1919* (London: King, 1938)

Edmonds, Brigadier-General James, *Military Operations: France and Belgium 1916*, vol. I (London: Imperial War Museum/Battery Press, 1993; originally published in 1932)

Griffith, Paddy, *Battle Tactics of the Western Front: The British Army's Art of Attack, 1916–1918* (London: Yale University Press, 1994)

Haig, Douglas, (eds. Sheffield, Gary and Bourne, John), *Douglas Haig: War Diaries and Letters*, (London: Weidenfeld and Nicolson, 2005)

Harris, Paul, *Douglas Haig and the First World War* (London: Cambridge University Press, 2009)

Middlebrook, Martin, *The First Day on the Somme* (London: Allen Lane, 1971)

Miles, Captain Wilfred, *Military Operations: France and Belgium 1916*, vol. II: *2 July 1916 to the end of the Battles of the Somme* (London: Imperial War Museum/Battery Press, 1992; originally published in 1938)

Philpott, William, *Bloody Victory: The Sacrifice on the Somme and the Making of the Twentieth Century* (London: Little Brown, 2009)

Prior, Robin and Wilson, Trevor, *Command on the Western Front: the Military Career of Sir Henry Rawlinson, 1914–1918* (London: Leo Cooper, 1992)

Prior, Robin and Wilson, Trevor, *The Somme* (London: Yale University Press, 2005)

Sheffield, Gary, *The Somme* (London: Cassell, 2003)

Sheffield, Gary, *The Chief: Douglas Haig and the British Army* (London: Aurum Press, 2011)

Simkins, Peter, *From the Somme to Victory: The British Army's Experience on the Western Front 1916–1918* (Barnsley: Pen and Sword, 2014)

SS 135, *Instructions for the Training of Divisions for Offensive Action* (December 1916)

SS 143, *Instructions for the Training of Platoons for Offensive Action, 1917* (February 1917)

Rogerson, Sidney, *Twelve Days on the Somme: A Memoir of the Trenches, 1916* (London: Greenhill, 2006; originally published in 1933)

Chapter 6

Bean, C. E. W., *The Australian Imperial Force in France 1916* (Sydney: Angus & Robertson, 1935)

Cook, Tim, *At the Sharp End: Canadians Fighting the Great War 1914–1916* (Toronto: Viking Canada, 2007)

Duffy, Christopher, *Through German Eyes: The British and the Somme 1916* (London: Weidenfeld & Nicolson, 2006)

Macdonald, Andrew, *On My Way to the Somme: New Zealanders and the bloody offensive of 1916* (Auckland: HarperCollins, 2005)

Nasson, Bill, *Springboks on the Somme: South Africa in the Great War 1914–1918* (Johannesburg: Penguin, 2007)

Pederson, Peter, *The Anzacs: From Gallipoli to the Western Front*, (Melbourne: Penguin, 2010)

Pugsley Christopher, *The Anzac Experience: New Zealand, Australia and Empire in the First World War* (Auckland: Reed, 2004)

Rawling, Bill, *Surviving Trench Warfare: Technology and the Canadian Corps, 1914–1918* (Toronto: University of Toronto Press, 1992)

Robbins, Simon, *British Generalship on the Western Front 1914–1918: Defeat into Victory* (London: Frank Cass, 2005)

Sheffield, G. D., 'The Australians at Pozières: Command and Control on the Somme, 1916', in David French and Brian Holden Reid (eds.), *The British General Staff: Reform and Innovation, 1890–1939* (London: Cass, 2002)

Stanley, Peter, *Bad Characters: Sex, Crime, Mutiny, Murder and the Australian Imperial Force* (Millers Point, NSW: Pier 9, 2010)

Stewart, Colonel H., *The New Zealand Division 1916–1919* (Wellington: Whitcombe & Tombs, 1921)

Chapter 7

Chatinières, Janet, Lefranc and Landousie, *Les Armées Françaises dans la Grande Guerre*, tome 4, vol. 1 (Paris: Imprimerie Nationale, 1927)

Doughty, Robert, *Pyrrhic Victory: French Strategy and Operations in the Great War* (Cambridge, Mass.: Harvard University Press, 2005)

Fayolle, Maréchal Marie Émile, *Cahiers Secrets de la Grande Guerre* (Paris: Librairie Plon, 1964)

Ferry, Abel, *Carnets Secrets, 1914–1918* (Paris: Grasset, 2005)

Foch, Maréchal Ferdinand, *The Memoirs of Marshal Foch* (New York: Doubleday, 1931)

Goya, Michel, *La Chair et L'Acier: L'invention de la Guerre Moderne, 1914–1918* (Paris: Tallandier, 2004)

Greenhalgh, Elizabeth, *Foch in Command: The Forging of a First World War General* (Cambridge: Cambridge University Press, 2011)

Jankowski, Paul, *Verdun: The Longest Battle of the Great War* (New York: Oxford University Press, 2014)

Neiberg, Michael S., *Foch: Supreme Allied Commander in the Great War* (Washington: Potomac Books, 2003)

Philpott, William, *Bloody Victory: The Sacrifice on the Somme and the Making of the Twentieth Century* (London: Little, Brown, 2009)

Chapter 8

7. Abteilung des Generalstabes des Heeres, 'Die Entwicklung der deutschen Infanterie im Weltkrieg 1914-1918', in *Militärwissenschaftliche Rundschau*, vol. 2 (1937)

Balck, William, *Entwickelung der Taktik im Weltkriege* (Berlin: Eisenschmid 1922)

Ehlert, Hans, Groß Gerhard P. and Epkenhans, Michael (eds), *The Schlieffen Plan. International Perspectives on the German Strategy for World War I* (Lexington: The University Press of Kentucky 2014)

Foley, Robert T., 'Learning War's Lessons: The German Army and the Battle of the Somme 1916' in *The Journal of Military History*, vol. 75 number 2 (2011)

Foley, Robert T., *German Strategy and the Path to Verdun* (Cambridge: Cambridge University Press 2005)

Groß, Gerhard P., 'Das Dogma der Beweglichkeit. Überlegungen zur Genese der deutschen Heerestaktik im Zeitalter der Weltkriege'. in Bruno Thoß and Hans-Erich Volkmann (eds.), *Erster Weltkrieg-Zweiter Weltkrieg. Ein Vergleich* (Paderborn: Schöningh 2002)

Gudmundsson, Bruce I., *Stormtroop Tactics. Innovation in the German Army, 1914–1918* (New York: Praeger, 1989)

Jessen, Olaf, *Verdun 1916. Urschlacht des Jahrhunderts* (Munich: C.H. Beck, 2014)

Reichsarchiv/Forschungsanstalt für Kriegs- und Heeresgeschichte/Bundesarchiv (ed.), *Der Weltkrieg 1914–1918*, 14 vols (Berlin/Koblenz: 1925–1956)

Samuels, Martin, *Command or Control? Command, Training and Tactics in the British and German Armies 1888–1918* (London: Frank Cass, 1995)

Stachelbeck, Christian, *Militärische Effektivität im Ersten Weltkrieg. Die 11. Bayerische Infanteriedivision 1915–1918* (Paderborn: Schöningh, 2010)

Stachelbeck, Christian, *Deutschlands Heer und Marine im Ersten Weltkrieg* (Munich: Oldenbourg 2013)

Stachelbeck, Christian, 'Taktik des Landkriegs' in Markus Pöhlmann, Harald Potempa and Thomas Vogel (eds.), *Der Erste Weltkrieg 1914–1918. Der deutsche Aufmarsch in ein kriegerisches Jahrhundert* (Munich: Bucher 2014)

Graeme C. Wynne, *If Germany Attacks. The Battle in the Depth in the West* (London: Faber and Faber 1940)

Chapter 9

Edmonds, J. E., *Military Operations France and Belgium 1916*, Vol. 1 (London: Macmillan, 1932)

Griffith, Paddy, *Battle Tactics of the Western Front* (New Haven: Yale University Press, 1994)

Griffith, Paddy, (ed.) *British Fighting Methods in the Great War* (London: Cass, 1996)

Lee, J., 'Some Lessons on the Somme: the British Infantry in 1917' in B. Bond et al, *Look to Your Front,* (Staplehurst: Spellmount, 1999)

Miles, W., *Military Operations France and Belgium 1916*, Vol. 2 (London: Macmillan, 1938)

Mitchinson, K. W., *The Territorial Force at War 1914–1916* (London: Palgrave Macmillan, 2014)

Samuels, M. *Doctrine and Dogma: German and British Infantry Tactics in the First World War* (New York: Greenwood Press, 1992)

Simkins, Peter, *From the Somme to Victory* (Barnsley: Pen and Sword, 2014)

Westlake, R., *British Battalions on the Somme* (London: Leo Cooper, 1995)

Wyrall, E., *The Fiftieth Division 1914–1919* (Uckfield: Naval and Military Press, 2006)

Chapter 10

Reichskriegsministerium (ed.), *Der Weltkrieg 1914–1918, vol. 10, Die Operationen des Jahres 1916 bis zum Wechsel in der Obersten Heeresleitung* (Berlin: Mittler, 1936)

Foley, Robert, 'Dumb donkeys or cunning Foxes. Learning in the British and German armies during the Great War', in *International Affairs* (90/2, 2014)

Hirschfeld, Gerhard et al (eds.), *Die Deutschen an der Somme 1914–1918: Krieg, Besatzung, Verbrannte Erde* (Essen: Klartext, 2006)

Sheldon, Jack, *The Germans at Beaumont Hamel* (Barnsley: Pen & Sword, 2006)

Sheldon, Jack, *The Germans at Thiepval* (Barnsley: Pen & Sword, 2006)

Jack Sheldon, *The German Army on the Somme, 1914–1916* (Barnsley: Pen & Sword, 2007)

Soden, Franz von, *Die 26. (württ.) Reserve-Division im Weltkriege* (=Württembergs Heer im Weltkrieg, vol. 6) (Stuttgart: Berger, 1939)

Stosch, Albrecht von, *Somme Nord, I. Teil. Die Brennpunkte der Schlacht im Juli 1916* (=Schlachten des Weltkrieges, vol. 20) (Oldenburg: Stalling, 1927)

Stosch, Albrecht von, *Somme Nord, II. Teil. Die Brennpunkte der Schlacht im Juli 1916* (=Schlachten des Weltkrieges, vol. 21) (Oldenburg: Stalling, 1927)

Strohn, Matthias, 'German Tactical Doctrine and the Defensive Battle on the Western Front', in, idem, *World War One Companion* (Oxford: Osprey, 2013)

Whitehead, Ralph J., *The Other Side of the Wire Volume 1: With the German XIV Reserve Corps on the Somme, September 1914–June 1916* (Solihull: Helion, 2010)

Whitehead, Ralph J., *The Other Side of the Wire Volume 2: The Battle of the Somme. With the German XIV Reserve Corps, 1 July 1916* (Solihull: Helion, 2013)

Chapter 11

Cailleteau, François, *Gagner la Grande Guerre* (Paris: Economica, 2008)

Chatinières, Janet, Lefranc and Landousie, *Les Armées Français dans la Grande Guerre (AFGG)* (Paris: Imprimerie Nationale, 1923)

Doughty, Robert, *Pyrrhic Victory: French strategy and operations in the Great War* (Cambridge, Mass.: Belknap Press of Harvard University Press, 2005)

Fayolle, Maréchal Marie Émile, *Cahiers Secrets de la Grande Guerre* (Paris: Librairie Plon, 1964)

Foley, Robert T. (2005), *German Strategy and the Path to Verdun: Erich von Falkenhayn and the Development of Attrition, 1870–1916* (Cambridge: Cambridge University Press)

Goya, Michel. *La Chair et l'Acier:L'invention de la Guerre Moderne, 1914–1918* (Paris: Tallandier, 2004)

Greenhalgh, Elizabeth, *Foch in Command: The Forging of a First World War General* (Cambridge: Cambridge University Press, 2011)

Joffre, Maréchal Joseph, *Mémoires du Maréchal Joffre (1910–1917)* (Paris: Librarie Plon, 1932)

Philpott, William, *Bloody Victory: The Sacrifice on the Somme and the Making of the Twentieth Century* (London: Little, Brown, 2009)

Porte, Rémy, *La mobilisation industrielle, « premier front » de la grande guerre?* (Cahors: 14–18 Éditions, 2005)

Chapter 12

Churchill, Winston, *The World Crisis*, vol. iii (London: Butterworth, 1927)

Dunn, Captain J. C., *The War the Infantry Knew 1914–1919* (London: Abacus, 2004)

Fussell, Paul, *The Great War and Modern Memory* (Oxford: Oxford University Press, 1975)

Hart, Peter, *The Great War* (London: Profile Books, 2013)

Keegan, John, *The Face of Battle: A Study of Agincourt, Waterloo and the Somme* (London: Jonathan Cape, 1976)

Keegan, John, *The First World War* (London: Hutchinson, 1998)

Levine, Joshua, *Forgotten Voices of the Somme* (London: Ebury Press, 2008)

Liddell Hart, Basil, *A History of the First World War* (London: Cassell, 1970)

Macdonald, Lyn, *Somme* (London: Michael Joseph, 1983)

Montgomery of Alamein, Field Marshal the Viscount, *The Memoirs* (London: Collins, 1958)

Philpott, William, *Bloody Victory: The Sacrifice on the Somme* (London: Little, Brown, 2009)

Prior, Robin and Wilson, Trevor, *The Somme* (New Haven and London: Yale University Press, 2005)

Sheffield, Gary, *Forgotten Victory. The First World War: Myths and Realities* (London: Review, 2002)

Strachan, Hew, *The First World War* (London: Simon & Schuster, 2003)

Terraine, John, *The Smoke and the Fire: Myths and Anti-Myths of War 1861–1945* (London: Sidgwick & Jackson, 1980)

Todman, Dan, *The Great War: Myth and Memory* (London: Bloomsbury Academic, 2007)

GLOSSARY AND ABBREVIATIONS

ANZAC	Australia and New Zealand Army Corps
AIF	Australian Imperial Force
Aéronautique Militaire	the French air service
AOK	Armeeoberkommando (Army Headquarters)
Augftragstaktik	the system of downward delegation of responsibility, allowing recipients of orders to act autonomously within the scope of the leader's intent
BEF	British Expeditionary Force
CEF	Canadian Expeditionary Force
chef d'état-major	Chief of the General Staff
CIGS	Chief of the Imperial General Staff
Corps d'Armée	army corps
Erster Generalquartiermeister	First Quartermaster General
Fliegertruppen des Deutschen Kaiserreiches	German Imperial Air Service, before October 1916
GHQ	British General Headquarters
GOC	General Officer Commanding
GQG	Grand Quartier Général (French General Headquarters)
Groupe d'Armées	Army Group
Groupe Provisoire	Provisional Army Group
Heeresgruppe	Army Group

Jasta	*Jagdstaffel* – German fighter squadron of 14 planes
Luftstreitkräfte	German Air Service, after October 1916
Materialschlacht	war of *materiél*
Menschenmaterial	'human material'
NZEF	New Zealand Expeditionary Force
OHL	Oberste Heeresleitung (Supreme Army Command)
OberOst	Supreme Commander East
RAF	Royal Air Force
RFC	Royal Flying Corps
RNAS	Royal Navy Air Service
Stoßtrupp	stormtroop
Zwischenstellung	intermediate position

British Empire	France	German Empire
Field Marshal	Maréchal de France	Generalfeldmarschall
General		Generaloberst
Lieutenant General	Général de Division	General der Infanterie, General der Kavallerie, General der Artillerie
Major General		Generalleutnant
Brigadier General	Général de Brigade	Generalmajor
Colonel	Colonel	Oberst
Lieutenant Colonel	Lieutenant-Colonel	Oberstleutnant
Major	Commandant	Major
Captain	Capitaine	Hauptmann
Lieutenant	Lieutenant	Oberleutnant
Second Lieutenant	Sous-Lieutenant	Leutnant

INDEX

References to maps are in **bold**.